Routledge Revivals

The Idea of the Soul

First Published in 1940, this book which is written not so much for the philosopher as for the ordinary educated man, is an account of the idea of the soul. It attempts to answer two questions-a) what is the idea of the soul; and b) why has it become 'unwelcome'? The first question is answered by tracing the actual historical development of the idea- from early myths of the soul up to Renaissance philosophy. The second question is dealt with by considering the idea of the soul as it is affected by modern scientific ideas, particularly biological ideas.

The book discusses themes like the physical psyche; the natural philosophers; Socrates; the Platonic immaterial real; rebirth of philosophy and birth of Christianity; Neo- Pythagorean method of biology; Behaviourism and nature and the organism. This will be an interesting historical reference work for students of philosophy.

The Idea of the Soul
In Western Philosophy and Science

William Ellis

First published in 1940
by George Allen & Unwin Ltd.

This edition first published in 2024 by Routledge
4 Park Square, Milton Park, Abingdon, Oxon, OX14 4RN

and by Routledge
605 Third Avenue, New York, NY 10017

Routledge is an imprint of the Taylor & Francis Group, an informa business

© William Ellis 1940

All rights reserved. No part of this book may be reprinted or reproduced or utilised in any form or by any electronic, mechanical, or other means, now known or hereafter invented, including photocopying and recording, or in any information storage or retrieval system, without permission in writing from the publishers.

Publisher's Note
The publisher has gone to great lengths to ensure the quality of this reprint but points out that some imperfections in the original copies may be apparent.

Disclaimer
The publisher has made every effort to trace copyright holders and welcomes correspondence from those they have been unable to contact.

A Library of Congress record exists under LCCN: 41001742

ISBN: 978-1-032-88043-3 (hbk)
ISBN: 978-1-003-53600-0 (ebk)
ISBN: 978-1-032-88047-1 (pbk)

Book DOI 10.4324/9781003536000

The Idea of the Soul

IN WESTERN PHILOSOPHY AND SCIENCE

BY

WILLIAM ELLIS
PH.D.

LECTURER IN EXPERIMENTAL ZOOLOGY
LIVERPOOL UNIVERSITY

LONDON
GEORGE ALLEN AND UNWIN LTD

FIRST PUBLISHED IN 1940

All rights reserved

PRINTED IN GREAT BRITAIN
in *12-Point Perpetua Type*
BY UNWIN BROTHERS LIMITED
WOKING

TO RAY

Rien ne retirera du tissu de la science les fils d'or
que la main du philosophe y a introduits
  Papillon, Histoire de la philosophie moderne.

FOREWORD

THE soul, according to an eminent philosopher of the last century, has worn out its welcome. Most modern philosophers would go further. Not only the soul, they would say, but all metaphysical ideas, have worn out their welcome.

This book, which is written not so much for the philosopher as for the ordinary educated man, is an account of the idea of the soul. It attempts to answer two questions. First, what *is* the idea of the soul; secondly, why has it become 'unwelcome'?

The first question is answered by tracing the actual historical development of the idea—from early myths of the soul up to Renaissance philosophy. The second question is dealt with by considering the idea of the soul as it is affected by modern scientific ideas, particularly biological ideas.

Of course, the anti-metaphysical trend of present-day thought is based on logical, not biological grounds. But, had it not been for the success of science, above all of the science of living things, no one would have thought of using logic as a stick to beat metaphysics. If Descartes had not said that animals are machines without souls, and if modern biologists had not worked on that assumption, we should have had no logical positivists to tell us that the idea of the soul is meaningless. (Between the 'linguistic' solipsism of modern positivism and the solipsism implicit in Cartesian philosophy, there is a closer connection than might at first sight be imagined.) In any case, the common reader cannot be expected to understand the modern analytical attack on metaphysics until he knows something of its scientific background. This must be my excuse for the fact that the second part of this book is about biology and not about logic.

Although written with a non-specialist audience in mind, it is hoped that the historical part will be of interest to biologists and that the account of biological theories may be of some use to philosophers. Philosophers nowadays are so intent on disguising themselves as mathematicians that they have no time to take an interest in biology. This is a great pity. There is, after all, some quite fundamental difference between human beings (or cats for that matter) and things like chairs and tables. The soul may have worn out its welcome, but this fundamental difference remains and is still, as it has always been, the proper study of philosophers.

No doubt the egocentric predicament, which besets every attempt to elucidate this difference, is ultimately inescapable. At least there are few to-day who still hope to find a way out through metaphysical theories, whether idealist or realist. But it does not follow that nothing significant remains to be said about the psycho-physical problem, still less that it is a problem which does not properly exist.

In the concluding chapters I have added some speculations on the shape which this problem may assume in the future. My intentions here are of the most tentative nature; there is much in these chapters which might be differently, and more fully, expressed. But I hope to develop these speculations more adequately elsewhere.

With the sincerest pleasure I offer my thanks to Professor Charles A. Campbell, Professor of Logic and Rhetoric, of the University of Glasgow, for his encouragement and criticism. I am deeply grateful to Mr. W. Somerset Maugham, who also read the manuscript, for his copious and penetrating critical notes. On his advice I have rewritten one chapter and numerous shorter passages.

CONTENTS

CHAPTER		PAGE
	FOREWORD	11
I.	*The Physical Psyche. The Cult of the Soul*	15
	INTRODUCTORY. THE SOUL IN PRIMITIVE THOUGHT. GREEK CULTS OF THE SOUL. ASIATIC INFLUENCES. THE CULT OF DIONYSOS	
II.	*Physis. The Nature Philosophers*	35
	THE DUAL PHYSIS. DIONYSOS AND THE PYTHAGOREAN NATURE PHILOSOPHY. THE FLOWING PHYSIS. HERAKLEITOS. THE STATIC PHYSIS. ELEATIC PHILOSOPHY. THE PLURAL PHYSIS. THE DECLINE OF THE MILESIAN TRADITION	
III.	*The Pythagorean and Ionian Conceptions of the Psyche*	62
IV.	*The Spiritual Psyche: Socrates*	67
V.	*The Spiritual Physis: the Platonic Immaterial Real*	79
VI.	*The Teleological Physis: the Aristotelian Entelechy*	95
VII.	*The Physical Logos: the Decline of Philosophy*	105
VIII.	*The Spiritual Logos: the Rebirth of Philosophy and the Birth of Christianity*	110
XI.	*The Christian Doctrine of Physis and Psyche: St. Augustine*	121
X.	*The First Renaissance of Platonism: the Carolingian Renaissance*	125
XI.	*The Second Renaissance of Platonism: the Italian Renaissance*	130
XII.	*The Para-Physical Psyche: the Neo-Pythagorean Philosophy of Descartes*	145

The Idea of the Soul in Western Philosophy and Science

CHAPTER		PAGE
XIII.	The Cartesian Traditions	165
XIV.	The Neo-Pythagorean Method of Biology	170
XV.	The Physical Schema of the Animal Psyche: the Conditioned Reflex	184
XVI.	The Physical Schema of the Human Psyche: Behaviourism	192
XVII.	The Drieschian Entelechy	215
XVIII.	The Physical Schema of Entelechy: Axial Gradients	230
XIX.	The Future of the Neo-Pythagorean Method	239
XX.	Physis, Psyche and Mechanism	255
	THE LIMITATIONS OF MECHANISM. THE PYTHAGOREAN ORIGIN OF THE LIMITATIONS OF MECHANISM	
XXI.	The Limitations of the Neo-Pythagorean Schema: 'Philosophical' Behaviourism	263
	NAÏVE EPIPHENOMENALISM. CRITICAL EPIPHENOMENALISM. THE PYTHAGOREAN ORIGIN OF EPIPHENOMENALISM. THE POSSIBILITY OF A DUALISTIC EPIPHENOMENALISM. THE INCREDIBILITY OF A DUALISTIC EPIPHENOMENALISM. THE HISTORICAL BACKGROUND OF DUALISM. THE NATURE OF PERCEPTUAL EXPERIENCE. 'MIND' AND 'MATTER'	
XXII.	Nature and the Organism	285
XXIII.	Nature and Psyche	294
	INDEX	307

> "*Wonder is above all the mood of the philosopher; for there is no other root of philosophy than this.*"
>
> PLATO

CHAPTER I

The Physical Psyche. The Cult of the Soul

METAPHYSICAL thinking is an arduous eccentricity for which few, in any age, have had inclination or leisure. But wonder and curiosity, the parents of all philosophy, are as universal as persistent thought is rare. Of all animals, only man has the genius to find cause for wonder in his surroundings and in himself. The *problems* of philosophy exist only for minds competent to create them. The mind which is not restless is empty. "*Because . . . thou hast eaten of the tree . . . in sorrow shalt thou eat of it all the days of thy life.*" The great cultures of the world have arisen, in various ways, out of this spiritual conflict which the author of Genesis traces to the curiosity of Eve.

The Hindu, believing that real knowledge, *samyagjana*, is unattainable by thought, that the seven veils of Maya are impenetrable to human reason, has evolved during the centuries a technique of ecstasy and symbolism for the exploration of worlds beyond thought and reason. And the Chinese, after building a Wall to shut out the world, burnt all their books and devoted the next thousand years or so to the perfection of their extraordinary aesthetic of living, a spiritual wall to shut out wonder. Even if their material wall had been impregnable, the spiritual one must eventually have fallen, for not even classicism, not even the supremely sophisticated classicism of the Chinese, can quite crush the philosophic spirit. Only the Greeks, because their minds combined uniquely the qualities of childlike naïveté and incomparable intellectual vigour, adventured freely in the realm of ideas.

The Idea of the Soul in Western Philosophy and Science

Because there is universal curiosity about ultimate questions, a philosophical speculation of one age may pass into the common thought of the next, may indeed insinuate itself so strongly into the general imagination as to become an universal and unconscious habit of thought, which only the abnormally reflective will think to question.

Even for those who know little of the thought of past ages, the word 'soul' owes the complexity of its modern meaning to a succession of great minds of the past. With the passing centuries, such words gain an increasing power of evocation, calling up in the thoughts of successive generations an ever-lengthening procession of thinkers, Socrates, Aquinas, Leibniz . . . passing through our minds like the ghostly lineage in *Macbeth*.

Nothing is more commonplace, even to the most illiterate European, than the notion that the body is actuated by this non-corporeal something called the soul. Not all Europeans believe this idea to be valid, but to all, sceptics and believers alike, it is a familiar notion, so familiar that few of those who adhere to it or reject it realise that it was once novel, still less that it was a comparatively late product of European culture, the flowering of several centuries of philosophical endeavour.

The idea of the soul as an animating principle has worked so deeply into our minds that, until lately, it was regarded as an essential feature, not of our own culture only, but of all cultures, no matter how primitive or strange, or how different, superficially, from our own.

THE SOUL IN PRIMITIVE THOUGHT

Until quite recently it was thought by anthropologists that a belief in *animism* was a feature of all primitive cultures. "An animistic philosophy," we are told, "is the distinctive philosophy of primitive culture. It is manifestly the outcome of

The Physical Psyche

that earliest analogical reasoning which concludes external agents to be animated with a life essentially similar to our own."[1]

Besides providing a convenient definition of animism this quotation may be taken as an epitome of the theory of 'universal animism,' the theory, due to Tylor and other anthropologists of the last century, that a belief in animism everywhere characterises the primitive mind. We shall see, however, that this notion of the universality of animism rests on the unconscious attribution of the concepts of European philosophy to the mind of primitive man.

It is indeed true that primitive man ascribes a soul not only to man, or to man and animals only, but also to rivers, pots and in fact to all kinds of inanimate objects.[2] That is the main fact on which the Tylorean theory rests. Now if the primitive idea of the soul were exactly, or even approximately the same as ours, this would be good reason for saying that primitive man believes inorganic things to be 'animated with a life essentially similar to our own.' Unfortunately, it cannot be assumed that the idea of the soul, as it occurs in primitive thought, is exactly equivalent to the idea denoted by such European words as *soul, âme, Seele.* . . . It would indeed be extremely odd if there were any such equivalence, seeing that the concept denoted by these words has a philosophical history extending over two millenia of Western thought! Even in translating from one European language to another it is sometimes a matter of extreme difficulty to find accurate equivalents: in the case of a primitive language, especially in dealing with such an abstract and complex idea as that of the soul, this difficulty is enormously increased.

If this had been properly appreciated by the Victorian anthropologists, they would not have offered us so simple and neat an explanation of the origin of the idea of the soul.

---

[1] From "Animism," *Encyclopaedia Britannica*, ninth edition.
[2] These examples are taken from Crawley's *The Idea of the Soul*.

The Idea of the Soul in Western Philosophy and Science

Primitive man, we were told, observed the phenomena of sleep and death, and concluded that the temporary or permanent cessation of vitality was due to the departure from the body of a vital principle, or soul, the cause of thinking, willing and feeling in animate beings.

Further, the theory went on, he was much given to seeing images of his friends in dreams and visions, and to meditation on the meaning of these visitations, with the result that he identified the ghost or dream image with the vital principle deduced from other evidence.

The primitive concept of the soul having thus been identified with the European concept of an animating principle, the rest of the so-called animistic theory follows naturally enough. Primitive man endows pots and rivers with souls . . . therefore he believes them to be bodies animated by spirits.

The absurdity of this conclusion should in itself have aroused the suspicion that the word soul might not hold quite the same significance for the primitive mind as it does for us! Later, in discussing the philosophy of Plato, we shall show that the belief in an animating principle is in fact a highly intellectual view which could not possibly be ascribed to primitive man.

But here it is much more important to realise that, from the philosophical point of view, the theory of universal animism commits an error even more fundamental than the ascription of European beliefs to the primitive mind. This more fundamental error lies in the uncritical assumption that the primitive mind formulates conscious beliefs of any nature whatever. Precise concepts, based on conscious ratiocination, such as Tylor and other anthropologists attribute to primitive man, appear only very late in the history of a culture, if they appear at all. The early workers in anthropology could hardly be expected to realise that the very existence of anthropologists implied a racial background so sophisticated, so far removed from the primitive, that only by means of a complete

The Physical Psyche

mental reorientation could the investigator hope to understand the primitive mind.

Beliefs are expressed in the form of language, and to understand primitive beliefs we must know something about the structure of primitive language. As soon as this is understood, the approach to the problem of primitive 'philosophy' becomes self-conscious, critical of its assumptions, in a way which was not possible in the days of the pioneer workers.[1] Here there is a significant parallel in the contemporary approach to our own philosophical beliefs, philosophers having become increasingly preoccupied with the study of words and symbols. (Incidentally, such studies might be greatly enriched by an enquiry into primitive languages.)

The most striking thing about language in its most primitive form is that, far from having evolved words for abstract and general concepts, it has hardly formed separate words of any kind whatever. In its most primitive form, language is *holophrastic*. Such a language consists, not of separate words corresponding to the abstractions of thought, but of holophrases, picturing, in all their richness and contingency, the events of everyday life. Thus, the Fuegan holophrase '*mamilapinatapai*' signifies "looking-at-each-other-hoping-that-either-will-offer-to-do-something-which-both-parties-desire-but-are-unwilling-to-do."[2] This situation, although highly contingent and complex, is not uncommon in life, so in primitive language it is denoted by a single, unanalysable holophrase. Even numerals are not abstracted, in the primitive mind, from the objects numbered, as may be seen from such a holophrase as 'boy-five-man' (five boys) or 'man-five-fingers' (five men).[3]

Isolated from its context, a holophrase is as meaningless as a square inch taken at random from a portrait. This is true, not only of such complex holophrases as those just quoted,

---

[1] For a fuller exposition of this point, see *The Idea of the Soul*, by A. E. Crawley, from which much of the material for this discussion is taken.

[2] Quoted by Crawley (op. cit.) from Payne's *History of the New World*.

[3] See Rickaby, *General Metaphysics*.

but even of the simplest. For example, the Waicuri had a series of holophrases: *bedare*, my father; *edare*, thy father . . . etc. But the common element -*are* was not intelligible to them. Similarly, primitive language has no one word corresponding to our verb 'to cut.' Instead there are many different verbs, according to what is cut, and how it is cut, and with what tool. So that even such a simple and definite action as cutting is not abstracted from its various contexts.

This discussion of language, which may seem to have led us far from the question of primitive philosophy, has in reality led us into the heart of it. For 'speaking in wholes' implies thinking in wholes, or to use the word coined by Crawley[1] *holopsychosis*. In real life one cannot cut without cutting something, in a particular manner, with some particular tool, and hence the bare abstraction 'to cut' is unknown in primitive thought and language. That a tree is a tree is clear from inspection, and hence even primitive language has names corresponding to such percepts. But a man is known to be a father, not in virtue of his appearance, but because of his participation in the father-child relationship. Hence early thought and language represent in a holophrase this concrete mutual relationship, not the abstraction which later thought isolates from its living context. Strictly speaking, even the word 'tree' denotes an abstraction, for in Nature no two trees are the same, or have the same 'context.' But even for primitive man, the abstraction is so slight that it is unconsciously made. To the reader acquainted with the Gestalt school of psychology these observations will suggest many parallels with modern psychological work.[2]

---

[1] In *The Idea of the Soul*.

[2] Particularly with Gestalt perception in animals. For example, if a hungry octopus is put in an aquarium with a crab, the crab will be captured and eaten only if it is in its natural relation to its surroundings, that is, crawling on the bottom. Even if starving, the octopus will not attack the crab if the latter be hung in 'mid-water' by a string. Removed from its natural surroundings, the crab is unintelligible to the octopus, just as the element -father, removed from the holophrase denoting its social context, is unintelligible to the primitive human mind.

The Physical Psyche

Now what is true of such an easy abstraction as 'father' applies with much greater force to the infinitely more elusive concept which we denote by the word 'soul.' For the essence of our concept of the soul, the concept of an animating principle, is that it is a division of the idea of a living thing into a pair of abstractions, the body and the *anima*. Certain characteristics (such as weight and impenetrability) which living things share with inanimate things are classed together as 'material,' while certain other characteristics (such as purposive action) which distinguish living things from inorganic objects, are classed together as 'psychical' or 'spiritual.' Then the material characteristics are referred to 'the body,' and the spiritual characteristics to 'the soul.' Having been given separate class names, the two groups of attributes are now thought of as separate beings, the one material, the other spiritual. So that, instead of talking of 'the group of attributes which collectively characterise living things' we simply say 'the soul.' And because it is denoted by an independent word, which can exist independently of the word 'body,' the soul is conceived as an independent entity which can detach itself from 'the body.'[1]

But primitive thought is simply incapable of such feats of abstraction as this. If the primitive mind is incapable of abstracting -father from holophrases of the type 'my-father.' 'thy-father,' still less is it capable of abstracting the common element from such holophrases as 'man-soul,' 'river-soul' and so forth. That is to say, primitive man does not think of 'the soul' as a separate being at all; he has not developed a notation or symbolism which would enable him to do so. This is what is meant by saying that the primitive idea of the soul, far from being a belief in the existence of an animating principle, is not a conscious belief at all. Primitive man does not sit down

---

[1] It may be as well, here, to point out that we are *not* advocating a materialistic, or any other metaphysical view of the nature of life. It follows, from the above discussion, that 'the body' is just as much an abstraction as 'the soul,' and for the same reasons.

The Idea of the Soul in Western Philosophy and Science

and take himself through a train of reasoning culminating in a philosophical concept of the soul. He simply formulates holophrases with a common element having some analogy with the European word 'soul.'

We have seen that the theory of universal animism rests on the fact that such holophrases refer, not only to living things, but also to pots and rivers. It is now clear that this fact implies something very different from a belief, conscious or unconscious, in animism. Just because the holophrastic element -soul may be linked with the name of any kind of object, we may infer, not that primitive man thinks everything is alive, but simply that the soul is not for him, as it is for us, an animating principle. To suppose that he thus confused the organic with the inorganic would be to under-rate his intellectual achievements as grossly as, in calling him an animistic *philosopher*, we should be over-rating them.

If the soul in primitive thought does not represent a vital principle, an *anima*, what does it represent? Obviously this is a question which only the anthropologist can hope to answer. Of the alternatives to the exploded theory of universal animism, by far the most interesting and suggestive is that due to Crawley, to whom we have already made constant reference. Before turning to his special findings, however, it will be of interest to look at the question from a very general point of view, again with particular reference to the structure of primitive language. It is obvious that a linguistic element which may appear in conjunction with the name of almost any object or situation must correspond to some common attribute, conceived, or rather felt by the primitive mind as inherent in all things, men, rivers or pots. (Just as fatherhood is the common factor unconsciously formulated in numerous holophrases.) This, and not an animistic philosophy, is the true significance of the *ubiquity* of the idea of the soul in primitive thought and language. Now the one element common to every situation in which a man may find himself

The Physical Psyche

is . . . himself. The ubiquitous nature of the element-soul must mean that it corresponds to something contributed by the observer himself to the bare perception of his surroundings.

Crawley, from a vast collection of facts which cannot be reviewed here, concludes that this universal attribute is simply the visual memory image, the copy left in the mind by every object which affects the senses. Now, however complete and accurate the copy in the mind, it must always differ from its prototype in one important respect. It is intangible. Hence the soul in primitive thought is always a thin, ethereal copy of the object or person, a 'shadow' or 'mist,' a 'vapour,' 'breath' or 'haze-being,' an 'image' or 'echo' which may be partially confused in thought with the reflection in water, with portrait reproductions, and very often with the miniature seen in the pupil of the eye.

The world of souls, then, is a private replica of Nature. It differs from Nature, not only in being intangible, but in another important respect. The 'real' objects in Nature can only be partially and indirectly controlled by the observer, but their replicas or 'souls' in the mind of the observer are controlled directly by the mind, as the creatures of a play are controlled by the dramatist, without physical intermediacy.

Primitive religion, with its magical practices, is the expression of the natural desire to widen that control from the copies to the things themselves, to traverse the bridge between the world of physical objects and the world of souls.

There are innumerable cults of the soul, and every one has flowered into its own complex ritual, its own elaborate mythology of phantoms, fairies and daemons, yet every one has its root in the fundamental fact that for every consciousness there are two worlds, the 'outer' world of objects and the 'inner' world of images: every cult, however deeply overlaid with irrelevancies, has the same object, to gain magical power over the material world through the inner world of images and ideas, the world of souls.

The Idea of the Soul in Western Philosophy and Science

That, in brief, is Crawley's interpretation of the idea of the soul. But, whether this interpretation be proved right or wrong, it is quite certain that the primitive mind does not separate the two worlds into matter and spirit, in the manner of European philosophy, or conceive of the spirit as an *anima*. For the savage, the soul is not spirit, but a special kind of matter, a rare, tenuous, even impalpable matter perhaps, but matter none the less. Hence in supposing that the primitive cults of the soul spring from an animistic philosophy, we should be expressing a fundamental truth in a misleading fashion. Magic is not philosophy.

But magic is the parent of philosophy, and of science and religion. And all these activities have one purpose in common, to gain power over the perceptual world by the manipulation of images and concepts. The sorcery of the Papuan islanders, Maori folk lore, the theology of ancient Egypt, the doctrine of the Holy Trinity, Chinese funeral customs and the theory of relativity all have their origin in the primitive philosophies which emerged from the still more primitive cults of the soul.

But, since we are concerned primarily with Western thought, only one of these philosophical traditions, that of the Greeks, is relevant to our theme. Until recently the influence of Oriental culture on Western thought was grossly underestimated or even ignored. "Except the blind forces of Nature," it has been said, "nothing moves in this world which is not Greek in its origin." That, of course, is simply an expression of Occidental arrogance. But it is nevertheless true that, even where we have borrowed from the Orient, we have more often than not borrowed through the Greeks. So that, in order to understand our own culture we must know something of the Greek cults of the soul and of the great philosophical tradition which, arising out of them, has moulded our own ideas and intellectual achievements. The unifying thread running through the history of European culture,

The Physical Psyche

whether in its religious, philosophical or scientific aspect, is the evolution of the Greek idea of the soul.

GREEK CULTS OF THE SOUL

Early Greek literature relates, although in a mythological setting different from that of Genesis, the world-wide story of the fall of man. Hesiod tells in his verses how the first god-like men of the Golden Age were succeeded by the inferior Silver race, and how after them came the yet more degenerate men of the Bronze age, and then, furthest removed from the Gods and most ignoble of all, the men of Hesiod's own day.

The beings of the far-off Golden age, after a long life of bliss on earth, became invisible Daimones, souls ruling the earth in the service of the Gods on Olympus.

It might be thought that such a myth must imply a view of the soul which, however latent or implicit, is not essentially different from, say, the Christian idea of the immortal soul. But in fact there is in Hesiod's myth no foreshadowing of later ideas of the soul.

For Hesiod ascribes no activity to the soul while the body is alive. After the death of the body the souls of the Golden race do indeed become agents so powerful that they are worshipped by men, but during the life of the body they have no such reality. The existence of the soul before death simply is not mentioned, because the idea that the soul could influence, still less control the body, had not yet occurred to the Greeks. Soul and body were not a dual being, a union of the life principle and its instrument, but separate and self-sufficient beings, each leading its own life in its own world, the body in the world perceptively known, the soul in the inner world of images and memories.

The soul worship which Hesiod describes, a practice persisting to his own day, arose no doubt in prehistoric times.

The Idea of the Soul in Western Philosophy and Science

But although the Greek cult of the soul was already old in the time of Hesiod, it was still a cult, a ritual, not a philosophy; the soul was not a speculative concept, but a dimly felt entity to be propitiated. The psyche came long before psychology.

For further evidence that the 'soul' we find in Hesiod has nothing in common with the word in its present meaning, we need only follow Hesiod's story of the ages after the Golden age. The men of the Silver age, because of their impiety and wantonness, were destroyed by the Gods and their souls were not permitted to rule on Earth. But they were allowed to reign in Hades, and as rulers of the underworld were worshipped by men. To the souls of the Bronze age even this honour was denied; they descended, unworshipped and without power, to Hades.

When we pass from the mythological period to historical times, the soul has dwindled to a feckless ghost that can do no more than twitter feebly in Hades. Thus, although great powers are ascribed to the souls of dead giants of a mythical Golden age, the souls of ordinary mortals are as negligible after as before death, images which can do little else but squeak and flit.

Hesiod's story thus leads us by transitions to the view of the soul which we find in the Homeric poems.

But between the helpless shades of Homer and the powerful souls of the Golden age there is no difference in principle. For Hesiod as for Homer the soul is a psyche in the primitive sense of the word . . . an air, or vapour, that is to say a mental image, visualised as some sort of thin material entity. A little introspection will show that it is most natural that $\psi\acute{\nu}\chi\eta$ should at first mean both 'soul' (image) and 'air,' or 'breath.' For most of us probably still picture a mental image as some sort of volatile copy, even when we know that it is 'not really' material.

Primitively, then, the soul is not in essence different from

The Physical Psyche

the body, it is just another body, less solid than the perceptual one, and therefore less potent.

Homer indifferently calls the soul an *eidolon* (image), *skia* (shadow) or a *psyche* (vapour), and these differ from the body only in being less tangible. Hence the soul is not in any sense the personality or the motive force of the body. Homer conceives of man, not as a spiritual person controlling a material body, but as two material entities, each with its own personality. Between the two personalities, that of the tangible body (or body proper) and that of the intangible (i.e. vaporous) body there is only the most slender connection. During life the soul acts only in dreams; while the body is active the *eidolon* is asleep. While the body sleeps, however, the *eidolon* may come to life and have the experiences which we call dreams. For Homer the events of dreams are real events, but they happen, not to the dreamer, but to another person . . . the *eidolon* of the dreamer.

The *locus classicus* for the Homeric view of the soul is, of course, the tenth chapter of the *Odyssey*.

Circe is giving Odysseus instructions before sending him on his long journey to the underworld:

> "Yet learn that your next journey will be to a strange destination, even so far as the House of Hades and the dread Persephone, to seek counsel of the spirit of Teiresias of Thebes, that sightless prophet whose integrity of judgement has survived death. For him, Persephone has ruled that he alone, though dead, should know: all the others of the dead are shadows that drift ineffectually."

In Hades Odysseus meets his dead mother. But she, being merely a soul, does not know her son, and he cries:

> "Before me is the ghost of my mother, dead. Lo there, how she crouches by the blood, and will not look upon me or address me one word. Tell me, King, how shall she know that I am her son?"

And he is answered:

> "Any of these ghosts of the dead, if you permit them to come near the blood, will tell you the truth."

The Idea of the Soul in Western Philosophy and Science

After she has tasted the blood of the sheep that he has flayed, in accordance with Circe's instructions, she knows her son again. Even the great Teiresias must drink of the blood:

"Stand off from the pit and put up your threatening sword, that I may drink blood and declare to you words of truth." [1]

Here we have the first glimmerings of a psychology. Or rather, an attempt to answer what we now call psychological problems, for a psychology which places no value on the psyche is hardly correctly so-called. Blood, not the soul, is thought of as the life principle. Or consciousness, νόμς, may be attributed to the midriff. Thus Achilles: "So then, ye Gods, there yet lives in Hades house a psyche and shadowy image of man, *but there is no midriff in it.*" That is, it is not alive; only the body is thought to be truly alive.

Thus, as soon as the intellect is mature enough to see psychological problems (and at this stage the soul and its cult are already ancient), the animation of the body is ascribed to a particular part of the body, not to the soul or any other non-material agency.

Homer's heroes do not of course suffer the semi-extinction in Hades that is the lot of common men. For them there is the beautiful Elysian plain, beyond the world's end, bathed in soft zephyrs from Okeanos, where with the fair-haired Rhadamanthys they dwell in immortal bliss. But their immortality is not of the soul merely, for, by the might of the Gods they are 'translated,' body and soul, to Elysium. Homer's Greeks could conceive of no real immortality without the body.

No doubt the Homeric description of the underworld is inspired by the ancient soul cults which peopled every cave with its own spirit or deity. Hades is a poetic and cosmopolitan transcription of a common element in innumerable local cults. The wider Homeric conception never quite replaced the

[1] From T. E. Lawrence's translation of the *Odyssey* of Homer.

worship of the local chthonic (subterranean) deities. But the revived chthonic cults involve no new concept of the soul, nor were they associated with any clear beliefs, for even from the earliest post-Homeric times we frequently find the view, more sceptical than anything in Homer, that nothing at all survives corporeal death.

Even the famous Mysteries, which spread from Eleusis to the confines of Greece, contained little which we should now call religious. Common belief, of course, gave the soul an everlasting but somnambulant existence in Hades. The Eleusinian Mysteries were a magic ritual to heighten the post-mortem consciousness of the soul; one might say an earthly substitute for the blood which Odysseus gave to the poor ghosts in Hades! This advantage was promised to all who would perform the required ceremonies, irrespective of moral beliefs or conduct. No moral responsibility, or indeed no power of any kind was attributed to the soul during this life.

ASIATIC INFLUENCES. THE CULT OF DIONYSOS

As early as Homer there appeared in Greece a strange God, Dionysos, who came from Egypt, or Crete, or India, but certainly not from Olympus. The extraordinary cult of the soul which he brought to the Thracian peninsula was not only to become a most powerful religious force throughout Greece: like a shuttle dancing through the ordered warp of Greek rationalism it wove through it a mysticism that was to colour the whole fabric of Western thought.

In every respect the Thracian cult was in contrast with the sober Greek worship of the Gods. For Dionysos was worshipped in dance, a mad vertigo on the mountain-tops at night. Horned, swathed in flowing fox-skins that broke the torch light into a fantastic swirl of shadows, the worshippers danced, hour after hour, until the pulse of the drums worked into the blood and the wild song of the flute, taking possession of the brain, replaced the exhausted will power and excited the limbs to a supernatural whirling.

Now the dancers enter into the divine ecstasy which is the object of the ritual. The soul, whirled free from its imprisonment in the body, soars to the celestial regions from which it came, and there enters into ecstatic union with the God. It has achieved '*enthousiasmos.*'

This strange 'enthusiastic' cult springs from the essentially Oriental doctrine of the divine origin of the soul. For the worshippers of Dionysos, the soul is no mere *eidolon*, but a captive God which can be freed from the body in orgiastic dance.

This cult of the soul, although so different from the native Greek cults, cannot be said to resemble the philosophical ideas which, arising much later in Greece, were so strongly influenced by the Dionysiac tradition. For the Dionysiac daemon, imprisoned in the body, is not in any sense the personality. Indeed, the soul, being ordinarily asleep, has nothing to do with normal activity. The use of the ritual dance was to induce the necessary abnormal conditions for the awakening of the soul.

But more important than the explicit thought is the new *way of thinking* which the cult awakened in the Greek mind. For Dionysos turned thought and ritual from the souls of the dead to the souls of the living. The soul has now become important and accessible during this life; and if it is still far from being the *anima* of later thought, it is infinitely more than an *eidolon*.

It is said by psycho-analysts that a vivid emotional experience in childhood changes the personality for life. Perhaps growing cultures are similarly moulded by the emotional crises of their youth. Certainly it is no exaggeration to say that this Oriental cult impinged on the Greeks with the intensity of an emotional storm.

Like a dervish or a cyclone the new cult danced, literally danced down the mainland through Boeotia and the Pelo-

The Physical Psyche

pennesus to the islands, sweeping valley after valley into the dance ecstasy.

Whatever the reason, Dionysos imparted to the still embryonic Greek culture an emotional twist that re-oriented its whole development. We read of men, long after the original dance madness had died down, of whole cities even, suddenly swayed by a mood as deep and mad as a wanderlust; of the strange state of κορυβαντιασμος in which visions and unearthly flutings lifted the soul to a restlessness that would not be stilled.

Wisely seeing that these new intoxications of the soul were not to be suppressed, the native priests of Apollo integrated them into their own cult by developing a ritual in which they could find outlet and expression. From the interplay of the native and the exotic cult came the new concept of purification or 'katharsis.'

The idea of katharsis is the paradoxical one that an inner malaise or disquiet of the soul can be exorcised only by drawing it out, by deliberately heightening it until it spends itself in action. In the new ritual, music was the chief kathartic of the Dionysiac power. By music it was made to discharge itself in dance, and the soul, thus finding consummation and tranquillity through action, was purified of its passion.

Although this dance ritual is in a sense little more than a revival, it is now modified, Hellenised by its new association with the idea of purification. As parents, after their death, live in their offspring, so the idea of katharsis, the child of Dionysos and Apollo, acquired its own individuality, in which the two cults were fused and perpetuated. Kathartic rituals multiplied until every event in life, birth, marriage, death, illness, bad dreams even, became linked to an appropriate ritual purification. During the centuries that led to the historic period, the Thracian cult was Hellenised almost beyond recognition, but the idea of katharsis remained in principle unaltered, although gaining in power and complexity.

The Idea of the Soul in Western Philosophy and Science

So closely had the kathartic idea welded itself into Greek life, that, in the sixth century, when the Orphics, the 'protestants' of the Dionysiac faith, founded societies for the revival of the primitive cult of Dionysos, they retained as an essential feature the rites of purification.

Orphicism arose at a most important time of transition . . . from the age of cult and mythology to the age of self-conscious philosophy. This transition is epitomised in the Orphic cosmogony, which, although less than a philosophy, is much more than a myth, despite its mythical form. Foreshadowed in it, as in the uncertain shapes of chaos on the eve of creation, are the great metaphysical problems to which Greek philosophy first gave definite form.

The Thracian God, in his earthly epiphanies still called Dionysos, but now also Zagreus, master of souls in the underworld, symbolises the Unity, or to borrow a phrase from a later age, the First Cause, underlying the apparent multiplicity of Nature. But the Unity, which is also identical with ultimate Good, is disintegrated by the forces of evil, represented in the myth by the Titans. The first disruption of Unity is symbolised by the reflection of Dionysos in a mirror given him by the Titans. Now the theme is amplified in other symbols. While Dionysos is gazing at his image, the Titans fall upon him and overpower him, although he tries to elude them by continually changing shape. In the form of a bull he is torn up and devoured. Evil has triumphed over Good: Unity is dispersed in multiplicity. But the triumph is apparent only, for Athene has snatched the heart of the bull and fled with it to Zeus. Zeus, by swallowing the heart, gives birth to a new Dionysos. Evil is only apparent: the manifold must always return to the One. Zeus then burns the Titans with his lightning, but from their ashes the first men are born. Because of the last meal of the Titans, the ashes are compounded of both Dionysos and the Titans. Therefore within man himself there is a fundamental dualism, for he partakes of both

The Physical Psyche

Titanic and Dionysiac elements, of body and soul, good and evil.

In Orphicism the dualism of the Thracian cult has acquired a moral aspect. Because of some transgression, not explained in the remaining fragments of Orphic literature, the soul is doomed to an endless Wheel of Birth, a series of purposeless incarnations and reincarnations in the bodies of animals and men.

Here we re-encounter the idea which, coming as it were between philosophy and ritual, yet extending deeply into both, forms the essential link on which depends the unity of the Orphic system.

We say 're-encounter,' because that link is the idea of katharsis which we have already met. For the teaching of Orphicism is that by katharsis the soul may escape from the monotonous round of incarnations, the evil cycle of Becoming, and, freed from the imprisoning body, attain pure Being. The restless flux of Nature which we know through our sense organs, the endless motion and multiplicity of the inorganic world and the growth and decay through which life achieves its perpetuation, in a word, all Becoming, is felt to be a mere appearance, a shifting smoke screen concealing the ultimate reality of changeless, eternal Being. Although the soul belongs to the Gods, to pure Being, it has been sucked into the vortex of appearances, caught up by the centripetal forces of Becoming from which only the centrifugal power of katharsis can whirl it free.

It is no doubt true that these ideas were felt, rather than thought, by the writers of the Orphic theogonies. Their poems were an emotional play of words around ideas as yet too unfamiliar to be caught in explicit statement. The ideas are, in the Aristotelian sense of the word, potential in the poems; their actuality will be realised later.

Thus, the soul is in every way contrasted with the body: the body is mortal, the soul immortal; the soul is one and changeless, living in a multiplicity of transitory bodies. Yet the step is not made from these particular notions to the universal concept that the soul and body are different in essence, the one material and the other spiritual, immaterial. The soul, which is good, is contrasted with the body and the Wheel of transmigrations, which are evil. But Orphicism does not infer from this that the soul is the seat of moral responsibility, an inference which would, in any case, hardly have been consistent with the idea of transmigration. (For if one soul can successively inhabit a number of different bodies, each with its own personality, it is the body, not the soul, which determines personality.) And in another respect the Dionysiac cult differs from the cult of the soul in its most primitive form: the Wheel of transmigration is a Wheel of Life. Souls inhabit all living things, but not inanimate objects. But although Orphicism thus associated the soul with life, it did not infer from this that the soul is the life principle.

It is characteristic of this age of transition that not only in the Orphic poems but even in common language there are hints of unborn ideas. For ψύχη, originally vapour or breath, is now the 'breath of life.' Breathing is the most obvious vital activity which ceases at death, and because of this, and the accident that the one word originally meant soul and vapour, the soul is now the breath of life. But, as in Orphicism, the symbols have run ahead of the ideas which they express, for no one yet dreams of making the (to us) obvious inference that the soul is the life principle.

Greek metaphysics was held in the fluid imagery of Orphicism, ready to materialise and grow, as a mass of crystals held in supersaturated solution will shower down at the least tremor of the containing vessel. The cult of souls has become charged with ideas to the point where it must crystallise into philosophy.

> La Tremouille: *And who the deuce was Pythagoras?*
> The Archbishop: *A sage who held that the earth is round, and that it moves round the sun.*
> La Tremouille: *What an utter fool! Couldn't he use his eyes?*
>
> BERNARD SHAW

CHAPTER II

Physis. The Nature Philosophers

ALREADY, in the Orphic theogonies, the nature and fate of the individual soul are becoming a lesser preoccupation, a mere aspect of a new, more abstract and grander problem that is now struggling for formulation in men's minds, the problem of the nature of ultimate reality, of the Being from which Becoming proceeds.

It is this great problem which reappears, although in a form very different from that given it by the Orphic poets, in the speculations of the so-called nature philosophers, the cosmologists of Miletos in Ionia, where, in the sixth century B.C., real philosophic and scientific thought first appeared. The distinction between Being and Becoming, between reality and appearance, which is pervasive but not explicit in the Orphic poems, emerges clearly in the speculations of the Milesians. And it is no mere accident that, historically, philosophy began with the recognition of this antithesis, for it is the beginning of philosophy in the profounder sense that it is the primal concept, the foundation, of all philosophic thought.

Precisely what is meant by saying that the object of Ionian philosophy was to discover the nature of the Being on which Becoming depends? To the modern mind it is perhaps a more intelligible way of putting it to say that the Milesians were looking for Identity in difference. That is, they felt that underlying the bewildering multiplicity of objects and processes which we call Nature, there must be one fundamental principle or essence which explains them all, a principle in the light of which all differences would be seen to be in some sense unreal, mere appearances of a fundamental reality or identity. And although the Milesian philosophies are no longer of intrinsic importance, the presupposition which underlies them, the concept of the One beneath the Many, is the most important in the history of thought, for this is the basic concept which has informed all philosophy and science down to our own day.

This may be illustrated by a concrete example from modern science. The fall of an apple to the ground, the paths of the planets and the motions of the tides are apparently different phenomena. But, as Newton showed by his concept of gravitational force, their apparent diversity can be grounded in the identity of a single law. By scientific explanation, in fact, we *mean* the demonstration of the identity in which apparent differences are united. We say that we have discovered an explanation when we have succeeded in showing that a number of apparently different phenomena are not 'really' different. And the greater the number of appearances or phenomena we can bring together within a single Identity, the greater is our intellectual satisfaction. Einstein's theory is more satisfying than Newton's, because it brings not only gravitational phenomena, but also those of inertial mass, as well as certain optical phenomena, within a unified system. In general, we may say that the aim of a scientific investigation is to produce the formal expression of identity in difference which mathematicians call an equation. In physics and chemistry this is obvious without further elucidation. But it is true even for the non-mathematical sciences. The biologist, for example, working on the anatomy of some obscure structure, has accomplished his work when he succeeds in showing that the mysterious organ in the animal investigated is merely a modification of one that is well known in other animals. A typical example of such a discovery is that the teeth of land animals are derived from

Physis

the scales of their fish ancestors. This statement, although not susceptible of expression in algebraic terms, is essentially an equation, in so far as it expresses identity within a system of apparent differences.

Two millennia of thought have shown that this desire for 'identity in difference' is the fundamental characteristic of the human intellect. The greatness of the Milesians lies in the fact that they were the first to give explicit expression to this desire. No doubt the savage mind has a strong desire to find 'explanations,' but it does not know what form it wants its explanations to take. Lacking that essential knowledge, it produces aetiological myth instead of philosophy or science. The Milesians were the first to see that the desire of the intellect is the desire to find Identity in the manifold: that is why they were the first philosophers, and why no science was possible before their advent.

Now if our desire to find Identity in the manifold corresponds to anything in the nature of reality (and the success of modern science has shown that it certainly does), then it follows that our sensory knowledge, which in itself tells us of the differences and not at all of the underlying Identity in Nature, must be in some sense illusory. The wider generalisations of science (the atomic theory is a particularly apposite example, since it is a result of the Milesian tradition which has been taken over and developed by modern science) contradict the findings of sense perception unaided by reason.

But the desire to find conceptual identity was so strong in the minds of the Milesians that when it led them to conclusions which were flatly contradicted by the evidence of their eyes, they believed in their reason and not in their senses. They steadfastly held to their basic principle that only in rational identity could the Real, or Being, be found, and that all else was mere appearance or Becoming. Their faith in this principle was all they had to support their reason against their senses. Of the experimental methods of modern science, by

The Idea of the Soul in Western Philosophy and Science

means of which rational principles may be experimentally verified, even when they appear to contradict the evidence of the senses, they knew nothing. And they knew nothing of the epistemological arguments invented by modern thinkers for the discussion of the relation between perception and Being. To-day, such arguments are quite widely, if somewhat superficially understood, for (largely through Berkeley's philosophy) they have attained popular currency. At this point it may be well to indicate, very briefly, the nature of these arguments. In doing so we shall be guilty of an anachronism. But Milesian philosophy is the seed from which all modern thought has grown, and we shall understand the root all the better by taking a surreptitious glance at the flower.

What, then, does a modern philosopher mean by the concept of the Real? Let us, in order not to remove the discussion too far from grounds which would have been familiar to the Milesians, consider physical reality, with which Ionian thought was primarily concerned.

Consider any physical object, a penny. To me, looking directly down on it as it lies on my writing table, it appears to be circular and moderately large. But to another person, viewing it from the far side of the room, it appears much smaller and not circular, but elliptical. We intuitively assume, however, that the penny cannot 'really' be both large and small, elliptical and circular. What, then, is the 'real' penny like? For the same person at different times, or for different persons at the same time, the perceptual penny is large or small, circular, or one of an infinitely numerous series of ellipses, varying from ellipses so narrow as to be little more than a straight line, to those scarcely distinguishable from a circle.[1] The perceptual penny is not one, but many things, a manifold of ellipses and circles. Yet we talk of *the* penny,

---

[1] For simplicity we have considered only the plane surface of the penny. The discussion would be complicated but unaltered in principle by bringing in the third dimension.

Physis

meaning the 'real' penny, which we somehow conceive to be one and immutable, in spite of its changing appearance.

As with the form, so with the colour of the penny. To me it is a certain shade of brown; to a colour-blind person it has quite a different colour. To my dog it has no colour; his world, like that of the early cinema, is all black and white, and intermediate greys. Often, a colour is perceptibly different, under suitable conditions, to the right and left eyes of the same person. And if we drug ourselves with santonin our whole colour perception changes. Which, of all the perceived colours, is the 'real' colour? The common-sense answer is that the real colour is that perceived by physiologically normal persons. But a very little reflection shows this to be an impossible position. For what reason have we for supposing that the sensations of colour-blind persons are less 'real' than those of 'normal' individuals? The eyes of certain insects are sensitive to regions of the spectrum which do not affect the human retina; the ears of the bat are sensitive to vibrations too rapid to affect the human ear. We must therefore suppose that such insects perceive colours, that bats perceive sounds, which for us are not 'there' at all. Compared with these insects, therefore, we are all colour blind, but our colour sense is not on that account less 'real' than theirs; it is merely different.

Questions such as these lead us to the more fundamental question underlying them: what do we mean by the 'real' penny? The answer is implicit in the above discussion. We mean the penny, not as seen by me, a fish, an insect, or Mr. Jones, but the penny as it is in itself, independently of being perceived. Not the manifold of sensations in myself and other organisms, but the one Being which we take to underlie all these appearances or becomings.

Bishop Berkeley's contention, that objects have no colour at all apart from their being perceived, has, as we have said, passed into popular thought, so that even those who, like Dr.

The Idea of the Soul in Western Philosophy and Science

Johnson, know nothing else of philosophy, are familiar with this central idea of Berkeleianism. The penny, he contended, has one colour *for* me, one *for* my dog, another *for* you. Physiologically, all these colours are the result of physico-chemical changes in the retinae of the three organisms concerned, and as such, all are equally valid, equally 'real,' but they belong to you and me and my dog, not to the penny *per se*. For if no one is looking at the penny, it is causing no changes in a retina, and hence no perception of colour. Such arguments, although now connected in popular thought with Berkeley's name, were well known to the Renaissance philosophers before him, and indeed to Plato, Berkeley's special contribution being the extension of this kind of reasoning to the so-called 'primary' qualities, notably to the attribute of 'extension.' For you the penny is elliptical, for me circular, but the penny in itself, Berkeley would have said, is neither circular nor elliptical; its 'spatiality,' like its colour, is supplied by the perceiving mind. In Kant's phrase, it is a 'form of intuition' in terms of which the real, non-spatial penny is perceived.[1] Much has been, and will be written about the problems which we have so briefly and superficially epitomised in our discussion of the 'real' and the 'phenomenal' penny. For our present purpose, however, the importance of our discussion is that it has established two points.

Firstly, that we commonly distinguish, however uncritically and naïvely, between Reality and Appearance, that on quite ordinary occasions we feel that there is one Real or Being beneath a given manifold of appearances or becomings. This is implied in the mere fact that we talk of 'the penny' and not of 'the manifold of variously coloured ellipses and circles'! Secondly, that 'scientific' thinking is based on a more critical and generalised form of this common intuition of unity within

---

[1] Kant, of course, infers the subjectivity of spatial relations from their necessity and universality, and not from the Berkeleian type of argument, of which, indeed, he is contemptuous.

Physis

diversity. The very fact that we ask 'why?', that we believe there is a reason for all things even if we only know the reasons for a few, is proof of our tacit assumption that Nature is not *merely* a manifold of isolated facts, of separate Reals, but one coherent *system* of facts, a Real in some sense one and indivisible. At the root of every scientific enquiry, no matter how difficult or abstract, is this basic intellectual desire for identity within difference; rational enquiry is always the search for the One beneath the Many. It was their faith in this primary rational principle which enabled the Milesian thinkers to translate human thought from the age of myth into that of philosophy and science. For they were the first thinkers consistently to believe, in spite of the apparent absurdities into which their belief led them, that in asking 'why?' of Nature we are asking a real question, that the facts of Nature are not separate or discrete from each other, that even if in our ignorance we take them to be so, they are in fact linked to each other in some underlying identity, and that this identity may be discovered by the human reason.

Religion, philosophy and science are all, although in different ways, concerned with this Identity, Reality or Being. For science the intrinsic nature of Being is of no interest; its task is to discover the concepts by means of which the perceptual manifold may be articulated into unity. To that end it has taken as its chief article of faith the well-known *mot* of the Franciscan philosopher: *Entia non sunt multiplicanda praeter necessitatem*, and goes on unifying more and more of the manifold in terms of ever less numerous and more general concepts. For religion the existence of the ultimate Being, which it calls God, and man's emotional reaction to his intuition of God, are the all-important facts. Philosophy, coming in a sense between science and religion, is concerned both with the nature of Being and with its relations to the manifold. Philosophy is the search for the Real: that is the great discovery which the Milesians made, the discovery which made philosophy, and ultimately science, possible. The mythologists looked for reality, for the origin of things, in the past; the thinkers of Miletos saw the origin of things in that which *is*, now, the eternal ground of becoming. Their philosophies all ask the same question. What *is* the origin of things? Thus Parmenides:

"Come . . . I shall tell thee . . . the only two ways of search that may be conceived. First, that *It is*, and that it is impossible for it not to be. This is the way of belief. Secondly, that *It is not*, and that it must necessarily not be. That is a way that none may tread, for thou mayest neither conceive nor utter that which is not; for that which can be thought and that which can exist are the same."

The '*It is*' of Parmenides is the Identity, or Real behind the manifold. If '*It is not*,' there is no Identity, and that, for Parmenides is unthinkable. Thought demands that there should be such an Identity, therefore it exists. This Identity, that which persists through the changing manifold, that which is *real* is denoted in early Greek thought by a technical term *Physis*, which may be translated Primary Substance.[1] That is to say, the Real, for the Milesians, was some kind of material stuff or substance. But they were certainly not what we should now call materialists; their Physis was not 'matter' in the modern sense of a non-spiritual substance, for the simple reason that no one had arrived at the notion of a spiritual substance; the *Psyche*, as we have clearly seen, was not that. Nor is it very helpful to call them *hylozoists*, for the name ($ὕλη$ matter, and $ζωή$ life) implies a denial of the separate reality of matter and the life principle. But no one had formed the concept of a life principle, unless indeed we say that blood was thought of as such, and as no one thought that blood was 'immaterial' or 'spiritual,' it is improbable that anyone would bother to deny it! If the Ionian thinkers must be labelled, it would be best perhaps to call them Naïve Monists, to indicate that their Monism consisted, not in the

[1] See Burnet, *Greek Philosophy*, Introduction vii.

Physis

denial of a (then non-existent) dualism, but in a simple assertion that only one Being exists.

For a time we shall hear a great deal of that Being, of Physis, and very little of the Psyche of pre-philosophic times. Later we shall find that, if the Ionian thinkers lead us away from the Psyche of the mythologies and the cults, they lead us towards a new Psyche, that of the philosophers.

Thales, the founder of the Milesian school, thought that the primary substance was water. Now water has just the properties we might expect of a primary substance, or Physis. First, it is the commonest substance in Nature; secondly, it is the most impressive example, in the whole of the natural realm, of a single substance having many appearances, of a manifold depending on a single 'real,' for it is the only familiar substance which is commonly seen in the solid, liquid and gaseous states; in addition it appears in the form of snow and hail, cloud and mist. It is necessary for life, and the main substance of all living things is watery. Further, water is practically a universal solvent, so that all things appear to be assimilable to it. And Thales, who, like the rest of the pre-Socratics, was specially interested in meteorology, must have had some conception of the circulation of water from the sea to the clouds, and thence back to the sea via rain and river.

What could have been more natural than to suppose that this multiform, ubiquitous substance, which in its ceaseless circulation through Nature included even the heavens in its ambit, was the Real that flowed through all Becoming, the Physis of which all other things were mere appearances?

There have been various speculations about the mathematical discoveries of Thales, but we cannot be sure of his precise achievements in this branch of thought. We do know, however, that one of the early Milesians, if not actually Thales, must have invented the *science* of geometry. The primitive meaning of 'geometry' is, of course, 'measurement of the earth.' And that was all it was, a series of rules of thumb for

The Idea of the Soul in Western Philosophy and Science

earth measurement, before the Greeks turned it into a science. In very early times the Egyptians had evolved a number of such rules for measuring fields and constructing pyramids, and there is no doubt that they knew a great deal of the properties of rectangles and of right-angled triangles. But they did not know why their rules were true, they did not understand, or enquire into, the rules of thought underlying their practical devices for mapping fields and building pyramid tombs. They knew, from experiments with knotted ropes, that a triangle having sides in the ratio of three, four and five is right angled, but they did not ask why this must be so. It did not occur to them that the properties of a triangle could be deduced from necessities of thought.

> "A new light flashed upon the mind of the first man (be he Thales or some other) who demonstrated the properties of the isosceles triangle. The true method, so he found, was not to inspect what he discovered . . . in the figure, and from this as it were, to read off its properties; *but to bring out what was necessarily implied in the concepts that he had himself formed a priori*, and had put into the figure in the construction by which he had presented it to himself."[1]

It was this discovery, the discovery of the concept of necessity and universality, which converted geometry from a series of rules of land measurement into the reasoned science which ultimately produced the Leibnizian calculus and Einstein's cosmology.

Anaximander, the next of the Milesians, maintained that the primary substance could not be water, or any of the specific forms of matter known to us. For, in so far as it is specific, it is limited, and the primary substance, if it is to contain the potentiality of all things, cannot be so limited. In order that it may give rise to all the substances in Nature, Physis must be more generalised than any of them; it must be a 'neutral' stuff, not partaking of any of the specificities

[1] From the preface to the second edition of Kant's *Critique of Pure Reason*, Norman Kemp Smith's translation.

Physis

of the particular stuffs we meet in Nature. Thus it cannot be moist, for, having that specificity, it could not give rise to the opposite specificity of dryness; conversely it cannot be dry, for that would preclude it from generating the moist. It must be neutral in this respect, so that both the moist and the dry may come out of it. Similarly it must be neither dark nor light, nor in any other way specifically limited. Therefore Anaximander called it *Apeiron*, the Unlimited or Boundless. The Boundless, by differentiating into pairs of opposites, heavy and light, hot and cold, gives rise to the endless specific substances of the natural manifold.

The clear insight of Anaximander's philosophy is seen again in the extraordinarily 'modern' outlook which informs his scientific explanations. He held that the earth, which he thought to be a cylinder, swings free in the Boundless, because there is no reason for it to fall one way rather than another. This means that he realised that there is no absolute up or down in space. He also discovered the true explanation of fossils. Most amazing of all, he said that all life comes from the sea, and that man must have evolved from a lower form of life. These flashes of intuition had to await two and a half millennia for their verification.

Anaximenes, the successor of Anaximander, identified the Boundless with air.[1] He said that air was a god, a statement which may appear merely fanciful, but which is in reality highly significant. It did not, of course, mean that air is a deity to be worshipped. It shows quite clearly, however, that Anaximenes was quite conscious that the personal deities of mythology had no place in Milesian philosophy; that the aim of philosophy was to explain the nature of things, not in terms of gods, but in terms of what we should call scientific principles. This point of view, that the ground of Becoming

---

[1] Theophrastos tells us that the primary stuff of Anaximenes is not unlimited, but specific, 'because he said it was air'; but this is an anachronism, for until the time of Empedocles, air was not taken to be a corporeal substance.

is immanent in Nature, is evident from the very beginnings of Ionian thought, as we may see from Thales's well-known statement that "All things are full of gods" (πάγτα πλήρη Θεῶν).

Anaximenes saw, what Anaximander did not see, or failed to see very clearly, that if all things are really made of one stuff, they can only differ from each other in one way. In a given space they may contain more, or less, of the primary stuff. Qualitative differences, such as redness and whiteness, must then be 'really' due to quantitative differences, or more correctly, to quantitative differences in the Real, differences in the tightness of packing of the primary stuff. Anaximenes said that air in its more rarefied state is fire; more tightly packed it gives water; compressed to the utmost it gives earth and stones. To-day, the belief that air is the primary stuff strikes us as very odd indeed. But that does not in the least detract from the value of Anaximenes' major postulate, that differences which are perceived as qualitative are due to quantitative differences in the Real. This postulate is the germ of the atomic theory.

A most curious, and illuminating, issue of Anaximenes' system is that his Physis, being air, is also Psyche, the breath of life. Because our souls are air, he said, they hold us together as the world is held together by the Boundless (air) encompassing it. Air is the soul of the world as it is of the living organism, and just as the world is a manifestation of air, so our own being depends on air, or soul. But the reason which led Anaximenes to say that our being depends on soul has nothing in common with the grounds on which that opinion might be based to-day.

THE DUAL PHYSIS. DIONYSOS AND THE PYTHAGOREAN NATURE PHILOSOPHY

Thus Ionian philosophy might have continued for centuries, developing its monistic assumptions. But now, by an historical

Physis

accident, the god Dionysos is to stride into the calm rationalism of Milesian thought, and henceforth philosophy dances to a different tune.

Pythagoras, a native of Samos in Ionia, fled in 532 B.C. from the Persian conquest and established himself at Kroton in southern Italy. There he found Orphic societies, and in his mind the ideas of the Milesian school mingled and fused with those of the Dionysiac cult of souls. From the union emerged a new philosophy, which, through its influence on Plato, gave rise to the main stem of European thought.

Three factors contribute to the development of the Pythagorean system; the Orphic idea of katharsis; the scientific study of music; and the Ionian tradition of the search for the Real.

With the Orphics, Pythagoras held that music purifies the soul, but he added this new idea to that of katharsis, that the most potent of all kathartics is intellectual activity. Only through philosophy, the disinterested activity of the mind, can man free his soul from the twin evils of the body and the Wheel of Birth. Katharsis, the liberation of the soul which long ago was the consummation of the dance on the mountain-tops, is now associated with the cooler activities of the reason.

The Pythagorean idea of katharsis gave a new shape to the dualism of the cult of Dionysos. From the idea that thought is the liberator of the soul came the fundamental concept of the new philosophy, that thought is *of* the soul. It is not certain that this concept, so important later in the philosophy of Socrates, was clearly in the minds of the early Pythagoreans. But there is no doubt that Pythagorean philosophy suggested the idea to Socrates.

Pythagoras' interest in music was not only in its kathartic power. His experiments with vibrating strings were the first laboratory experiments in history. By means of a sounding-board and a stretched string with a movable bridge or stop, he discovered a law of physics. The movable bridge enabled him to vary, without altering the tension of the string, the length which was put into vibration by plucking. He found that the pitch of the note is numerically related to the length of the vibrating part of the string. For instance, halving the length gives a note an octave higher; to sound the note a fifth higher the length must be decreased by a third, and so on.

To-day everyone knows what is meant by a scientific 'law' and therefore it is not easy for us to picture the effect of this discovery on Pythagoras. But twenty-five centuries ago the realm of physical law was an unknown universe. Not only were the simplest scientific principles unknown, but even the general notion of natural law was only nascent in a few contemplative and exceptional minds. Such was the world into which Pythagoras' discovery was born.

Pythagoras was that rarity, a discoverer with the vision to see the general implications of his discovery. If music, the intangible kathartic of the soul, is subject to numerical laws, then must not all Nature be so ruled? Must not all matter, and all material configurations and processes, be determined by Number? Must not Number, in fact, be the formative influence which, sculpturing raw matter, creates Form out of amorphous substance, shapes the primary stuff into the manifold we call Nature? This is the idea symbolised in the Pythagorean doctrine of *Apeiron* and *Peras*. Following Anaximander, the primary stuff is thought of as the Boundless or Unlimited, the *Apeiron*. But, for Pythagoras as for Anaximander, the primary stuff is neutral, homogeneous and formless, with nothing of the diversity, the 'manifoldness' of the matter we actually find in Nature. *Peras*, the Limit or Number, by imparting form and diversity to the featureless primary stuff, turns it into the world we know. The great question which the Milesians ignored. . . . "How does variety emerge from the formless?" is the central problem of the Pythagorean system.

Physis

"Thales or some other" had discovered how to reason about geometrical entities. In the hands of the later Ionians, Pythagoras above all, that discovery had developed into the substance of the first, second, fourth and sixth books of Euclid,[1] including, of course, the famous 'Pythagorean' proposition about the square on the hypotenuse. No wonder that the author of that proposition, discovering the mathematical laws of music, should become obsessed with Number. His hypostatisation of Number was justified in the important sense that reasoning about abstract numerical data gives us correct information about concrete events. Translated into modern idiom, that is the central idea of Pythagorean thought. To the modern mind, which does not like to mix poetry and science, the idea may not be enhanced by the half poetic, half scientific symbolism of Peras and Apeiron. But it must not be forgotten that in the time of Pythagoras, science and poetry had hardly emerged from the womb of mythology.[2]

By combining his own ideas with concepts borrowed from the Milesians, Pythagoras created a new doctrine of the Real. For instead of the one Real of the Milesians, Pythagoras presupposes two. The Pythagorean universe arises, not from a primary stuff alone, but from the interaction of *Peras* and *Apeiron*, Matter and Form. Apeiron is the passive stuff, Peras the active sculptor of the universe.

The Pythagorean system was also much concerned with ethical beliefs, which were united to the cosmological theory, in an unexpected way, through the concept of the limit, Peras. Because it creates Form, Peras is considered to be superior to Apeiron. The form created by the sculptor is, *because of its limitations*, aesthetically superior to the 'unlimited' quarry

---

[1] See G. J. Allman, *Greek Geometry from Thales to Euclid*.

[2] There is much less to be said in extenuation of those pseudo-Pythagoreans of to-day (eminent physicists) who tell us that God is a mathematician and Nature a creature of the human mind, or, more ingeniously, a set of differential equations, or most ingeniously, a bundle of pointer readings.

The Idea of the Soul in Western Philosophy and Science

from which the stuff of the form is taken. Similarly, said Pythagoras, human behaviour which is 'limited' by ethical considerations is superior to that which knows no such restraint.

Although the Pythagorean philosophy consists of two seemingly independent lines of thought, that concerning man and that concerning the cosmos, each ends in a dualism. On the one hand, the mystical body-soul dualism of the Dionysiac cult is combined with the idea of katharsis and turned into a metaphysical idea. The doctrine of Number, on the other hand, leads to the cosmological counterpart of the dualism of man, the dualism of formal and material causes.

And it is the formal cause, Peras, which is the ancestor (through Socrates and the Platonic concept of the immaterial Real) of the Christian doctrine of the soul. It is strange indeed that the most pregnant idea in European culture should spring from an Oriental cult of the soul and a string with a movable bridge.

THE FLOWING PHYSIS. HERAKLEITOS

If Pythagoras was the most significant of the pre-Socratic philosophers, Herakleitos of Ephesos was the most profound, the most fascinating, and his influence on the thought of Plato (and hence on the European tradition) was only less than that of Pythagoras. Because his mind burned with an ardour too passionate to express its thoughts in the conventional systematic form, he was called Herakleitos the Obscure. His writings are obscure for two reasons: not only because they are in the form of disconnected aphorisms, thrown up, as it were, from the poetic ferment of his mind, but also because of the nature of the aphorisms themselves, which are paradoxical:

"God is day and night, summer and winter, peace and strife, hunger and repletion";

Physis

or even frankly self-contradictory:

> "Good and evil are one."
> "It rests by changing."
> "The upward and downward directions are the same."
> "We are and we are not."
> "Fire is hunger and repletion."
> "It is the opposite which is good for us."

But the poetical and metaphorical flights of Herakleitos spring from the firm ground of logical insight; his whole philosophy is based on a simple logical discovery, which, once understood, is the key to all his paradoxical sayings.

He took from the Milesians the doctrine of the one ultimate Real; but he discovered in that concept a difficulty which they had not seen. If all the diverse forms and substances of Nature are 'really' modifications of a single primary stuff, what is it that causes the primary stuff to change into any of its modifications? If water, air or neutral stuff is the primary stuff, why does it not remain for ever in its primary condition; how does the One become the Many? Given that it does not so remain, what cause makes it leave its state of rest at *this* moment rather than *that*? We have seen that the Pythagorean system dealt with this difficulty by positing a second Real, which by interaction with the first, produced the Many from the One. But Pythagoras probably resolved this problem without seeing it, for his concept of the two Reals grew out of his mysticism of Number, not from a conscious desire to improve the logic of Ionian thought. Herakleitos, if he was to account for change within the framework of the Ionian doctrine of the one Real, was left with only two alternatives: (1) That change cannot be rationally explained, that it just happens 'when it likes' causelessly and capriciously; (2) that change *is* the Real.

The first alternative was one that could not be seriously considered by any Greek thinker: the essence of Greek thought was a passionate faith in reason, even to the extent of believing

The Idea of the Soul in Western Philosophy and Science

in rational deduction when it contradicted perceptual knowledge. What is the meaning of the second alternative . . . that Change *is* the Real? This may best be shown by an analogy. Consider a fountain. As long as the pressure of water remains unchanged, the pattern of the fountain also remains fixed. But that fixity is only apparent; it is not a static fixity, but a dynamic equilibrium between the uprush of the water and the downward pull of the earth. The fountain *rests by changing*. If it ceases to change it ceases to *be*, because change is a necessary condition of the existence of a fountain, the *essence* of a fountain. Remove the essence, and the being is removed too. If we substitute Physis, the Real, for the fountain, we have the Herakleitan doctrine of reality. Change is the essence of the Real. That is to say, change is a necessary condition of the existence of the Real, as it is of the fountain. The Real cannot cease from changing, for if it did it would simply disappear like a fountain deprived of the hydrostatic pressure which is the source of its change. Hence the philosophy of Herakleitos, far from having to explain change, which it assumes in the very quiddity of things, is faced with the converse difficulty of explaining absence of change. In the Herakleitan world fixity is an inconceivable notion; it is inconceivable for the same reason that a triangle with three right angles is inconceivable in the Euclidean world, because it is a self-contradictory notion. Therefore when we appear to observe rest, absence of motion, it must be an illusion, as the fixity of the fountain is an illusion. The pattern which we observe, like that of the flowing fountain, may remain fixed, but the Real, the ultimate stuff or Physis, must change ceaselessly, or suffer annihilation.

Hence the Herakleitan Physis must be the very epitome and symbol of flux, of perpetual change, instability, Becoming. That symbol Herakleitos found in Fire. The Herakleitan Real is a restless flame that never is (itself) but is always becoming (something else). In a still air the flame of the candle is static, but its fixity is as illusory as that of the fountain. It must burn

Physis

and change, or die. Just as one can never say of a moving object that it *is* at this or that point at a given instant, so we cannot with truth predicate anything of the Real, for it has become *that* before one may say that it is *this*. The Real is an unseizable flux of which 'It is' and 'It is not' are equally true, or false. "We are and we are not," and all our attempts at predication are fruitless attempts to write the choreography of a dance which is ever new and in which we ourselves must perforce take part.

Fire in the Herakleitan sense has a wider significance than we give the word to-day. It was not merely flame, but heat in general, and warm vapour, including the breath, ψύχη. Hence the Psyche of Herakleitos, being part of the divine World Fire, is also, like the Psyche of Anaximenes, one with the ultimate stuff, Physis. Therefore the very nature of the soul, like that of the flame, is change; the pattern of the soul, like that of the fountain or the flame, is alive; it is a dynamic tension of warring opposites; it rests by changing. The flame of life must be incessantly fed, and must as incessantly consume itself, for only through self-destruction can it live: *it is the opposite which is good for us*: like the water of the fountain, it must strive upwards, but the striving must always be defeated, and out of that perpetual flux of assault and defeat arise the perfection and living tension of the soul.

"Homer was in error when he said, 'Would that there might be no more strife among Gods or men.' He did not understand that he was praying for the annihilation of the world, for were his prayer answered, all things would vanish."

It is in the writings of Herakleitos that the word Logos is first used in the special philosophical sense which later was to be of such importance in the shaping of Christian philosophy. The ordinary meaning of the word, is of course "word, speech, discourse or reason."[1] Now Herakleitos tells us that it is not he who speaks in his writings, but the Logos, speaking through him and using him as an instrument. That is to say, he is

[1] *Oxford English Dictionary*.

thinking of the Logos, not just in its ordinary sense, as the faculty of reason possessed by himself or any other individual man, but in the philosophical sense of a divine force from which all individual men derive the power of reason. "There is," he tells us, "but one wisdom, to know the knowledge by which all things are guided through all."

It is reasonable to see the origin of this notion, or at least some hint of it, in the Pythagorean doctrine that all things are ruled by Number. Both the Pythagorean Number and the Herakleitan Logos are in a sense similar to the conception of 'natural law' in modern science. The 'laws' of physics, like the ultimate principles of Pythagoras and Herakleitos, constitute an immanent order which is in conformity with, and accessible to, human reason. If we find that the behaviour of the external world is such that we may predict it by the use of reason, this means that in some way human reason is an aspect of an immanent principle which regulates the whole universe. It is this principle which Herakleitos calls the Logos. "All things come to pass by way of the Logos." But he does not think of the Logos, as would a modern thinker who talked of immanent Reason, as an immaterial principle. In fact, he identified the Logos with the ultimate *stuff*, Fire, as we may see from his comparison of the soul with a mass of glowing embers which glows more brightly when it is near the divine Fire, but ceases to glow if taken away. The Logos, then, is not only the ultimate unity, in which all opposites are reconciled, but the ultimate rational, yet material force which regulates the Cosmos.

No philosophy of any worth can arise merely from reasoning about the nature of things. As well might one sit down to reason out an ode. Philosophy, like poetry, must spring from a personal vision of the kind that no amount of mere learning, or thinking, can produce. Few philosophers have been inspired by so intense a vision as that of Herakleitos, a vision so vivid and personal that it is more akin to the mystic's than that of most philosophers.

Physis

THE STATIC PHYSIS. ELEATIC PHILOSOPHY

It is in keeping with the paradoxical nature of all we know of Herakleitos that, by following out the logical implications of Ionian monism, he should have arrived at the antithesis of that doctrine. Faced with the alternatives of spontaneous or inhesive change, he chose the latter. But there was a third alternative which he did not consider. The philosophy of his successor, Parmenides of Elea, is based on that alternative, namely, that there is no real change, that our apparent perception of change is always illusory. Now this postulate is really the logical outcome of the Milesian doctrine of the One underlying the manifold. Herakleitos, reasoning that if the One is, and if change is real, then the One is change, was thereby led to the paradox that the One both is and is not. Unless we deny the reality of either the One, or of change, we must accept the Herakleitan paradox, if not exactly as he propounded it, then in some other form. The Herakleitan antinomy is but the explicit expression of a contradiction latent in the theories of all his predecessors. We have seen, for instance, how Anaximenes tried to derive the manifold from the One by his theory of condensation and rarefaction, which asserts that the apparently qualitative differences of the manifold are due to quantitative differences in the One, to differences in its density or tightness of packing. He failed to notice that, if the One is to be more tightly packed in some places than others, it must have parts which can be loosely or tightly interrelated:

DIAGRAM I

If, however, it has parts, it is no longer one, but many (atoms). And this, of course, is a restatement of the Herakleitan antinomy. Therefore, if we rigidly and unequivocally hold to the idea of the One, we must follow Parmenides and say that it is a continuum. It cannot have parts; therefore there can be no empty space, and therefore no motion, since a moving body must have space into which it may move. And this illusory nature must apply to motion in the very widest, in fact in the Aristotelian sense of the term. In the continuum of Parmenides there can be no growth or decay, or change of any kind.

Now, not only the monism of Parmenides, but all the theories we have considered, have this in common, that they reject the evidence of the senses as at least partially unreal. If the view that the world is air or neutral stuff conflicts with our perceptions, still more so does the Herakleitan conception of a fluent Real, and the static physical plenum, in which all change is illusory, is so patently and flagrantly contradicted by the evidences of the senses that, on this ground alone, one is tempted to reject it as what a certain modern philosopher would call a 'silly theory.'

But we must not forget that the denial of the reality of the sense manifold, which appears in such an acute form in Eleatic thought, is the outcome of an authentic attempt to grapple with a very real intellectual problem, the problem of the ontological status of the perceptual or phenomenal world. Any attempt to resolve this problem is bound in some way to incorporate the fact that the brown ellipse given in sense perception is *in some sense* dependent on the observer, and to that extent, therefore, 'illusory.' And the appearance we call motion is, presumably, dependent on the observer in just the same way as other physical appearances. But in exactly what sense perceptual appearances are dependent on the observer is still, of course, a fundamental problem over which philosophers may and do differ. The phenomena given in perception

Physis

cannot, however, be dismissed as *merely* illusory; even the grossest hallucination—the pink rat seen by the drunkard—is not *merely* illusory, for since people really do have such sense data, they are perfectly real sense data. Therefore the philosophical problem of perception is to discover in just what sense the phenomenal world is illusory, although not merely illusory. The Eleatic concept of the static Physis is inadequate, therefore, not because it asserts the unreality of motion, but because it is content to assert its mere unreality, without analysis of the concept of 'reality.' As a theory of the ontological status of phenomena the Eleatic theory is not so much fallacious as incomplete; it stops short just where a modern philosopher would begin. And this, considered in the light of the history of thought, is understandable enough; the important fact about the Ionian thinkers is not that they gave inadequate answers to modern philosophical problems, but that they had the genius to discover those problems for us.

As it happens, Parmenides' method of stating the doctrine of the static Physis does seem to involve fallacious, or at least ambiguous, beliefs, for it would appear that he regarded the universe as a *physical* continuum. We know this, because he said it was a sphere,[1] for the reason that a sphere *is* equally in all directions. If, for example, it were not a sphere but an ellipsoid, there would *be* more of it along the long than the short axis, and this would lead us back to some form of the Herakleitan paradox. Now the universe may well be a continuum of some kind, but it can hardly be a physical continuum, otherwise our perceptual knowledge, in which Nature appears as a collection of separate material objects, would be a *mere* illusion.

Faced with the concepts (1) that the One is a continuum,

---

[1] Or at least that it was '*like* a sphere.' The analogical nature of this phrase may, as some have contended, indicate that Parmenides was reaching towards the idea of an immaterial soul.

The Idea of the Soul in Western Philosophy and Science

and (2) that the material world is not a continuum, Parmenides should have inferred that the One must be immaterial. He does not appear to have made that inference. We must always bear in mind, however, that for Parmenides and his predecessors the One was not material in the modern significance of 'non-spiritual,' for such a distinction had not been made. Parmenides held that only that which can be thought can *be*, and in that sense at least it may be said that his One was spiritual. But until this distinction was made, philosophy was incapable of further advance. Eleatic monism was not only the logical culmination of the Ionian tradition but the cul-de-sac in which it ended.

The Eleatic position may in fact be summarised in Parmenides' brief aphorism ἔστιν εἶναι, 'That which is, is.' This proposition rivals in terseness the products of Chinese literary art, but, as the culmination of a century and a half of thought, it may be considered a disappointment. However, this philosophical impasse was only temporary, and on the road to it the Ionians had arrived at conceptions which lived on not only in Greek thought, but survive to-day in European thought.

THE PLURAL PHYSIS. THE DECLINE OF THE MILESIAN TRADITION

Parmenides had raised an impenetrable wall across the hitherto uninterrupted path of the monistic-physical tradition. For a period, philosophy became as it were a groping around that wall, a groping towards the Platonic philosophy that lay beyond. As if here and there a ray penetrated some chink in the wall, the philosophy of this time is full of isolated illuminations, flashes premonitory of Plato.

The dialectic of Parmenides left only two immediate alternatives for speculation. Either philosophy must abandon the idea of the One, that is, become pluralist, or, on the other hand,

Physis

base itself on the idea of an immaterial, non-physical Real. In fact, the monistic position was abandoned, to be replaced, not by simple pluralism, but by pluralism trying to reconcile itself with those premonitions, to which we have referred, of a new approach to philosophical problems.

Physical pluralism originated in Empedocles' doctrine of the 'elements.' An element, according to Empedocles, is a being which cannot be transformed into anything other than itself; it can be mechanically mixed with other elements, but is itself unchangeable. That is to say, an element has the same nature as the One of Parmenides; it is real, immutable and eternal. But in place of the One, Empedocles has four Beings or elements. Three of these, Fire, Air and Water, we have already encountered; to these Empedocles added Earth. The manifold arises, not by condensation and rarefaction of the One Real, a conception which Parmenides had shown to be untenable, but by the intermingling, in various proportions, of the four 'Reals.'

Since an element cannot change into another, Empedocles postulated that the elements are full of pores, so that they can interpenetrate mechanically. This conception was further developed by Democritus, who said that the elements were divided, not by pores, but into numerous particles or atoms, so small that they cannot be separately distinguished by the eye. Each atom is like the One of Parmenides. Within it there can be no motion or change of any kind. From this it follows that an atom is impenetrable and indivisible. The (apparently qualitative) variety of the manifold is due to the combinations of pattern into which the atoms may be arranged.

We have briefly indicated the rise of atomism, although it is rather away from our main theme, because of its peculiar interest in the history of human thought. The atomic theory was taken over by Galileo and Dalton from the Greeks and, as everyone knows, has since been amply verified by experi-

The Idea of the Soul in Western Philosophy and Science

ment. The Greeks, however, did not arrive at it by experiment, but by a process of reasoning based on the minimum of observation. Moreover, the reasoning was of the type which, since Aristotle, has been called metaphysical. It is difficult to see how it could have been otherwise. From mere observation no one would suppose matter to be atomic, and until the theory was formulated no one could devise experiments to verify it. If such historical examples were kept in mind, one might hear less of the prevalent notion that philosophy should become merely the logic of the special sciences.

Despite its great importance as a 'scientific' theory the atomic theory is in philosophy a forgotten backwater of thought. Nor must we suppose that the atomists were entirely satisfied with their physical pluralism; for there are many signs that they were striving towards the idea of an immaterial Real.

Empedocles, for example, supposed that the elements were mixed and separated by the cosmic forces of Love and Hate. Love brings the atoms together, Hate draws them apart. The variety of the manifold is created out of the interplay of these two forces in the four elements. It is curious that at this time philosophy should have been so near, and so far from the notion of a spiritual principle. In spite of their names, Love and Hate in the philosophy of Empedocles are not spiritual, as we know from the fact that he discusses their spatial dimensions, and even their weight, compared with the corresponding properties of the four elements.

In the speculations of Anaxagoras we find the same half-formulated dualism. Like Anaximenes, Anaxagoras supposed that the manifold arises from a separation of opposites in a primordial matrix. This separation he attributes to the activity of an all-ruling Nous or Reason. The Nous imparts a rotary motion to the primordium, and the opposites are 'centrifuged out,' as it were, at various places on the great whirling mass. But, like the Love and Hate of Empedocles, the Nous of

Physis

Anaxagoras is only quasi-spiritual, for Anaxagoras talks of it in specifically material terms.

Despite their vague and ambiguous character these speculations are really a great advance on anything that preceded them, for, with the possible exception of Pythagoras, no one had yet even tried to form the idea of anything but a purely physical principle.

"The world and life are one."

LUDWIG WITTGENSTEIN

CHAPTER III

The Pythagorean and Ionian Conceptions of the Psyche

OF the products of Ionian thought, one of the most important was its concept of the Psyche. This is unexpected, because, as we have seen, the Ionians were not primarily, or indeed hardly at all, interested in the Psyche; their interest was not psychological but cosmological. What is the ground of Becoming *in Nature*, was always the question they asked. But it was just on account of their intense and all but exclusive interest in cosmology that the Ionians gave a novel orientation to the concept of the Psyche. For when they did happen to enquire into the nature of the Psyche, they invariably saw this question as a subsidiary aspect of their major preoccupation with Being. That is to say they always, as a matter of course, regarded the Psyche as a part of Physis, the eternal Being of Nature.

In the philosophy of Anaximenes, air is the Physis of Nature and also the Psyche of the organism. But it is only secondarily the latter; primarily it is the ontological ground of phenomena. Because the thought of Anaximenes, in common with that of the other Ionian thinkers, proceeded from the idea of the Being underlying phenomena, the Psyche became the Being and cause of animation of the body. As in Nature all process has its origin in Physis, so the activity of the organism springs from its Psyche. The Psyche has become the life principle. But it is still very different indeed from present-day (e.g. Christian) conceptions of the soul as a life principle, not only because the Ionian Physis is first the life principle of Nature

Pythagorean and Ionian Psyche

and only derivatively that of the organism, but also because it is a material life principle. After these distinctions have been made, however, the central fact remains that the Psyche of Milesian thought is an organic life principle, and that the Milesians were the first to formulate this idea. This is the idea implied in the famous statement of Thales that the magnet and amber have souls, because they attract, or as it were, animate, other bodies. The Psyche is here conceived, not merely as the principle animating living bodies, but as the universal principle of natural animation. Only in the light of such a world view could Anaximander have ventured to propound his theory of organic evolution, which, in common with modern biological theory, held that life first arose in and from the sea, and that land vertebrates, including ourselves, are descended from fishes. Now a theory of this kind is very difficult to reconcile with a supernatural view of the soul, as was shown by the ecclesiastical opposition to the Darwinian theory. The essence of the supernatural view of the Psyche is that it must insist on a fundamental discontinuity between the living organism and the rest of Nature, or even (in its Cartesian form, for instance) between the human organism and the rest of animal life. But the concept of organic evolution fits very readily into the 'natural' Ionian view of the Psyche. Indeed, it may almost be said to follow logically from the Ionian metaphysics: Anaximander's theory was something more than a fortuitous guess.

As with the 'air' of Anaximenes, so with the Herakleitan Fire. Fire is the eternal Being and the soul is just a fragment of the universal Fire, imprisoned in the body. Its imprisonment, however, is only partial. Just as the Pneuma or 'Air-Psyche' of Anaximenes is a cosmic reservoir which maintains a constant (respiratory) circulation through the organism, so the Herakleitan 'Fire-Psyche' maintains communication with its mother, the external Fire or Logos. It does this partly through the intermediacy of the sense organs and partly

The Idea of the Soul in Western Philosophy and Science

through respiration. The life of the soul depends, not only on this communion with the Logos, but on a balanced 'tension of opposites' within itself. This tension is conceived, however, in purely material terms, as a balance between fire and water.

It is pleasure to the soul to become moist, but excess of pleasure is evil. For instance, the drunkard has so moistened his soul that he loses his normal faculties and may then be 'led by a beardless boy.' Carried beyond a certain point, moistening of the soul puts out the inner fire, causing death. But excess of fire is also fatal. The fiery death, however, is a noble one, the death accorded to those who die bravely in battle. Through such a death man becomes god-like, for then the soul, leaving the body in the form of fire, is reunited with the divine Logos. This death is contrasted with the ignoble end of those whose souls perish from excess of moisture; such souls sink miserably into the earth.

But although material, the Herakleitan Psyche is a real life principle, for it is only in virtue of the Psyche, or inward Fire, that we have intelligence and life; the soul is like a heap of embers, glowing in the radiant warmth of the divine Fire. In sleep, the sense organs no longer mediate between the Logos and the individual Psyche, and the Psyche, now maintained only by the residual activity of respiration, glows dimly, suspended as it were between life and death.

In the Pythagorean philosophy, the psychology does not spring from the cosmology with the same inevitability as in the Milesian doctrines. Indeed, the central doctrine of the Pythagorean system, that the soul differs from the body in having a divine origin, is borrowed from the Orphic-Dionysiac cults. To this, however, the Pythagoreans added the important idea that thought, being the most perfect, or god-like, activity of the organism, is of the soul. Like the Ionians, the Pythagoreans were primarily concerned with problems of cosmology. On account of this, perhaps, they failed to see the

Pythagorean and Ionian Psyche

full potentialities of their concept of the Psyche. Even its dualistic implications appear to have been only dimly understood, as we may see from the Pythagorean doctrine (derived, like so much else in Pythagorean thought, from musical and mathematical studies) that the soul is a harmony or attunement of the bodily functions. In the sense that it is an attunement, or numerical harmony, but not in any wider sense, the Pythagorean Psyche may be said to be an immaterial being.

Thus the Ionian and the Pythagorean traditions have each given birth to a new concept of the Psyche, and each of these concepts differs from the Psyche of primitive cult and mythology. Also, each contributes something to the Psyche of later philosophical tradition. On the one hand, the Pythagorean Psyche, although quasi-immaterial, is not a life principle; the Milesian Psyche, on the other hand, is a life principle, but not an immaterial, or spiritual being.

The Ionian Nature philosophy has now worked itself out. In atomism there were hints of new developments, but these were the last flickerings of a dying tradition, an uncertain mirage of the new regions towards which philosophy was going.

By the fifth century many of the conceptions of the Milesians were passing into popular thought. This may have been largely helped by the philosophy of (the Cretan) Diogenes, of which the central principle, taken from Anaximenes, is that air is the life principle. Diogenes was a skilful interpreter, rather than a leader, of popular thought, for everyone had by then assimilated the idea that air is the soul and the life principle, and that when we die we give back our souls to the upper air whence they came. That this was virtually a canon of popular belief we can infer from the fact that it was not only a favourite sentiment for inscription on private tombs, but that it even appeared in an official epigram, that in memory of those who fell at Poitidea:

The Idea of the Soul in Western Philosophy and Science

αἰθὴρ μὲν ψύχας ὑπεδεξάτο, σώματα δὲ χθὼν

(Their souls to the Air, their bodies to Earth return . . .)

This was also the epitaph of the Milesian thinkers, written not on stone, but on the mind of the Greek man in the street, and on the development of European culture.

> "*There is surely a piece of divinity in us, something that was before the elements, and owes no homage under the sun.*"
> SIR THOMAS BROWNE

CHAPTER IV

The Spiritual Psyche. Socrates

WITH the death of the Ionian tradition philosophical speculation did not cease, but it took on a completely new orientation. The Ionians had been primarily interested in Nature, and only secondarily in man: for their successors the proper study of mankind was man. Philosophers were no longer nature philosophers, but students of human institutions and morals, 'Sophists.' The reason for this change of interest is to be found in the Ionian tradition itself. From the outset it had been implicit in the principles of Ionian thought that sense perception gives us no knowledge of the 'real' outside world; towards the end that implication became increasingly explicit. And the Sophists, lacking the genius to find a more valid basis for knowledge, seized on the purely sceptical aspect of this position. If the world of sense perception is not the real 'external' world, it is at least the real *human* world. If we cannot know things in themselves, or find outside ourselves any fixed or objective standards by means of which we may test the validity of our ideas, then let us be frankly anthropocentric, let us take as the basis of our speculations, not an inaccessible Being outside ourselves, but . . . ourselves. The saying of Protagoras the Sophist that 'Man is the measure of all things' must have come from some such train of thought as this. This famous saying has been the subject of much commentary and argument, but there seems little doubt that it means that absolute truth is unattainable by the human mind, that at most we can arrive only at conceptions which are socially workable, and in that sense, the purely pragmatic sense, 'true.'

Scepticism may be of two kinds. There is the scepticism which is the result of a desire to avoid hard thinking. Most of the Sophists, who were less interested in abstract truth than in their fees for instructing the youth of Athens in 'virtue,' were sceptical in this facile sense. There is also, however, a scepticism which springs from a real desire for truth, based on a determination to accept nothing that will not bear critical examination. The scepticism of the greatest of the Sophists, the famous Socratic irony, was of this deeper kind.

There are few figures of Socrates' fame about whom so little is certainly known. We may at least, however, from Aristotle's evidence, suppose that the aim of his philosophy was to define ethical universals, such as justice and courage, by means of a dialectical method. And although Socrates left no writings, we may be reasonably sure that the nature and scope of his thought are truly represented in Plato's early dialogues, particularly since Xenophon, a very different personality from Plato, gives us a substantially similar impression of the Socratic dialectic. Not only is the subject-matter of the Socratic dialectic always ethical, but the argument itself, whatever aspect of ethics it relates to, always conforms to the same general pattern. The discussion starts with an attempt to define some ethical concept. Justice, for example, is held to consist in not practising deceit.[1] It is then shown that the definition holds only for a limited number of concrete instances. For instance, it must be allowed that it is not unjust to employ deceitful tactics against an invading army. The definition is then modified to meet the objection. Justice consists in not deceiving one's friends. But, by testing it against a still wider range of examples, the second definition is also broken down. Consider the action of a father who deceives his ailing son by concealing medicine in his food:

[1] The examples are from Xenophon and from the *Republic*.

The Spiritual Psyche

such deceit is surely justifiable; similarly it would be just to deceive a homicidal maniac, searching for his victim.

So the dialectic proceeds; definition after definition is suggested and refuted, until it becomes clear that every attempt at abstract definition of justice, or of whatever ethical universal is under discussion, is inadequate when tested against the concrete variety of human experience. Now we do not meet the same difficulty in defining all universals. Swiftness, to take an example of a non-ethical universal, is always 'the accomplishment of many things in a short time' whether it be swiftness in running, learning, speaking or anything else.[1] Justice consists sometimes in honesty, sometimes in deceit; sometimes it is more courageous to fly from the enemy than to hold one's ground. But swiftness does not sometimes consist in the accomplishment of few things in a short time.

Socrates' solution of the dilemma is that, whereas a universal like 'swiftness' is derived from simple observation, the moral universals are *concepts* grounded in objective *knowledge*, on an intuitive grasp of *meaning* which is ultimate in the sense that it cannot be stated in terms of anything but itself. Just as the percept 'yellow,' as given in sensory experience, cannot be described in terms of anything else, so the concept of justice is given to the mind. To define justice is like trying to explain what yellow is like to a person born blind: the concept 'justice' is as ultimate for the mind as the percept 'yellow' is for the senses. An infinite variety of different actions may be informed by the same meaning, but it is impossible to know the identity common to those actions until we have grasped that meaning. Consider, for example, the great variety of actions performed by the doctor in the exercise of his science. It would be futile to try to find the identity in that manifold of actions by mere observation (as we would find the common factor 'swiftness' by observation of change) unless we had

[1] See the Laches, where Socrates asks for a definition of courage modelled on this definition of swiftness.

already grasped the meaning of the concept 'health.' The difference is not merely one of complexity, but of principle, for the actions of the doctor do not invariably result in health, but swiftness is invariably the accomplishment of many things in a short time. And the doctor cannot restore health by following a stereotyped set of rules; it is necessary that he should have grasped the *concepts* he was taught as a medical student. The identity in his actions springs from the application of those conceptual principles; it is not in his actions, *qua* physical actions, but in the knowledge which informs them. Sometimes he may bleed a patient, sometimes transfuse new blood into him, sometimes prescribe rest, sometimes exercise, sometimes give stimulants, sometimes soporifics, but the knowledge which leads him to do all these different things is a real unity. Similarly, the identity in a given number of examples of justice is not this or that action (e.g. deceit or its opposite), but the knowledge which informs the actions.

It will be seen that the Socratic dialectic has this in common with Ionian metaphysics, that it is the search for unity in diversity, identity within manifoldness. But there is this fundamental difference between Ionian and Socratic thought. The Ionians sought for *physical* unity in difference: Socrates was concerned with *conceptual* unity in difference. It is a conceptual, not a physical unity, which informs the manifold actions of the doctor, or the manifold of apparently diverse actions which we call just. Socrates' great contribution to philosophy is the discovery of the concept. And the concept is a spiritual unity, an immaterial Identity in difference, the One within the Many which the Ionians vainly sought in matter, in Physis. The Socratic concept is, moreover, the first appearance in European thought of the idea of a non-material, spiritual entity as we understand that idea to-day. The nature philosophers, for all their intellectual brilliance, never quite succeeded in discovering this idea, although, it was struggling for formulation, in the minds of Anaxagoras and others, in the last days of the

The Spiritual Psyche

Ionian tradition. In the *Phaedo*, for example, we read how Socrates, as a young man, fell in love with 'science' (i.e. nature philosophy) and worried himself

"with all kinds of problems, such as whether it is blood that makes all things possible, or whether it is air or fire, or perhaps none of these things but rather that the brain produces knowledge from the various perceptions that it generates. . . . In the end, however, I only became convinced that I had no aptitude for such speculations. Indeed they seemed merely to cloud my mind, so that I became involved in confusion even over the simplest questions. . . .

"But one day I heard a man reading from a book, written, he told me, by Anaxagoras, in which it was asserted that everything is ruled by Intelligence. Now here was an idea which enchanted me; in Anaxagoras, I thought, I have really found what I am after. . . ."

But Socrates did not find what he hoped for in the philosophy of Anaxagoras,

"For, as I read through the works of this man, I found that he made no use at all of a ruling Intelligence, but purported to explain everything in terms of air, ether and water, and similar infantile notions. It was just as if someone were to say 'The actions of Socrates are ruled by his Intellect' and were then to describe my behaviour at the moment by saying 'Socrates is now sitting here because of the properties of his bones and sinews, of which his body is constructed. The bones, sinews and sockets are arranged in such and such a way, and the nerves, by relaxing and tightening the bones, have brought him into his present posture.' Or again, it was as though he should explain in the same way the reason why I am talking to you now, saying it were all due to sound, air and acoustics, and completely ignoring the real reason, namely that the Athenians have seen fit to condemn me, and that it seems to me best that I should submit to their sentence. For, heavens above, these bones and sinews of mine would long ago have arrived in Megara or Boetia, *propelled there by the concept of that which is best*, had it not seemed to me more just and honourable to submit than to run away. . . ."

Or it was as if Anaxagoras should purport, like a modern behaviourist, to explain the manifold actions of the doctor in terms of the physical chemistry of the doctor's nerves and muscles, 'completely ignoring the real reason,' namely, that the physical diversity of the doctor's actions is ruled by the spiritual, or conceptual unity which we call volition, or, as Socrates puts it, by 'the concept of that which is best' for the health of the patient.

The *Alcibiades*, a dialogue which, although probably not Platonic, was used by the Academy as an introduction to Socratic philosophy, devotes considerable attention to showing that our knowledge of good and evil, that is, of ethical universals, is not acquired but innate. Looking back on our lives, the argument goes, we cannot remember any precise time when we acquired a knowledge of good and evil. Nor do we learn the concept of Justice, as we learn to speak, from our teachers. About the meaning of the words of our language everyone is agreed. "Do the people appear to differ as to what is stone and what wood?" asks Socrates. But about what is just and unjust there is no such unanimity:

> *Socrates*: But upon questions of justice and injustice, how bitterly they differ I know well. . . . Did not battles and deaths take place among the Greeks and Trojans, and amongst the wooers of Penelope, and Ulysses on account of just such a difference?
>
> *Alcibiades*: You speak what is true.
>
> *Soc.*: Shall we say then that those persons had a knowledge on the question about which they differed with such vehemence?
>
> *Alc.*: It appears not.
>
> *Soc.*: Do you not then refer to teachers of such a kind, as you confess yourself to know nothing?
>
> *Alc.*: I seem to do so.[1]

Our social environment, then, does not cause, although it occasions, our knowledge of good and evil. Particular social happenings lead us to compare our intuition of universal justice with the degree of justice of any particular happening: similarly, the doctor would not know how to set about his work unless his innate ability to grasp concepts had been brought into relation with observation of the human body.

We are now in a position to summarise the Socratic doctrine of ethical universals. Ethical universals are real; we know

---

[1] From the translation by George Burges, Bohn's Classical Library.

The Spiritual Psyche

quite well what we mean by justice, courage and so forth. Yet they evade formal definition. This is because goodness is knowledge. In the exercise of any science, the actions of the 'scientist' take the most diverse forms, and these actions are only comprehensible in terms of the concepts (i.e. knowledge) of the science. When we say that goodness is knowledge, we mean exactly the same as when we say that chemistry or mathematics is knowledge, namely, that goodness is a principle of thought, a concept, which explains actions in the sphere of morals, just as knowledge of the conceptual principles of chemistry explains the actions of the chemist. The ability to know good from evil, however, is not acquired, but innate knowledge.[1]

Now it is from this doctrine of the concept, which as we have seen is a spiritual, not a physical, identity in difference, that Socrates derives his idea of the Psyche. Already the material or physical Psyche of the Ionian philosophers (and in particular the Air-Psyche of Anaximenes) was beginning to be looked on as the cause of life, and hence of consciousness. It was therefore quite natural for Socrates to suppose that not only our ordinary consciousness, that is to say our knowledge of the material world, but also this new kind of knowledge which he had discovered, comes to us from the Psyche. Hence Socrates conceives the Psyche as the controlling power, not merely of the physiological functions which we call 'life,' but also of our moral concepts. And since the Socratic Concept is not physical but spiritual, the Socratic Psyche, because it is the seat of conceptual knowledge, is a spiritual being. The Psyche of primitive thought and of the Greek culture of the soul, even the Ionian Psyche, are material principles: the Socratic Psyche is truly spiritual, the first clearly formulated idea of a non-physical being. As such it is

---

[1] The Platonic doctrine of *anamnesis* (which may, of course, be Socratic in origin) breaks down even this distinction between moral and scientific knowledge, maintaining that all knowledge is really innate.

The Idea of the Soul in Western Philosophy and Science

only less epoch-making than the Ionian principle of Identity in difference. Indeed, it is through the Socratic idea of a spiritual Psyche that this principle was transformed into the basic concept of all subsequent religious and philosophical thought in Europe, the concept of the immaterial Real.

Now, as Plato is always insisting in the Socratic dialogues, moral consciousness is a highly individual matter. Because he so clearly realises this, Socrates conceives of the soul as a *personal* being, in marked contrast with the universal 'nature-soul' of Ionian thought. Differences in moral outlook and behaviour, he maintains, are due to the varying capacities of our souls for moral knowledge. We do not choose the good or evil course; if we do not follow the good, it is not that we have consciously chosen the bad, but because we have not really (i.e. clearly) seen the good. If the Psyche has very little knowledge of the ethical universals our moral behaviour will be imperfect, just as the performance of a chemist would be inadequate if his grasp of the principles of chemistry were incomplete.

Of course, Socrates' theory of the soul was not entirely grounded in his discovery of the Concept, although that discovery is the crucial element of his metaphysics. We have already seen that the Socratic idea of the Psyche is in one aspect an extension of the Ionian view; the Psyche of Ionian philosophy is the seat of ordinary consciousness, the Socratic Psyche possesses, in addition, moral consciousness.

There is little doubt, too, that the Dionysiac-Pythagorean view of the Psyche must also have influenced the Socratic conception. It will be recalled that the Dionysiac soul, unlike the Ionian, was individual; each of us has within us a soul which is really a separate person, the separate personality of the soul being symbolised in the notion that it is a fallen god, held captive in the body. But because it is a *separate* person, the Dionysiac soul, although individual, is not personal; it is not, that is to say, our own personality. Also (and here again

The Spiritual Psyche

it differs from the Ionian Psyche), the soul of Dionysiac cult is not the life principle; on the contrary, the highest intensity of life could only be attained by voluntarily losing one's soul

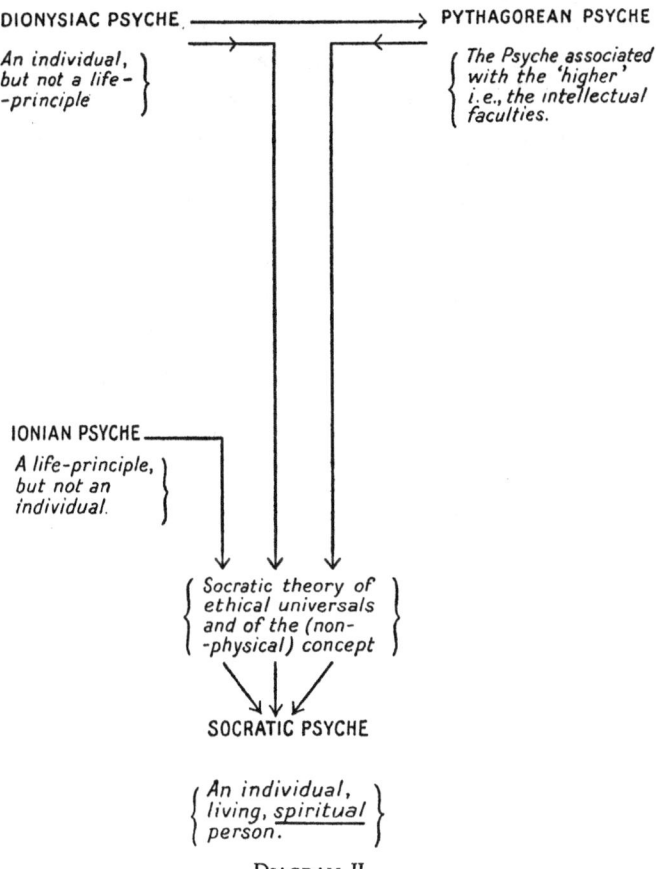

DIAGRAM II

in the dance ecstasy. The Socratic conception of the soul takes from Ionian thought the idea of the life principle, from the cult of Dionysos the notion of individuality. In the Pythagorean development of the Dionysiac view we find a further suggestion of the Socratic theory. The doctrine of katharsis, which had

The Idea of the Soul in Western Philosophy and Science

its origin in the dance ecstasy, was transformed by the Pythagoreans into the idea of intellectual katharsis, and from this came the Pythagorean notion that the soul is associated with the 'higher' or intellectual capacities of man. To Socrates, who regarded moral, rather than purely intellectual faculties as the highest, this would no doubt suggest the association of the soul with moral intuition. But the Socratic idea of the soul, although in one sense a synthesis of these earlier views, is an organic synthesis, not a mere mechanical eclecticism. As an organism creates itself out of materials taken from the environment, so the dead ideas which Socrates takes from earlier thought are transformed, through his discovery of the Concept, into a new and living whole.

The Psyche has become the living, individual and *spiritual* entity, the 'personality' which uses the body as its instrument.

Soc.: This, then, I was lately asking, whether the person, who uses a thing, seems to you always to be different from the thing which he uses?
Alc.: He seems so.
Soc.: What, then, shall we say of the shoemaker? That he cuts with his tools only, or with his hands likewise?
Alc.: With his hands likewise.
Soc.: He uses them too.
Alc.: Yes.
Soc.: And does he not use his eyes too, when he is cutting leather?
Alc.: He does.
Soc.: Now we are agreed, that the person who uses, is different from what he uses.
Alc.: Yes.
Soc.: The shoemaker, then, and the harp player, are different from the hands and eyes with which they work.
Alc.: It is apparent.
Soc.: And does not a man use also his whole body.
Alc.: Certainly.
Soc.: Now the thing using is different from what it uses.
Alc.: True.
Soc.: A man, therefore, is a being different from his body.
Alc.: It seems so.
Soc.: What sort of being, then, is a man?

The Spiritual Psyche

Alc.: I cannot tell.
Soc.: But you can tell that it is some being making a use of its body.
Alc.: Yes.
Soc.: Does any other being make use of its body but the soul?
Alc.: None other.
Soc.: And does it not do so by ruling the body?
Alc.: Yes.[1]

A man's soul is his essence, his real self, the spiritual unity which informs the diversity of his actions as the Psyche of the Ionian philosophers was the unity-in-diversity of Nature. Therefore a man can have no higher duty than to care for his soul: that is what the Socratic philosophy amounts to in practical life.

The idea that the Psyche is something that we should care for was, as that famous classicist, Burnet,[2] has shown, very startling to Socrates' contemporaries. For, even though the Psyche were already regarded as the life principle, that did not mean that anyone thought it necessary to bother overmuch about it. On the contrary it was a natural force, immanent in all of us, but of no personal significance; it was as impersonal as gravitation or any other natural phenomenon. But if, as Socrates maintained, the Psyche is the essential and individual self, that spiritual essence in us which by its feeling, willing and thinking controls our moral behaviour, nothing can be of closer personal interest to us than the Psyche. By acting against the principles of justice we damage the Psyche, the self. And from Plato's *Apology* we know that Socrates did hold that the care of the soul, as the source of our moral being, should be the first concern of everyone.

"I will not cease from philosophy and from exhorting you, and declaring the truth to every one of you I meet, saying, in the words I am accustomed to use: 'My good friend . . . are you not ashamed of caring for money

---

[1] From the translation by George Burges.
[2] See *The Socratic Doctrine of the Soul*, Burnet, Philosophical Lecture to the British Academy, 1916.

and how to get as much of it as you can, and for honour and reputation, and not caring or taking thought for wisdom and truth, and for your soul, and how to make it as good as possible?"[1]

If the sentiment of this passage seems quite commonplace to the modern reader, that is because the Christian view of the soul came down to us, through Plato, Aristotle and the Fathers, from Socrates. But it seemed revolutionary to the Athenians of Socrates' day. They were indeed so bewildered by it that they killed him, mistakenly thinking that thus they would be rid of him.

[1] Quoted from *The Socratic Doctrine of the Soul*.

> "And swear that Beauty lives, though lilies die."
>
> FLECKER

CHAPTER V

The Spiritual Physis; the Platonic Immaterial Real

THE Sophists with their 'practical' philosophies had tried to cut the Gordian knot into which Parmenides had tangled the strands of Milesian thought, for Sophism was essentially a sceptical denial of the possibility of metaphysics.

Socrates, interested in the same problems as the Sophists, yet dissatisfied with their easy scepticism, created a positive philosophy of life and thereby gave to metaphysics an orientation which it still retains.

The philosophy of Plato is a synthesis of Ionian and Socratic thought. Because his intellect combined a concern for human problems as deep as that of Socrates with an interest in Nature not exceeded by that of the nature philosophers, all philosophy since his day has been Platonic, if only in the sense that no serious philosophy can henceforth be exclusively 'scientific,' like that of the Milesians, or, like that of Socrates, exclusively ethical.

Although a purely sceptical attitude is necessarily barren, all positive knowledge must have a basis in scepticism, not of the facile kind practised by the Sophists, but in that creative scepticism which consists in a thorough examination of assumptions and premisses. In this sense, Platonism is sceptical. In the scepticism of the Protagorean epigram, 'Man is the measure of all things,' and in the more profound negation of the Heracleitan antinomies, it finds the necessary resistance, as of stone against a chisel, out of which it moulds its positive form.

The Idea of the Soul in Western Philosophy and Science

'Man is the measure of all things.' What is the meaning of this cryptical saying? In the *Theaetetus*, Plato tells us that it is based on the concept of the relativity of sensation, which was always implicit in Ionian thought and gradually came to be more and more clearly understood. The penny has one colour for me, another for you, no colour at all for my dog, and for insects, perhaps, a colour that we cannot see or even try to imagine. But all these colours are equally 'real,' or unreal, because none of them is 'really out there' in the sense of belonging absolutely to the surface of the physical object. So that there is no criterion by which we may say that one of these appearances is a truer representation than any other. For what possible meaning could be attached to the statement that the chemical reactions in my retina are 'truer' than those in yours? Even if you are colour blind, and I am not, all we may say is that the chemistry of your retina is less complex than that of mine. All sensory representations, then, are equally 'true' or false. That, in rather different language from Plato's, is a brief epitome of his discussion of the relativity of sensation in the *Theaetetus*.[1] There we are told that the 'Man is the measure . . .' of Protagoras really amounts to this, that perception is knowledge. That is to say, since the perceptions of A are as valid as those of B, the *individual* man is the measure of all things. The scepticism of this position lies in the fact that, if perception is knowledge, there is really no such thing as knowledge; there is only *opinion*. For if I say 'This is yellow' and you 'This is white,' or you 'This is sweet' and I 'This is sour' (and as descriptions of what we perceive they are indeed equally true), then we must give up the notion of *truth* altogether. If perception is knowledge, the distinction between truth and falsehood is meaningless, a mere invention of the human fancy, and the only statements we can make with any

---

[1] Plato, of course, does not talk of retinae: he was presumably unacquainted with the physiology of vision. But he had grasped the essential point, which is all that matters for philosophy, that sensations are in some sense 'subjective,' or somatocentric.

The Spiritual Physis

certainty are those of the type: I am now having a perception with which I connect the word white, or sweet, etc. If your perceptions are different, all we may say is that your perceptions are different. We must not try to go beyond this, we must not try to say, the object as it is in itself, independently of being perceived, is 'really' like this or like that, for there is no criterion by which percepts are corrigible, or in the light of which we may hope to penetrate through the world of appearances, of 'becomings' to that of Being. The changing manifold of appearances, which is different for each of us, is all we may ever know, and with that we must be content.

Not only do different persons at the same time, and the same person at different times, perceive differently (the wine which is sweet when I am in health is sour when I am ill), but the world of things in themselves is, according to Herakleitos, fluent and therefore indefinable. Of the body in motion we may never say that it *is* at this point or that; the green leaf changes to yellow and man himself, whose life is but a perpetual change culminating in death, is as fluent as the leaf. Even where things seem static, this is but an illusory equilibrium, the flame-like fixity which is really perpetual flow. The flux of appearances is but the fluent appearance of a flux. How can we have any knowledge if all our consciousness is but a stream of personal becomings, based on nothing solid or immutable, but on a flowing and therefore indefinable Real. The answer is that we cannot; there is no difference between truth and falsehood; there is no knowledge, but only opinion.

That is the scepticism which is the opposite pole of Platonism, the dark background against which we may most clearly see its light. The famous theory of Forms is a continual argument for the existence of the ultimate truth or reality denied by Protagorean subjectivism. The essence of the theory is simply this. There must be truth which is ultimate in the sense that it is independent of the opinions of any individual. If there is not, then not only philosophy, but science, and in

The Idea of the Soul in Western Philosophy and Science

fact all human judgments are just nonsense. No one, in fact, denies this. Even Protagoras was not really able to deny it, for he thought his own theory (that there is no such thing as truth) was true! It is therefore impossible to deny that there is ultimate truth, for in the very attempt to deny it, one is forced to assert it. But, as Plato freely admits, the Protagorean argument is incontrovertible as far as it goes. My perceptions, or for that matter those of a pig, a lunatic, a drunkard, or those of a man drugged or dreaming, are as valid, in the perceptual world, as yours. From this it follows, not that nothing is ultimately true, but that ultimate truth cannot be grounded in perception.

Plato's philosophy is in fact an attempt to answer the question: what is the ground of truth, if it is not perception? And his answer was that truth is grounded in the entities which he called Forms, that the Forms exist whether anybody is having perceptions or not, that the Forms are not affected by the nature of these perceptions, if anybody is having them.[1]

What are the Forms? Plato was a mathematician, and a pupil of Socrates, and he approached this question from two directions, the Socratic and the mathematical.

Consider any proposition of mathematics, say the statement that the sum of the three angles of a triangle is always two right angles. Now suppose that the angles of this or that diagram of a triangle, or of this or that triangular surface, are measured with a protractor. I find, say, that the sum of the three angles is $178°$: on another occasion, or if another person measured the angles, the sum may come to, say, $180\frac{1}{2}°$. Now, according to Protagorean subjectivism, all we may say is that for a given person on a given occasion the sum of the three angles of a triangle was $x°$, while, for another person, or on another occasion, the sum was not $x°$, but $y°$. Apparently

---

[1] This, and not the various forms of Cartesian dualism which have been anachronistically foisted on Plato, is what I take to be the true meaning of the statement that the Forms are separate ($\chi\omega\rho\iota\sigma\tau\acute{\alpha}$).

The Spiritual Physis

Protagoras would in fact have said this, for he said that the propositions of geometry are not true for 'reality' (meaning perceptual reality) because 'tangents do not touch the circle merely at one point' . . . that is, Euclidean one-dimensional lines do not exist in the perceptual world.

But how do we arrive at the truths of geometry? Not by measuring angles but by reasoning about them. It is not possible to draw a Euclidean triangle, but even if it were, we should not investigate the properties of the triangle by measuring it; we should still follow the method of reasoning about a *conceptual* triangle. For suppose it were possible to draw 'perfect' triangles, and to measure their angles with perfect accuracy; suppose we drew a million such and found that in each of the million instances the sum of the angles was two right angles. We should still have no means of knowing that the sum of the angles of the million and first triangle would not be, say, 1·99 right angles, or, for that matter, half a right angle, or thirty right angles. But by *a priori* reasoning about a conceptual triangle we may say that the sum of any triangle, large or small, scalene, isosceles or equilateral, is just two right angles. "A new light flashed upon the mind of the first man (be he Thales or some other) who demonstrated the properties of the isosceles triangle. The true method, so he found was . . . to bring out what was necessarily implied in the concepts which he had himself formed *a priori*."[1]

But 'Thales or some other,' like most pioneers, was doing much more than he knew, or could have known. Had he seen the full implications of his achievement he would not have found in water the Identity in difference which he and his successors sought. The Milesians were looking for the right thing in the wrong place. Because they were the first thinkers to look for the right thing, Ionian philosophy is the most significant episode in the history of thought; because they

[1] From the preface to the second edition of Kant's *Critique of Pure Reason*, Norman Kemp Smith's translation.

sought it in the wrong place, their tradition came to an end in the logic of Parmenides.

The Being, or Identity in difference that the Ionians were seeking is not to be found in water, fire or air or in any other physical substance, but in the *conceptual* unity discovered in intellectual activity. That is the fundamental discovery underlying the Socratic dialectic and the discovery to which Plato gives expression in the theory of Forms. In the Forms discovered by the mind there is unity and identity which we look for in vain in the perceptual world. Within the limits of that world, but only there, the subjectivism of Protagoras and the Herakleitan paradoxes are completely applicable. In that world all things do indeed flow, evading definition. In it there is no universality; my sensation is as good as yours, though yours be the opposite of mine. 'It is, and it is not' is as descriptive of the scepticism of Parmenides as it is of Herakleitan mysticism. But the conceptual triangle is not a flux, whose angles may sometimes add up to this, sometimes to that, according to its own caprice or that of the observer. It is an eternal object of knowledge, a mathematical Form. It is not an evanescent Becoming, a mere appearance generated between object and observer, but a self-subsistent Being, existing in and by itself, regardless of whether it is known to any individual observer. It is not, like the individual appearances which participate in it, scalene, isosceles or equilateral, large or small, but non-spatial and universal. Unlike yellowness, bitterness, weight, or any of the other qualities of the perceptual world, its essence is not in being perceived, but in itself.

The unification of the material world is not to be found in itself, that is, in a φύσις or material Real, but in the Forms, the 'common notions' or κοιναὶ ἔννοιαι in terms of which the modern scientist expresses his so-called laws of Nature. A stone flung at random may fly in one of a million paths, but the infinite diversity of possible trajectories is embraced in the

The Spiritual Physis

unity of the equation of the stone's path, namely, the parabola. And the equation of the parabola is a particularised expression of those 'common notions' or necessary and universal concepts, without which mathematics, or any other valid thought, would be impossible. In this example, which we have taken from the modern science of dynamics, the equation of the parabola is as it were a link between our *conceptual* knowledge of the world of necessary and universal truth (the world of Forms) and the perceptual world of contingent events. Only in so far as we have knowledge of the Forms may we predict the course of natural phenomena; man is the measure only of those things of which he has seen the Forms, which are the ultimate measure of all things. Protagorean, or indeed any other, subjectivism is quite unable to account for prediction based on reasoning.

The position of the flying stone, of the swinging planet, is constantly changing, but the equation of the parabola or ellipse does not change, and in virtue of its immutability the position of the stone or of the planet may be calculated for any given instant. In Platonic language, we can predict, that is, make true judgments about future time, when we have seen the Forms which do not change with the passage of time. Prediction is knowledge of the Forms which are 'outside' space and time. If there were no such Forms beneath phenomenal change, if, as Herakleitos said, the Real were a flux, prediction would be impossible.

In so far as the world of sense perception participates in the Forms it is not wholly 'unreal.' We measure the perceptual triangle and find that the sum of its angles is not exactly two right angles; the triangle of perception is participating in, or imitating, the immaterial Form. The Forms, although never completely present in any individual material object, are immanent in the material world.

This brings us to the central feature of the theory of Forms, the analogy between the mathematical and the moral Forms.

The Idea of the Soul in Western Philosophy and Science

We have ascribed to Socrates the argument, developed by Plato in the early dialogues, for the 'separate' existence of the ethical universals. But how much of this is really due to Socrates and how much to Plato is not, of course, known with any certainty. The essential point is that the discovery of the concept underlies both the Socratic and the Platonic philosophies, and that for Plato the moral universals have the same status as the mathematical Forms. The moral Forms are immanent in human nature as the mathematical Forms are immanent in Nature. Just as the universal, conceptual triangle is a perfection to which individual objects of perception may approximate, but can never quite reach, so in the moral sphere the ethical Form is a standard of perfection towards which we may strive but never attain. And as the mathematical Forms are the real Identity in which the apparent differences of the physical manifold are grounded, so the manifold of human activities, in its social aspect, is grounded in the identity of the ethical Forms. The Form of justice is an objective unity, underlying the infinite diversity of human actions; the mathematical Forms are an analogous unity in the physical manifold. Like the mathematical Forms, the ethical Forms are not subjective; we do not and cannot 'make them up' for ourselves, any more than we can make up the laws of Nature. Concepts are objective entities which we discover.

Other Forms are derived from the conception of these two basic types. There are Forms of genera, of man, fire, or horse, for example. My perceptual knowledge of an individual horse is private to me and may be very different from yours. And a change in my physiology, such as may be occasioned, for example, by drugs of various kinds, may induce radical changes in the group of percepts which I call 'this' (individual) horse. But, whatever may happen to my sense organs, the group of percepts which I call 'this' horse will change in the same way as the group which I call 'that' horse. That is to say, we know that horses have something *objective* in common, even though,

The Spiritual Physis

owing to the relative and somato-centric[1] nature of sensation, we cannot know that objective entity, the Form of the genus 'horse,' as it is in and by itself. This Form, or universal in which individual horses more or less imperfectly participate, is real whether I am looking at a horse or not, it is real even though the individual horse, as given in my perception, is an evanescent becoming whose *esse* is in my perception.

How do we come by our knowledge of universals? Whence do we derive our standard of perfect justice, in a world where injustice, at the best of times, is more in evidence than its opposite? How do we recognise beauty in a multiplicity of physical objects and situations? Beauty of colour, of sound, beauty in poetry, in human character, plastic beauty or the beauty of flowing line, the beauty of an 'elegant' mathematical demonstration . . . the common factor is obviously indefinable in merely physical terms; it is a conceptual, not a physical unity in diversity, not φύσις but εἶδος, a Form, the Form of beauty. The *Form* of beauty (as distinct from the individual physical object in which we see beauty) is not perceptually known, any more than the Form of the triangle is perceptually known: in relation to the Form of beauty, individual objects stand in the same relation as the individual diagram to our conceptual knowledge of the geometrical proposition which the diagram represents. To what, then, is our knowledge of the Form of beauty due, if not to perception? And why does the human intellect strive to find the mathematical Forms? What faculty of the Psyche tells us to look for mathematical unity in Nature, the conceptual unity which the Ionians vainly sought in φύσις, when our sense organs tell us only of diversity?

It is this faculty which Plato calls ἀνάμνησις or 'recollection' in order to account for the fact that man strives to create beauty, to attain justice, to find conceptual unity in the material manifold. Until we have found an example of con-

[1] That is, dependent on the body (soma) of the observer.

The Idea of the Soul in Western Philosophy and Science

ceptual unity (e.g. a 'law' of Nature), we cannot be said to have any present experience of it. Yet we cannot find such an example until we have the urge to discover it, that is, until we have already a *belief* in its existence. (This applies above all to the mathematical Forms; only one Form, the Form of beauty, shines clearly through the physical veil.) By calling this belief *anamnesis*, Plato means that the soul, having seen the Forms in a previous existence, dimly recollects them in this life and strives to find them again. This is illustrated in the *Meno* by the dialogue with the slave, who, although he knows no geometry, is led, solely by being questioned, to work out a geometrical proposition for himself. That he is able to do this means that the questions remind him of the Forms. How, for example, do we know the Form of equality; that is, how do we know that equals of equals are equal? Not by measuring equal objects, for how, without an *a priori* concept of equality, should we know which objects to measure and compare? It is intrinsic, therefore, in the nature of ideal equality that the notion of it cannot be derived from sensory experience, although sensory experience is the occasion which reminds us of it in particular instances. It is a Form which the soul remembers because it has seen it in the world of Being, before it became united to the body in the world of Becoming. In the world of sense perception we may believe A to be equal to B, and B to C, and yet, through some error, find that A is not equal to C. Such errors are in principle corrigible by more careful perception. In fact, what we now call scientific research is largely the development of a technique for the 'correction' of sense data in the light of concepts. But in the conceptual world, the world of Forms itself, there is nothing corrigible, or conditioned by the observer. Our perception of beauty in individual objects is the subject of endless conflict of opinion, but Beauty in itself, the Form in which all beautiful objects participate is . . . "eternal, unproduced, indestructible; neither subject to increase nor delay: not, like other

The Spiritual Physis

things, partly beautiful and partly deformed; not at one time beautiful and at another time not; not beautiful in relation to one thing and deformed in relation to another; not here beautiful and there deformed; *not beautiful in the estimation of one person and deformed in that of another*; nor can this supreme beauty be figured in the imagination like a beautiful face, or beautiful hands, or any portion of the body, nor like any discourse, nor any science. Nor does it subsist in any other that lives or is, either in earth or in heaven, or in any other place; but it is eternally uniform and consistent, and monoeidic with itself. All other things are beautiful through a participation of it, with this condition, that although they are subject to production and decay, it never becomes more or less, or endures any change."[1]

In a famous passage in the *Phaedrus* the logic and epistemology of the theory of Forms, and of the Psyche and its anamnesis of the Forms, are interwoven with Dionysiac mysticism to give a mythical description of the Psyche as it exists in the world of Being before it descends to the body. There the soul is described a charioteer (Reason) driving a pair of winged steeds in the realm of Forms, the realm of "Real existence, colourless, non-spatial and intangible, visible only to the intelligence which sits at the helm of the soul. . . ."[2] If nothing more had survived of Plato than these words, we should still know that he was the greatest thinker of antiquity, and the father of modern philosophy. For in this half sentence from the *Phaedrus* is the fruition of two centuries of Greek thought, and the quintessence of the thought that has dominated Europe for twenty-five centuries. There, clear and explicit, is the logical outcome, always latent in Ionian thought, of the Ionian search for identity in diversity. If there is identity beneath the spatial manifold, if the universe is anything more than a meaningless plurality, the 'real existence' is not material

---

[1] *The Banquet*. Shelley's translation.
[2] ἡ ἀχρώματος τί καὶ ἀσχημάτιστος καὶ ἀναφὴς οὐσιά, etc.

The Idea of the Soul in Western Philosophy and Science

or perceptual. The perceptual world is a limitation of the real 'non-spatial and intangible' immaterial world of concepts, the world of Forms discovered not by the senses, but by the rational faculty of the Psyche.

Although Plato's idea of the Psyche is largely a development of the Socratic idea, it is in certain ways more akin to Ionian concepts. The Ionians were primarily interested in Nature, and in man and his Psyche only as an aspect of Nature. For Socrates, Nature was a teleological background for the spiritual drama of the life of man. Plato, like Socrates, took man as the starting-point of his thought, but like the Milesians, he saw organic life as a fragment of the pattern we call Nature. Because it was concerned solely with ethical universals, the Socratic dialectic was necessarily limited to man. The essential feature of Platonism, that the ethical Forms which determine human behaviour are in essence the same as the mathematical Forms which pervade inorganic Nature, transforms the Socratic Psyche by bringing it into dynamic relationship with the world outside man. It is in virtue of this crucial analogy that the Platonic Psyche, although a willing, feeling, and thinking essence, that is, a truly spiritual being, is nevertheless conceived to be connatural with the inorganic world, like the physical Psyche of the Ionians. Only, of course, the Platonic Psyche is not a part of a material continuum, but of a spiritual Real. Like the Socratic Psyche, the Platonic Psyche is the spiritual source of all action and passion in living beings, but, like the Ionian Psyche, it is also the source of all activity in the inorganic world. It is a matter of common experience that only living things have the power to move themselves, and it is of course this power of self-movement that Socrates and Plato ascribe to the soul. Now, individual objects in the inorganic world have no such intrinsic power of motion; they move only when impelled extrinsically. Therefore it is not to the individual objects in Nature that we must attribute a Psyche, but to Nature as a whole. That is to say, there is a universal

The Spiritual Physis

Psyche, a world-soul which moves the whole of Nature as the individual Psyche moves the whole organic being. The universe is a "living organism," a soul which is the "visible image of God, who can be conceived only in thought."

Adapting the epigram of Protagoras, we might define Plato's God as the 'Measure of all things,' the ultimate Identity in which all objective truth is grounded. And as it is the essence of Platonism that it conceives reality to be immaterial, spiritual, it follows that God, too, is spiritual, a Psyche like the soul or visible image of himself which he put into the world to move it. In the famous description of creation, in the *Timaeus*, Plato tells us that the first act of the Creator was to give the world a soul. "And therefore, using the language of probability, we may say that the world became a living spirit and truly rational through God's providence." But nowhere more clearly than here does Plato realise that his language can only be "the language of probability." He is perfectly well aware that in his account of the creation he is attempting to describe the indescribable. The distinction between God and the world soul is therefore intended less as an ultimate distinction than as a descriptive and mythical device. In other dialogues, God and the world soul are not so explicitly distinguished. All that Plato seems to regard as certain is that the force which moves the universe, which causes the motions of the heavenly bodies, of the winds and the tides, and all the ceaseless interplay of natural phenomena, is akin to the spiritual force which moves in us, and in virtue of which we are living beings.

This, however, is nothing but . . . animism, in a subtle and complex form perhaps, but nevertheless, in essence animism. Further, it is really the first appearance in history of the doctrine called animism, which the Victorian anthropologists attributed to the most naïve stage in the development of the human mind! At the beginning of this essay we endeavoured to show that this attribution was mistaken, basing our argument on Crawley's analysis of primitive beliefs. Now we are

The Idea of the Soul in Western Philosophy and Science

at a stage when we may see that animism, in the sense of a belief in the spiritual nature of the universe, is not a naïve, but on the contrary, a highly sophisticated view; indeed, the mere conception of *spirit*, as we understand it and as the anthropologists of the last century understood it, was unknown before Socrates discovered it. Even the Ionian Psyche was material, the very antithesis of the Platonic, or Christian, idea of the soul. Animism, in the sense which we have defined, could not in fact have existed before the Socratic discovery of the immaterial Concept.

Why, then, did the anthropologists of the last century attribute animism to savages? The answer is, that being literate modern Europeans, brought up in the Christian tradition, they were necessarily, if unconsciously, Platonists. To borrow a conception from a distinguished modern anthropologist, our cultural configuration, our European 'pattern of culture' is Platonic.[1] Of course it has long been recognised that our culture conforms to an unified pattern, and by common consent that pattern has been called Christianity. But what we call Christianity is in effect Platonism. Later we shall elaborate this bare assertion: here it must suffice to point out that the social pattern we are born into, the very language we learn, is impregnated through and through with the Socratic-Platonic idea of an incorporeal soul and of a God who is in essence akin to the human soul. As soon as we learn to use words we become verbally conditioned to the idea, so that we take it for granted long before we can even understand it; Platonic animism is almost as deeply rooted in our mental make up as the grammar of our native tongue, and anthropologists are not exempt from this rule. Further, the primitive beliefs which they study, although different from animism, are not altogether inconsistent with it. Indeed, we have endeavoured to trace the evolution of Platonism from the concept-percept dualism of which the savage seems to be subconsciously aware, and which

[1] Ruth Benedict, *Patterns of Culture*, Routledge 1935.

The Spiritual Physis

he expresses in his cults of the soul. This being so, it should seem no longer curious, but almost inevitable that anthropologists should at first assume that the primitive concept of the Psyche was the same as their own, for their own was too deeply implanted in their minds to be dragged into the daylight for analysis. The result was that the 'animism' they attributed to the unfortunate savage was neither animism properly so called, that is, Platonic animism, nor primitive religion, but a weird chimera compounded of primitive ritual and of the Socratic-Platonic idea of the Psyche which has integrated itself into our cultural pattern through Cartesian philosophy.

In our account of Platonism we have omitted all reference to the Platonic doctrine of immortality, for the reason that it is very difficult to say which parts of it are intended as scientific truth, and which as illustrative myth. Plato offers more than one 'proof' of the immortality of the soul; but, as he himself points out, it follows from the very nature of the Psyche as he conceives it that it is in a certain sense immortal. For that which moves itself must be without beginning and therefore eternal. But this immortality of the soul as an essence is not incompatible with its mortality as an individual. It is in this restricted sense that Buddhism takes the soul to be immortal, and it is difficult to be sure that Plato believed in a more extensive immortality than this.

It has been asserted, by one of the most profound modern students of Plato, that Plato had no system, or that if he had, it is not disclosed in his essays.[1] And although this view would no doubt be repudiated by other authorities, it can hardly be denied that Plato's philosophy was not systematic in the same way as that of Aquinas, say, or Kant. His writings raise many questions which they do not answer. Of these unsolved questions, one at least is fundamental; we refer to the much discussed question of the relation of the perceptual world to the Forms. The modern commentaries on this problem would

[1] Professor A. E. Taylor, *Plato*, vii.

probably run to a bulk many times that of the dialogues themselves, yet it can hardly be maintained that they have clarified the matter, far less resolved it. It is possible that Plato's ambiguity on this point is more profound than the optimism of modern scholars who write elaborate discussions on the meaning of μίμεσις, μετάληψις, and the numerous other terms by which Plato designates the relationship of the Forms to the perceptual world.

The positive content of Platonism, as it has come down to us in the dialogues, is after all simple enough to be epitomised in a few words. Truth, beauty, virtue, the Psyche; these are the eternal essences which are ontologically prior to the physical world, and of which the physical world is in some sense a limitation. It is possible that Plato believed that reason cannot take us much beyond this, or can only take us beyond it in poetry and mysticism. In the later dialogues there is more than a hint of the 'super-rationalism' which was to become the dominant feature of neo-Platonism. Thus, in the *Republic* we are told that the Form of the Good is supreme among Forms; that it is the unconditioned ground of all Being, and is itself 'beyond mind and Being,' an *ens realissimum* more like the One of the neo-Platonists than the God of the *Laws*. On such a view the ultimate identity in which differences are grounded would be unknowable, and the relation between the Forms and the manifold one that cannot be adequately expressed in either a monistic or a dualistic setting, or in any way comprehended by the human mind. Plato's philosophy ends, as it begins, in scepticism. But because his scepticism is more profound and ironic than that of Protagoras, or than that of any of our little modern sceptics and agnostics, Platonism is the richest and most positive of all elements in European culture.

> " '. . . and I am so clever that sometimes I don't understand a single word of what I am saying.'
>
> " 'Then you should certainly lecture on Philosophy,' said the Dragon-fly; and he spread a pair of lovely gauze wings and soared away into the sky."
>
> OSCAR WILDE

CHAPTER VI

The Teleological Physis; the Aristotelian Entelechy

IN the lecture notes which are all that has come down to us of Aristotle's philosophy there are no fundamental concepts which are not taken from Plato, and Aristotle's handling of these concepts adds little but verbal subtlety to the thought of his master.

The basic principle of Aristotle's, as of Plato's thought, is that there is objective truth which is independent of varying personal opinions and sense perceptions. Knowledge is, in fact, not grounded in sense perception, nor can there be any true knowledge of the individual appearances given in sense perception. Following Plato, Aristotle asserts that science is grounded, not in the individual, but in the universals or Forms. Now if knowledge relates to what *is*, as opposed to opinions and perceptions which are grounded in appearances merely; if, in other words, we mean by knowledge 'objective truth,' and if the object of knowledge is the universal, it follows that the universal, or Form, is *real*. It is real and separate ($\chi\omega\rho\iota\sigma\tau\acute{\alpha}$) in the sense that it still exists in and by itself, independently of the nature, or even of the existence of sense perceptions. These premisses, and this logical deduction from them, are the central element of Plato's thought. The essential feature of Aristotle's philosophy is that he accepts these premisses, but refuses to accept the (really inevitable) conclusion that only the universal is real. It is a curious irony that the man who created formal logic by his discovery of the syllogism should have refused to apply his discovery to the assumptions of his own philosophy.

In flagrant contradiction to his basic assumptions, Aristotle maintained that only the individual is real, and the greater part of his metaphysics resolves itself into a really superb attempt to reconcile verbally what is irreconcilable in thought. Indeed, the tradition of verbal pattern making, which the Sophists initiated, and of which Aristotle is the supreme master, has done much to bring metaphysics into disrepute. There is, however, this great difference between Sophism and Aristotelianism. Beneath the verbiage of the former there is nothing substantial; strip the latter of its verbal subtlety and one finds . . . Platonism.

We have seen that it is fundamental to Platonism that the phenomenal world, which exists only in the perceptions of individuals, is derived from the real and objective world by *limitation*. The phenomena arise by limitation of the Forms, and the principle of limitation is variously called: not-Being ($\mu\grave{\eta}$ ὄν), the Receptacle ($\pi\alpha\nu\delta\acute{\epsilon}\chi\epsilon\varsigma$), Space ($\chi\acute{o}\rho\alpha$) or Mass ἐκμᾰγεῖον).[1]

The Real is immaterial, and the material world, because it arises by limitation of the immaterial, "rolls about between Being and not-Being." Space, because it splits up the unity of the Form into a diversity of individuals, individuals because of their separate positions in space, is the *principium individuationis*, and hence the cause of all subjective uncertainty, since the individual by itself is unintelligible, and intelligible only in so far as it participates in the universal. The principle that the individual, by itself, is unintelligible is, of course, the basic assumption of all philosophy, even from its first dawning

[1] It has often been pointed out, of course, that Plato's identification of space and materiality is remarkably suggestive of modern physical concepts.

The Teleological Physis

in Miletos. For the goal of all the Milesian systems was, as we have seen, the discovery of the One beneath the Many, the universal Unity which alone renders the multiplicity of individuals intelligible.

But Aristotle could never really accept this principle, because he could never quite rid himself of the 'naïve realist' view (to which, as a naturalist, he was temperamentally inclined) that the phenomenal world is 'really out there,' in the sense of existing as we perceive it independently of our perception. But if he was by temper a naïve realist, he was by reason a Platonist. He found it impossible to reject Plato's discovery that the true object of knowledge is the conceptual universal. Therefore he compromised by asserting that the phenomenal world of individuals arises, not by the limitation of the world of Forms, but by the union of Form with a limiting Being, which he called Matter. Plato's matter is a negation; that of Aristotle a Being with the property of negation. This, of course, converts Plato's incorporeal monism into a dualism of Form and matter, a dualism which Aristotle tries to avert by saying that neither Form alone, nor matter alone, but only the union of Form and matter is real or 'substantial.' By this ingenious verbal device he tries to combine the immaterial Real of Plato with the common sense 'couldn't he use his eyes' view towards which he was instinctively inclined.

Because of its indissoluble substantial union with matter, the Aristotelian Form is very different from the Platonic conceptual universal from which it is derived. It has become simply the structure of the individual, as opposed to its stuff. A vase and a statue, say, both of bronze, are made of the same stuff, but the structure, or Form of the two is different. Logically, this conception requires that the basis of Being is a structureless (i.e. formless) stuff, on which Form is imposed. Such a structureless stuff is, however, inconceivable, a difficulty which Aristotle evades by saying that matter and Form are purely relative terms. Consider, for example, a statue in process of being sculptured. First, there is the rough block of marble, out of which the artist might cut the likeness of almost anything, an animal, a man or any other form. The rough block, although not devoid of form, is formless relative to these potential Forms or perfections. In the early stages of the sculpturing it might be possible to see that the figure was, say, a human form, but not possible to say whether it were intended to represent a male or a female. Later, though it may have become apparent that the form was that of a male, it might still be impossible to say that it resembled any individual prototype more than another. Finally, the model attains its definitive Form, a representation, say, of Zeus. Aristotle would say that each of these stages in the realization of the end or definitive Form (τέλος) is *matter*, relative to the stage above it, but *Form*, relative to the preceding stage. Completely formless matter, which stands logically at the foot of the series, is an abstraction which does not exist, and never has existed. Matterless Form, which stands at the other end of the series, is equally inconceivable: it is this which Aristotle calls God. This God is not an immanent principle, but an individual among others.

The Aristotelian universe is a scale or ladder of individuals stretching from formless matter below, to matterless Form (God and the spirits of the heavenly spheres) above. All change is as it were a teleological movement from one rung of the ladder to the next, and this is brought about by the action of Form on matter. Form contains its perfection or end (τέλος) in itself: Telos is actual in Form. Matter contains its end or perfection only potentially: Telos is potential in matter. This may be illustrated from the analogy of the statue. In a sense the statue is already within the material before the sculptor sets to work on it. The Form is there potentially. When the sculptor has done his work it is there actually. Similarly the Form of the animal is potential in the egg, actual in the adult. Aristotle continually returns to these analogies, of biological

The Teleological Physis

development and of human purposive action; they give us the essential clue to the personal vision by which he interpreted the world.

The Aristotelian concept of Form should be compared with the Platonic conception of Formal Reality, from which it is derived. The Form of triangularity is (1) the perfection, and (2) the universal, or undetermined genus, of all individual triangles, which are but limitations of the universal Form. The Aristotelian Form is the perfection of a given individual, and is completely determined and actual in the individual. The individual attains any given Form, which is its perfection relative to the stages which lead up to it (e.g. the stages in the sculpturing of the statue) by motion, or, as a modern philosopher would prefer to say, by process. Process of any kind is a motion from the potentiality which is in matter to the actuality of Form. Because Form contains its Telos, or actuality, within itself, it is the Entelechy of matter.[1] Entelechy transforms potentiality into actuality. The Entelechy of the statue is the concept of it in the mind of the sculptor; the motion of the material under his chisel is the process through which the Entelechy passes into the marble.

Now, as Plato pointed out, inorganic matter does not move itself. It is only moved intrinsically. But living beings move themselves. That is to say, the living being is that in which Entelechy is intrinsic; this intrinsic Entelechy is the Psyche. The Entelechy of inorganic matter, which causes motion in it, is energy; the Entelechy of the living being, which causes motion and development in it, is the Psyche, the ἐνέργεια σώματος. And since the energy cannot be conceived apart from the matter which it moves, so the Psyche, the energy or Entelechy of the body, cannot be conceived apart from the body. Like the moving body and its motion, the soul and the animal body are different yet inseparable. Like motion, the soul is immaterial, yet inseparable from matter.

[1] ἐντελέχεια—from τέλος, perfection and ἔχειν, to have.

The Idea of the Soul in Western Philosophy and Science

Entelechy is the central concept of Aristotelianism, as the Forms and the Psyche are the central concepts of Platonism. And Entelechy is essentially both Form and Psyche. For Plato the Forms were the perfect prototypes, towards which our souls strive and the ideal patterns after which God fashioned the world. The world-soul was the mover of the world as the individual soul was the mover of the individual organism. For Aristotle, Entelechy is both pattern and motive power. The Psyche, which is the Entelechy of the body, is the perfection which is actualised in the development of the individual from the egg. God, the highest Entelechy, is the perfection and prime mover of Nature, as the Psyche is the perfection and *mobile* of the body.

The doctrine of Entelechy may at first sight seem very different from Platonic animism, a doctrine which Aristotle, in fact, explicitly rejects. But, as with most of the Platonic doctrines which he repudiates, after much discussion he puts forward as his own a restatement of the Platonic theory. Because of his personal vision and orientation, however, Aristotle transforms Platonism in restating it. Plato was a mathematician, and a poet; Aristotle was a biologist, and more common-sensible than poetical. Only a mind of Plato's type, combining poetical vision with the analytical powers of the mathematician, could have discovered the concept of the immaterial Real, and since Plato's day countless poetical minds have found in his philosophy an expression of their own intuitions.[1] But Aristotle was temperamentally unsympathetic to Plato's spiritual and immaterial Real. Like the sensuous ghost of a modern poet's conception he, "loved the veins of the leaves, the shapes of crawling beasts . . . the feel of wood and stone." Yet, since he could not escape the logic of Platonism, he took the immaterial Real and tempered it to his own desire by welding it, like an earthbound spirit, to the shapes

[1] For an interesting account of the influence of Platonism on English poetry, see James Adam's *Vitality of Platonism*, Cambridge University Press, 1911.

The Teleological Physis

of the crawling beasts that he spent his life in observing. Thus he was led to consider it as a part of the eternal process of birth, growth and decay that we call life, the cause of the process, yet real only as a part of the process. He could not conceive that the Real was in any sense 'separate' from the sensual world that he loved, and his philosophy is one long effort to unite the two worlds that he (probably mistakenly) thought Plato had divorced.

And by a strange irony, the effect of his philosophy was to bring about just that separation which it was its object to avoid. By changing Plato's matter, a limitation of Form, into separate principle opposed to Form, Aristotle was unwittingly laying the foundations of metaphysical dualism, a dualism which he himself vainly tried to avoid by his insistence on the substantial unity of matter and Form.

In the Aristotelian psychology the potentialities of dualism are even clearer. To the Ionian physicists the possibility did not even occur that there could be any fundamental discontinuity between man and Nature. Therefore, when they speculated about the soul they saw it as part of the Physis which they conceived to be the substratum of Nature. And Plato, although the concept of the spiritual Psyche which he takes from Socrates is so different from anything in Ionian thought, nevertheless preserves this continuity of man with Nature in his doctrine of a world soul, immanent in Nature as the individual soul is immanent in the body, a prime mover which causes all inorganic motion as the soul initiates physiological motion. Aristotle, seeking to simplify and clarify Platonism, by combining in the notion of Entelechy the two concepts of Form and Psyche, succeeded in doing the opposite. The two attributes of Entelechy, namely, its perfection (derived from the Platonic Form) and its motive power (derived from the Platonic Psyche) are really incompatible. For if Entelechy is, by definition, that which has its end or perfection within itself, what need has it to complete itself by acting on matter?

The Idea of the Soul in Western Philosophy and Science

Aristotle evades this difficulty by one of his most breath-taking verbal feats.

Form, he says, does not act on matter actively, but purely passively, as a loved one acts on a lover! Matter 'desires' Form, and moves towards it, as a lover desires and seeks out his loved one. Of course, by endowing matter with 'love' of Form, Aristotle, like the modern 'materialist,' is really attributing to it just those spiritual qualities which he excludes from it by definition. For Plato, matter is an aspect of a larger whole, a subaltern or incomplete Being included in a more ultimate teleological ground; for Aristotle it is the 'matter' of the naïve realist, matter as given in sense perception, which is itself teleological. Unfortunately it is impossible to reconcile this account of the relation between Form and matter with their substantial unity, which Aristotle is so anxious to preserve.

And when he comes to apply this formula to the relation between God and the world, the results are even more disastrous. Since we cannot attribute to God any of the limitation (στέρνησις), which for Aristotle, as for Plato, is the essential characteristic of matter, God must be pure Form, absolute Being in whom there is no potentiality which seeks actualization through Becoming or Process. God must, however, be a substance, not a mere predicate of substance; therefore he is incorporeal substance, pure thought. Now if God is pure Form or Entelechy, he is as incapable as any other Form of real action. Even the thought which is his only activity cannot be directed to anything outside himself, for if it were, that would imply that his perfection was not entirely intrinsic, and then he would no longer be pure Entelechy. Therefore, in God, thought and its object must be an eternal, self-sufficient identity; his activity is the thought of thought. From this it follows that God is so wholly separate from the world that he does not even know of its existence. Just as the immanent Platonic Form has become a determinate individual, God him-

The Teleological Physis

self has been deposed from the status of an immanent spirit to that of one among many individuals. By the same device whereby the individuality of the Form is reconciled with its motive power, the individuality of God is reconciled with his function of prime mover. He moves the world, not by acting on it, but because the world is drawn towards him by its desire for perfection, as all matter is drawn towards Form.

Aristotle's interpretation of Plato is a philosophy in which the poetry and grandeur of Platonic animism have been degraded to a meaningless verbal quibble, in which the immanent motive spirit of the universe has dwindled to a remote and incredible individual, devoid even of the dignity of a Jehovah. The Aristotelian doctrine of God is indeed scarcely distinguishable from atheism, and although it is in questionable taste, it is by no means untrue to call Aristotle the "godless bulwark of the papists."

Worse, the Aristotelian universe is a world split in two. Hitherto it has been the assumption of all philosophic thought that beneath the perceptual manifold there is a 'real' Identity. Different philosophers have put forward different conceptions of that Identity, but all have agreed that it must exist. For the Ionians the Identity, whether Fire, Air or Water, was material. In the Pythagorean philosophy we find the first attempt to formulate the notion of an immaterial Real. Plato, by availing himself of the Socratic discovery of the Concept, was able to convert the vague, semi-mystical presentiments of the Pythagoreans into an explicit and self-conscious philosophy, logically grounded in experience. Now the One of Platonism, the immaterial Real, is the very antithesis of the material Real, the φύσις of the Ionians. The two conceptions are grounded in mutually incompatible visions. Aristotle's encyclopaedic mind set itself the hopeless task of reconciling, and combining these contradictory points of view. His boast, that his own philosophy is a synthesis of all previous thought, is well known. Inevitably the outcome of this impossible effort of synthesis was the opposite of synthesis . . . cleavage. Aristotle's world is a self-contradictory dualism of material and immaterial, precariously bound together by the strained threads of Aristotle's verbal subtlety.

Not content with thus separating Physis and Psyche, Aristotle proceeds to divide the Psyche itself into sections like those of an encyclopaedia. He distinguishes three kinds of Psyche. The plant Psyche is purely nutritive and reproductive; the animal Psyche is in addition sentient. Only the human soul is cognitive, because in it mind or thought (νόυς) is added to the animal soul. He tells us that the animal soul comes into being with the body and dies with it, but that a part of the human soul is immortal. This immortal part he calls the active *nous*, which he distinguishes from the passive *nous* (νούς παθητικός). In the individual man, thinking arises from a combination of these faculties, so that the mind of the individual is not, as such, immortal. It has an immortal part, the universal or active *nous*. This exists before the birth of the body and continues to exist after its death. It is not affected in any way by the death of the body, and indeed is incapable of suffering any kind of change. The active *nous* is a curious remnant of the Platonic immaterial Psyche.

"I . . . smile . . . like a Stoic . . . and let the world go by."
TENNYSON

CHAPTER VII

The Physical Logos: The Decline of Philosophy

PHILOSOPHY, or any other disinterested activity of the mind, can only come into being in a stable pattern of culture which ensures, for some of its members, a life relatively free from the material necessities which determine the lives of most.

The conquests of Alexander, the pupil of Aristotle, threw the Mediterranean world into a social and political turmoil in which it was impossible that philosophy, at any rate in the form in which it was previously understood, could survive. For the essence of philosophy is that it is an attempt to transcend the personal, even the purely human, point of view, by striving to discover the Real which is not affected by human opinions. Human problems have, of course, a large and indeed prominent place in philosophical thought, but only as an aspect of that more ultimate reality in which they are believed to be grounded. But the period which followed the Macedonian conquests, a period in which the civilisation of the Mediterranean became a whirlpool of clashing and mingling cultures and religions, was one in which immediate social problems forced themselves into the centre of man's consciousness. The voice of philosophy was drowned in the thunder of the Macedonian cavalry sweeping across three continents, the light of reason an imperceptible candle beside the flames of Persepolis and Thebes.

The philosophical problem "What is the ultimate meaning of life?" was forgotten, in face of the practical immediacy of

The Idea of the Soul in Western Philosophy and Science

the problem "How shall we live?" The popular religions had answers ready made to that question, but men were becoming dissatisfied with these answers, all the more dissatisfied, perhaps, because the world had suddenly turned into a clamouring rabble of religions, spreading this way and that from their native lands to which, for centuries, they had been confined. Egyptian deities were worshipped, not only in Sicily, Syria and India, but in Athens itself, eventually in Rome. Like mushrooms, synagogues sprang up on all coasts. The Babylonian books of magic, the literature of the Jews, even parts of the mystical books of the Hindus, were translated into Greek. Small wonder that, surrounded by a thousand competing systems of belief, in a world in which it was difficult to know what the next day might bring, men found it difficult to believe in anything.

It was inevitable that under such conditions the more sensitive and reflective should seek refuge in quietism, in a simple philosophy which taught that peace, so obviously absent from the outer world, could only be found within, a philosophy which set a greater value on patient endurance than on intellectual curiosity, and which required one to believe in little but the practical value of unbelief.

There was, of course, a limit to the retrogression which philosophy could undergo. The subtleties of Plato and Aristotle might be too difficult for a tired and harassed generation, but, however great the practical stress of the times, it was impossible for thought to go back to a prephilosophical, mythological, pattern.

Accordingly, even Stoicism, essentially a 'practical' philosophy, a way of living rather than a system of thought, had to find some intellectual basis for its moral precepts, and it found that basis in the simple physical monism of the Ionians, particularly in the mystical system of Herakleitos. Not that Stoicism was entirely without later affinities, particularly with Aristotelianism.

The Physical Logos

The basic feature of Stoic, as of Aristotelian, thought, is that all knowledge arises from sense perception. And in maintaining that only matter is real, the Stoics were merely carrying to its logical conclusion the Aristotelian principle that only the individual is real. Even the Stoic monism is partially derived from Aristotle's dualism. Instead of a dualism of matter and form, Stoicism postulates a dualism of matter (or world) and Logos (God). Matter in itself (like the Aristotelian πρώτη ὕλη) is formless, completely without qualities. The qualities of the manifold are due to the Logos which permeates matter. The dualism of this doctrine is, however, only apparent. For the Logos is not spiritual, or in any way immaterial. It differs from the rest of the material world only in being a very finely divided form of matter, variously described as Fire, Air or Ether, penetrating every part of the cosmos. This material Logos, obviously derived from the Heracleitan Fire-Logos, is God. God himself, then, is material, and, in the sense that he is not Being, but just one material being among others, individual. Unlike the Aristotelian God, however, and like the Platonic world soul, the Stoic Logos is immanent in all things, although only an individual. And although material, the Logos is conceived as a Mind or Generative Reason (λόγος σπερματικός) diffused throughout the universe. It is the rational soul of the world, and the world is the body of God. In spite of the obvious Platonic origin of this conception, it is soul in the old, naïve Ionian sense of the word, a physical soul. It is in fact a contradiction in terms, a material Platonic world soul. The Stoics even went so far, or rather, so far back, as to 'explain' the world after the manner of the Ionian cosmologists, in terms of space, time and matter. Their cosmology was in fact but a slightly modified form of that of Herakleitos. They said that the world arose from God by condensation: God, the primal Fire, formed the world out of himself by condensing a part of his fiery substance into air, water and earth. Out of these he made the world, and the remaining part of him, the uncondensed primal Fire, is the Logos which permeates the world.

It is difficult to believe that, barely a century after Plato, philosophy could have descended to such absurdities. Nevertheless, Stoicism survived, in one form or another, for nearly half a millennium.[1] It survived mainly on account of its ethical appeal, an appeal which, in an age such as we have described, was perhaps strengthened, rather than impeded, by the puerility of the metaphysics on which it was based.

The Stoic ethics was derived from the metaphysics in the following way. Herakleitos, from whom the Stoics borrowed so many of their notions, had said, following Pythagoras, that all things happen according to law. This idea was quite widely familiar by the time of the Stoics, who made it the central feature of their materialistic philosophy. They saw the cosmos as a vast machine. Even God, in forming the world out of himself, was only obeying inviolable material laws. Every event in the universe, from the first beginning of the condensation of the primal Fire, down to the smallest happening in the completed world, was for the Stoics a link in an unalterable chain of cause and effect. They believed that human actions were no exception to this universal rule; that every detail of human life was but a predestined part of the great pantheistic scheme.

> "Yea, the first Morning of Creation wrote
> What the Last Dawn of Reckoning shall read."

Consequently the highest virtue is submission, in subordination of the self to the universal law of Nature, and since the universal law is none other than the Logos, or divine Reason which permeates the soul of every man, to live according to Nature is to lead a completely rational life, unaffected by the

---

[1] Finally dying out in the repulsive moral *schwarmerei*, called *Meditations of Marcus Aurelius*.

The Physical Logos

passions. Only in complete 'apathy' can one find freedom from the instability and changes of the world, and this inner peace is the only true good, the only real wealth. A man may have many possessions, but without the peace which comes from wisdom he is poor. Because the fate of all men, rich or poor, is impartially determined by the Logos, all men are equal in the light of the Logos. Therefore all mankind, irrespective of nation, class or wealth, is a community of equal brothers, and every member of that community has an equal right to sympathy and love, whether he be a slave or a prince. Even to our enemies we owe good will, not less than to our friends. True happiness, therefore, lies in the suppression of the passions; only thus can the 'Wise Man,' living in an over complex and too passionate world, find peace and simplicity.

The fundamental defect of Stoicism, from the metaphysical point of view, is that, since everything is determined by the Logos, it simply is not possible, whether one wants to or not, to oppose it: one *can* only do that which has been preordained by physical law. Therefore the injunction not to oppose it is meaningless. But the men of this time found comfort in the quietist ethic of Stoicism, without looking too closely at its metaphysical foundations.

"In the beginning was the Word . . ."

ST. JOHN

CHAPTER VIII

The Spiritual Logos: the Rebirth of Philosophy and the Birth of Christianity

IN the complex pattern of intermingling cultures which made up the Mediterranean world of this time, the interaction between the Greek and Hebrew cultures was by far the most significant.

In the sixth century B.C. the kingdom of Judea had been conquered, its temple destroyed, and Jerusalem "that was great among the nations" now became "as a widow," and its people were led to captivity in Babylon. There the Jews felt that they had but one remaining fragment of their civilisation, one symbol, to which they could yet cling, of their racial and spiritual integrity. That symbol was the Torah, the sacred written record containing the Mosaic law, the prophetic writings and the Psalms. This, the Word, was all they had. "They had no state, holding them together, no country, no soil, no king, no form of life in common. If, in spite of this they were one, more than all the other peoples of the world, it was the Book that sweated them into unity. . . . Sometimes the Book was overgrown by the weeds of life, but it stuck fast in each of them, and in the hours when they were most themselves, at the highest points of their lives, it was there, and when they died it was there, and what flowed out from one to the other was this Word. They bound it with phylacteries round heart and head; they fastened it to their doors; they opened and closed the day with it; as sucklings they learned the Word; and they died with the Word on their lips."[1]

[1] From *Jew Süss* (A Historical Romance), by Lion Feuchtwanger. The English translation by Willa and Edwin Muir.

The Spiritual Logos

Three centuries after the Babylonian captivity there were in Alexandria so many Greek Jews, Jews who had forgotten their native tongue and could think only in Greek, that the holy Scriptures, the very symbol and essence of Jewish nationality, had to be put into Greek in order to be intelligible to the Alexandrian community.

One of the most remarkable results of the fusion of Greek and Hebrew cultures was the sect (from whom many believe that Christ derived much of His teaching) known as the Essenes. Although they adhered to the sabbath and to the sacred books of the Jews, the Essenes went to Greek sources for their most fundamental beliefs. They regarded the soul as a captive spirit, held in the body as in a prison, and believed that after the death of the body the souls of the good would live beyond the ocean in endless bliss, in a beautiful land continually swept by a warm west wind. A curious combination of Pythagoreanism with Jewish ethics and the Greek myth of the Islands of the Blest! And the ascetic and communistic way of life of the Essenes, the division of their society into intellectual orders or castes, of which the highest were celibate, remind one strongly of Plato's Republic, and are undoubtedly to be traced to neo-Pythagorean origins.

In the curious Hebrew-Alexandrian writing known as the Book of Wisdom there recurs continually the doctrine which was to be so important in the history of Christianity, the doctrine of the Logos.

"For Wisdom is more moving than any motion: she passeth and goeth through all things by reason of her pureness.

"Wisdom reacheth from one end to another mightily: and sweetly doth order all things.

" . . . what is richer than Wisdom, that worketh all things?"

Compare these texts with the Herakleitan fragments:

"There is but one Wisdom, to know the knowledge by which all things are guided through all.

"All things come to pass by way of the Logos."

The Idea of the Soul in Western Philosophy and Science

The affinity is too striking to call for comment.
And in the text:

> "For I was a witty child, and had a good spirit
> Yea, rather, being good I came into a body undefiled"

it requires little penetration to recognise the Socratic-Platonic identification of the personality, the "I," with the soul, and the Platonic idea of the pre-existence of the soul. There is even a reference to one of the more abstract Aristotelian concepts:

> "For thy Almighty hand, that made the world of *matter without* form. . . ."

While the extent of Greek influence on Hebrew culture can hardly be overestimated, it must not be supposed that the individuality of Hebrew culture was lost. On the contrary, it was invigorated by the Hellenic ideas which it assimilated. In spite of all the impacts of foreign cultures on their own, the Jews remained . . . Jews. They remained a race dominated by their own peculiar spiritual ideas, obsessed with the notions of sin and repentance, living in the perpetual hope of the Messiah. The Greeks felt no need of a Messiah, or of repentance, since they had no consciousness of sin. What would they have made of the idea that Repentance and the name of the Messiah were among the seven things created before the world began? Such an idea was as typically and peculiarly Hebrew as the Pythagorean proposition, or Plato's dialogues, were typical of Greek civilisation. It was, above all, the hope of a Messiah, created by the great prophets of the eighth century B.C., which came more and more to dominate not only the popular religion, but also the philosophical speculations, of the Hebrews. And although the Messiah legend is long since dead, its name, attached to a religion which is no longer a cult of the Messiah, still lives, although in Greek translation. The name by which the Nazarene became known, and by which He is still known, is a symbol of the synthesis

The Spiritual Logos

of Greek and Hebrew cultures which was active at the beginning of our era. We speak of the founder of our religion, not by His Hebrew designation of Messiah ("the anointed" of the Lord) but by the Greek translation χριστος . . . Christ.[1]

But, in spite of the Greek name by which it was known from very early times, Christianity was at first an essentially Jewish cult, a cult of the Messiah. A Christian was one who believed that the Hebrew Messiah had appeared on earth in the person of Jesus. The first Christian community regarded their cult, not as a departure from the Jewish cult of Jahveh, but rather as a new expression of it, foretold, moreover, in its ancient prophecies, so that it seemed to them entirely natural that they should meet for prayer in the Temple.

But the divergence between the new cult and the traditional Hebrew religion began very early. Even before it took its name from the Greek language, Christianity was assimilating Greek ideas. Already, in the lifetime of Christ, the way was being prepared for this assimilation by the Jewish philosopher, Philo.

His philosophy is the culmination of those sporadic incursions of Greek ideas into Hebrew culture which had already been going on for centuries. His avowed aim was to bring the revelations found in the holy Scriptures into conformity with Greek philosophical ideas, in particular with those of the Pythagoreans, Plato and the Stoics.

The two essential features of God, in Hebrew theology, are His goodness and His transcendence. "The Holy One, blessed be He, is exalted . . . above the whole universe."[2] The very name of God was felt to be ineffable, so that its use came to be restricted to the Temple, and later it became the custom, within the Temple, to drown the divine name in singing. Philo finds a Greek parallel for this in Plato's statement that

---

[1] Actually, the word Messiah itself is a Greek transliteration of the Aramaic, Meshisha.
[2] Chagighah 13b. Quoted from Cohen's translation, *Everyman's Talmud*.

the Form of the Good is "beyond Being and knowledge." But the God of the Hebrews, for all the remoteness of His Throne of Glory in the seventh heaven, is omnipresent in the world. "How ever high He be above His world, let a man but enter a Synagogue, stand behind a pillar and pray in a whisper, and the Holy One, blessed be He, hearkens to his prayer. Can there be a God nearer than this, Who is close to His creatures as the mouth is to the ear?"[1]

The doctrine of the Logos, in which Philo reconciles these paradoxical attributes of God, is the means by which Christianity was transformed from a minor Hebrew sect into an universal religion. The Logos, in Philo's philosophy, was an intermediary between this world and a transcendent God. Although he gives it this Herakleitan-Stoic name, the Logos as Philo conceives it is really much closer to the Platonic world soul than to the *Logos spermatikos* of the Stoics, or the Fire Logos of Herakleitos. For, unlike the Stoic Logos, Philo's Logos is an immaterial essence, a soul in the truly Platonic sense of the word.

Why, then, did he call it Logos, a word which had come to be identified, in Stoic thought, with a materialistic modification of Plato's doctrine of the world soul? Because it thus became identified with the Hebrew 'Word.' Like the Word or Logos of the Book of Wisdom, the Logos as Philo conceives it is the Reason or Word of God, the divine Mind which moves in all things. Therefore, although he took the name from the Stoics, Philo returned for the concept to Plato. His Logos, or universal Reason, like Plato's rational world soul, is not God Himself but the first creature created by God. Even Aristotelian concepts are reconciled within the unity of Philo's all-embracing Logos. Aristotle conceived the world as a scale of beings, ranging from the utter privation of formless matter to the complete perfection of God, Who is matterless Form. Philo identifies the Aristotelian scale of beings with the angels,

[1] Berachoth, 13a, ibid.

The Spiritual Logos

demons and demigods, and other spirits, of Hebrew mythology, maintaining, however, that all these are hierarchic manifestations of a single Logos. These manifestations of the Logos, like the emanations from the Stoic primal Fire, are 'outflowings' from God, but their essence is not material, like that of the Stoic Logos. They are immaterial, like the Platonic Forms. (This is the basis of the later neo-Platonic identification of the Forms with ideas in the mind of God.)

By adhering to the Pythagorean idea of the fall of the soul, which, having become imprisoned in the body, may only be released from it by purification, Philo was able to identify the Dionysiac-Pythagorean idea of katharsis with the Hebrew ideas of sin and repentance.

In its original Hebrew form, Christianity was a simple doctrine of quietism, with even less intellectual pretensions than Stoicism, the other great quietist movement of the time. Nor could it have been foreseen at the time that Christianity would displace Stoicism, which then dominated the Mediterranean world. It had none of the universal appeal of Stoicism. It is true that its ethical doctrine of submission and brotherly love was almost indistinguishable from that of Stoicism. But with this teaching of universal love it combined the specifically Hebrew cult of the Messiah, the Hebrew reverence for the Mosaic law, the practice of circumcision and many other Hebraic elements which could not hope to evoke sympathy outside Jewish circles.

It was Philo, who, although not himself a Christian, laid the foundations of European, as distinct from the original Hebraic form of Christianity. European Christianity has so completely identified itself with the philosophical outlook expressed in his writings that it is almost impossible to believe that certain passages are not the work of a Christian. We have seen that Philo describes the Logos as the image of God (εἰκὼν Θεοῦ). That might be the language of any Platonist. But when he also calls the Logos the "archetypal man" ('ὁ κατ' εἰκονα ἄνθρωπος) or "the man of God" (ανθρωπος Θεοῦ) and even "the son of God, and the first-born Son" (πρωτόγονος) he is speaking a very different language.

Christ the Messiah found little favour among the Jews, the only people for whom the concept of the Messiah had any significance, yet the cult of the Messiah was too parochial, too intimately Hebrew, to develop into a cosmopolitan religion. Nor could the severely intellectual creed of Philo hope to appeal to any but the sophisticated. But from the combination of these two elements, from the identification of Christ the man with the Son or Logos of God, the creation of a philosopher who did not know Christ, arose the new religion which conquered Europe. The Mediterranean world was well prepared for such a religion. Stoic quietism, in essence the same as the quietism of the Sermon on the Mount, was already an ancient and widespread doctrine, of which, moreover, the Logos was the central conception. But the Stoic Logos was a purely intellectual notion; the popularity of Stoicism rested rather on its ethics. Once they had identified the metaphysical Logos with the man Jesus, the Christians had created a doctrine which, while retaining the noblest features of Stoicism, transformed its central conception from a remote abstraction into something infinitely more vivid, emotional and personal. The very contradictoriness of the concept of the Christ-Logos, which identifies the image of God, the immanent Reason or world soul, with an individual man, appeals to a deep intuition which tells us that ultimate reality somehow transcends the cut-and-dried antinomies of reason.

The identification of which we speak had yet, however, to be made. Jesus was still the Messiah, the Logos still only the metaphysical, not yet the flesh and blood Son of God. Nor did the synthesis of the two concepts take place rapidly. It was the result of centuries of evolution. But, even before Christianity was well launched on its missionary career, the germ of the new Christ was born, in the mind of St. Paul. It was

The Spiritual Logos

he, the greatest of the missionaries, who gave Christianity the potentialities of an universal religion, by tacitly dropping its specifically Jewish aspects. Only those Hebraic features were retained, such as the ban on idolatry, which were considered essential for any transcendental religion; while features such as circumcision, and the Mosaic law and ritual, were jettisoned.[1] Above all, the Messiah concept is discarded. St. Paul, like Philo, was steeped in both Greek and Hebrew culture. In addition, he was a Christian, so that in identifying Philo's Logos with the historical Christ he was probably not conscious of any great innovation, certainly not of the tremendous importance of the concept he thereby created. In the Epistles he refers to it casually, as though it were almost too obvious for mention.

"In whom the god of this world hath blinded the minds of them which believe not, lest the light of the glorious gospel of Christ, who is the image of God, should shine unto them."[2]

In the Epistle to the Colossians the idea is expounded at more length, but with the same air of a lecturer reminding his audience of an elementary truth.

" . . . his dear Son . . . who is the image of the invisible God, the first-created of all creation, by whom all things were created."[3]

If for 'Son' we were to substitute 'world soul' the passage might be from the writings of any Alexandrian Platonist.

Just as the culminating discoveries of Greek philosophy were really latent in its initial assumptions, so the history of Christian thought consists in an unfolding of the potentialities of the Logos doctrine, which in the Pauline literature is an attitude of mind rather than an explicitly stated theory.

In marked contrast with Paul's treatment of the Logos is the formal summary of the doctrine which we find in the fourth Gospel. The Logos is unmistakably the centre of

[1] See The Acts of the Apostles, chapter 15.
[2] 2 Corinthians iv. 4.
[3] Colossians i. 15.

John's religious faith; the Logos, not Christ, is the subject of the opening paragraphs.

"In the beginning was the Word, and the Word was with God, and the Word was God."

Like the Platonic world soul, it is the image of God; it is by this that "all things were made," and it is this of which Christ is the personification. "And the Logos was made flesh."

The first stage in the Hellenisation of Christianity is already complete; the Messiah is all but forgotten, its place taken by the Logos. In the second and third centuries the process goes even further. In the writings of the ante-Nicene fathers, not only does the conception of the Logos become more and more central and important, but there is even a tendency for the Christ Logos to become simply . . . the Logos. Justin Martyr, for example, asserted that the Logos manifested itself, before the advent of Christ, in such sages of the ancient world as Moses, Pythagoras, Socrates and Plato. Although they did not know Christ, these men were Christians because the Logos which was fully revealed in Christ appeared, only in a less perfect form (λόγος σπερματικός) in them. Clement of Alexandria draws conclusions of a similar, though even more far reaching, kind from the doctrine of the Logos. It is not enough, he maintains, merely to assent to the teaching of Christ. He who does this has faith, but this is less valuable than *gnosis*, or understanding. True *gnosis*, the full revelation of the Logos, can only be attained through the study of philosophy. It was later asserted by the Patriarch Photius that Clement did not even believe in an incarnation. That is, of course, a mistaken interpretation of Clement's writings, but the mere fact that such an interpretation was possible is a proof of the extraordinary changes which the Logos doctrine had effected in Christian thought by the third century.

This period, from about the middle of the second to the middle of the third century, is the crucial one in which the

The Spiritual Logos

pattern of subsequent European thought is determined, down to the Middle Ages and, to a degree, down to our own times. In the apologetics of the time the Hellenic-Hebrew form of the Logos concept broadens into a systematic doctrine of Christian Platonism. As in the philosophy of Philo the Jew, the materialistic associations of the Stoic Logos are dropped: the name Logos is retained, not because of its Stoic associations, but rather in spite of them, and because of its similitude with the Hebrew 'Word.' In everything but name, the Logos has become identical with the Platonic world soul. The ante-Nicene fathers did not, and could not, in the nature of the case, produce a unified body of thought, for they were the pioneers who were laying the foundations of Christian thought. But, when we have stripped from their writings the fragmentary and often contradictory doctrines which have since been rejected from the Christian canon, there remains a concept common to all their philosophies, the Platonic concept of the immaterial soul. This is the central core which remains the same beneath numerous differences of emphasis and expression, and it remains the core of Christian doctrine now that the differences of the primitive fathers are forgotten. It is the Platonic philosophy of the immaterial Psyche and the immaterial God, welded to the Hebrew revelation by Philo and adapted by the fathers to Christian apologetics, which turned Christianity from a local cult, subject, like others, to the vagaries of fashion, into a religion with an intellectual basis. A mythology may grip the imagination of a people for centuries, a mystical cult may sweep a whole nation, as the cult of Dionysos swept Greece, into an emotional fervour, but all mythologies, and all purely emotional or magical cults, are bound to be discarded in the end, because they have little intellectual justification, and the intellect outgrows them. Christianity derives its peculiar vitality from its dual nature: it is a synthesis, unique in history, of mysticism and logic. Henceforth the history of Christian thought is the history of

The Idea of the Soul in Western Philosophy and Science

the Platonic renaissance, and in spite of the endless modifications of expression imposed on it by the special requirements of Christian theology, by Aristotelianism, by Hebrew and Arab speculation, this reborn Platonism nevertheless remains an unchanging essence beneath the flow of its modes.

The bridge over which Platonism passed from the ancient to the modern world was, as we have seen, that most rickety of philosophical structures, the Stoic doctrine of the material Logos. But for this peculiar name which the Stoics gave to their debased version of the world soul, Greek thought and the cult of Christ might not have met. For this word, with its dual significance of Reason and Scripture, is the essential link, in Philo's philosophy, in the Pauline writings, in the fourth Gospel, and in the writings of the ante-Nicene fathers, between Hellas and Judaea. Without that synthesis there could have been no Christianity. Christianity *is* that synthesis, and Christianity is the history of Europe.

And the catalyst which brought about that synthesis, thereby determining the course of European history was . . . a pun, the most perfect of all puns, Philo's magnificent and immortal pun on Logos.

> "*Augustine, who as an artist and philosopher, was so explicitly dualist and tragic. . . .*"
>
> REBECCA WEST

CHAPTER IX

The Christian Doctrine of Physis and Psyche: St. Augustine

THE philosophies of the ante-Nicene fathers were the preliminary excavations in which St. Augustine built the foundations of Christian dogma. In his philosophy, Christian thought emerges as a clear and unified doctrine from a long period of conflict and experiment.

Augustine accomplished his work only just in time. Even during his lifetime, Roman civilisation was disintegrating. Twenty years before his death the barbarians had entered Rome, and he died in Hippo during its siege by the Vandals. The growing ignorance and fanaticism within the Church reflected the civil disorder without. St. Augustine was still a young man when the bishop Theophilus caused the destruction of one of the great libraries for which Alexandria was famous. And a decade later, also in Alexandria, a fanatical Christian mob showed its contempt for philosophy by dragging the philosopher Hypatia to the Caesarium, where, on a Christian altar, they tore her to pieces. This act, intended to celebrate the destruction of pagan thought, might have symbolised, rather, its final and irrevocable transubstantiation, through the metaphysics of St. Augustine, into the body of Christian dogma. For it was his philosophy, a synthesis of the exploratory Platonism of the early fathers, which imparted a solid structure to the hitherto fluid and adolescent tradition of Platonic-Christian thought. Thus the Church was provided, just when

The Idea of the Soul in Western Philosophy and Science

it most needed it, with a definite and authoritative doctrine, a rock which stood firm under the waves of barbarism which now swept over Europe. It emerged, three centuries later, in the Carolingian renaissance of learning, as the foundation of scholastic thought.

Into the development of Augustine's thought it is hardly necessary to go: it is sufficient to point out that, like his predecessors in the Church, he founded his thought on that of Plato. His arguments for the existence of God are essentially the same as Plato's arguments for the existence of the Forms. Augustine's God, like Plato's world of Forms, is that in which truth is grounded, the necessary immutable basis for the existence of objective truth, truth which is independent of the changing and conflicting opinions of individuals. For Augustine, however, the world of Platonic Forms or eternal prototypes to which the ectypes of the perceptual world approximate, is not God Himself, but the Logos or divine Wisdom, which is also the Son of God. Therefore in Augustine's philosophy the Forms are a proximate, rather than the ultimate, ground of truth. The Forms were created by God in order that the soul, through contemplation of them, might rise to knowledge of Him. The two essential concepts of Plato's thought, the Forms and the immaterial soul, have now become a trinity, God; the Logos of God in which the Forms have their being; the immaterial soul.

From the historical point of view, however, it is not the Platonic core of Augustine's philosophy which is important, for this was in any case an accepted feature of Christian thought. Of more importance are the modifications which Christian Platonism acquired in its passage through Augustine's mind. These modifications are of great significance for the development of Christian theology, because Augustine, in much the same way as Aristotle before him, misinterpreted Plato's thought as a dualistic philosophy. He rejected Plato's doctrine of a world soul, maintaining, like Aristotle, that the

Christian Doctrine

soul is individual. Therefore he introduced into his philosophy the same discontinuity between living organisms and the rest of Nature which we have remarked in Aristotle. In Platonic, as in Ionian thought, life and Nature were one. Nature was *alive* for Plato, as it had been for the Nature philosophers, for like them he regarded the principle of life as one with the power which moves the whole of Nature. Of course, he differed radically from them in his discovery of the incorporeal nature of that principle. In one form or another, this discovery has been fundamental to every serious philosophy since Plato's day; also, it was the discovery which made Christianity possible. But Plato's concepts, suffering the common fate of intellectual discoveries, have been made the basis of doctrines of which he certainly would not have approved. Once the immaterial Psyche becomes, as it does in the philosophy of Aristotle, an individual strictly confined to the living organism, dualism becomes inevitable. The material world, no longer explicable as a limitation of the 'real' immaterial world, becomes an independent world, set over against the immaterial. And the two worlds, the physical and the psychical, can never interact, because, by definition, they are a pair of independent 'Reals.' Interaction would involve interdependence, a common ground, and this would destroy the separate reality of the two principles, spiritual and material. This is a fundamental difficulty in St. Augustine's, as in Aristotle's thought. Aristotle sought to evade it by the concept of the substantial unity of Form and Matter. Augustine sought another, less subtle, way out, saying that the soul acts on the body through an intermediate essence which partakes of the nature of both soul and body. Of course, the introduction of this intermediate substance really destroys the dualism which it seeks to bolster up. If such a substance is necessary, then two others must be required, one to come between the first intermediate substance and the body, another to come between it and the soul. This in turn demands the introduction of four more intermediate substances, and so on, *ad infinitum*, until body and soul become a continuum, and the original dualism becomes a monism.

It is significant that Augustine follows Aristotle in separating man from the rest of life, as he separates life from Nature. Brutes, he said, have only irrational souls; man has, in addition, a rational soul, and only the rational soul is immortal.[1] But although Augustine retains the Aristotelian distinction between man and all other organisms, he relies on Plato's arguments, which Aristotle rejected, for the immortality of the soul.

[1] Cp. Aristotle's doctrine of the νοῦs.

"There are, it may be, so many kinds of voices in the world, and none of them is without signification."

ST. PAUL

CHAPTER X

The First Renaissance of Platonism: The Carolingian Renaissance

A CENTURY after Augustine's death the barbarians, Goths and Visigoths, Vandals, Franks, Burgundians, Angles and Saxons occupied Europe, from Britain to Greece. The study of philosophy survived only where barbarian influence did not reach. In the fourth century, Themistius, the 'many-tongued' and Prefect of Constantinople, had expounded Aristotle there, thus founding a tradition of Aristotelian studies which not only persisted for centuries in Byzantium, but spread throughout the Mohammedan world. And on the opposite border of Europe, in the remote monasteries of Ireland, the study of Plato and the ancient languages went on quietly, century after century, undisturbed by the distant noise and stress on the Continent. An unexpected fate for Plato's philosophy, the flower of Greek rationalism, to be transplanted from the clear sun of Greece to the remote mists of the land of Cuchulain. When, in the ninth century, the desire for learning reappeared in Europe, it was to Ireland that Europe had to go for instruction. Or rather, Ireland went to Europe, Irish monks taking their books and knowledge to every part of Charlemagne's great empire.

Except for Boethius' translation of the *Categoria*, the first schoolmen knew very little of Aristotle. But they had the *Timaeus* of Plato, the works of the neo-Platonists, and the Platonic philosophies of Clement and Origen. Above all, they

The Idea of the Soul in Western Philosophy and Science

had the works of St. Augustine, the culmination of the Platonic-Christian synthesis begun by Philo the Jew. Thus the ninth century took over the Platonic tradition practically at the stage of development which it had attained in the fourth century, almost as if the intervening years of intellectual sterility had not been. In fact, because the cultural gap had resulted in the loss of the *corpus aristotelicum*, and in the removal of Christian Platonism from the semi-Oriental environment of its youth, the pattern of mediaeval Christian culture was more purely and radically Platonic than the Alexandrian tradition of which it was a development. The religion of the mediaeval Christians was, in fact, nothing but a peculiarly modified form of Platonism. When their thoughts turned to God, it was of Plato's immaterial Demiurgos that they thought, and of Christ as the Demiurgos made flesh. When they thought of the soul and of its fate in the world to come, it was no cabbalistic Hebrew imagination, but the immaterial Psyche of Plato that was in their minds, and their belief in its immortality was founded on Plato's philosophical arguments which St. Augustine had handed down to them. The whole orientation of their culture was, as has often been said, 'other-worldly,' and the other world to which they turned their thoughts and aspirations was none other than the Platonic world of 'real existence, colourless, non-spatial and intangible,' the world of Forms which had come down to them through the concept of the Logos. When they argued about their beliefs, and they argued indefatigably for centuries, they argued about problems which Plato had invented for them: even those who were nominalists, in opposition to Plato, were Platonists, for nominalism is only intelligible, only came into being, as the antithesis of Plato's philosophical realism. The history of Christian thought, from Erigena in the time of Alfred the Great to Alexander of Hales in the thirteenth century, is the history of a four-hundred-year-long controversy over Plato's theory of universals. In the West, Greek intellectualism had assimilated and reorganised

The First Renaissance of Platonism

the quietism of Christ as in the East Buddhist philosophy had usurped the quietism of Laotzu.

During this time the works of Aristotle were making their way back to Europe by a devious route. As early as the fifth century the Syrian Christians had made translations of the Aristotelian texts of the Byzantine schools, and in the ninth century the Syriac versions were translated by Mohammedan scholars into Arabic. The Arabic texts followed Mohammedan civilisation into Spain, where in the twelfth century the works of Aristotle were known and studied in their entirety. The Latin translations of these texts, which now appeared in Europe, were, however, banned repeatedly by the Church, even as late as the second half of the thirteenth century, since the interpretations of Averroes and other Arab commentators were incompatible with Christian teaching. But, after the capture of Constantinople,[1] the Christian world gained access to the original Greek texts, and new interpretations, compatible with Christian dogma, were made, and new philosophies, based on Aristotelian thought, were created.

Of these new philosophies, the most famous and inspired was, of course, that of St. Thomas Aquinas, which brought about a brief revival of Aristotelianism in the thirteenth and fourteenth centuries. In Aquinas's philosophy the thought of Plato again goes through the paradoxical transformation which it has twice before experienced. Like Augustine and Aristotle, Aquinas developed the Platonic idea of the incorporeal Real in a way which was contrary to the spirit of Platonism. Following Aristotle, Aquinas regarded ultimate reality as a compound of material and immaterial essences. Like Aristotle, he tried to evade the consequences of this ontological duality by saying that soul and body, matter and form, are inseparable aspects of a substantial unity, neither being capable of existence independently of the other. To use a simile of which Aristotle was fond, soul and body are like the concave and convex

[1] By the Crusaders in 1204.

The Idea of the Soul in Western Philosophy and Science

aspects of a curve; they are different, but mutually dependent. As Aquinas was not only a philosopher, but also a Christian apologist, this doctrine led him into difficulties which did not exist for Aristotle. For it is very difficult to reconcile this view with the Christian dogma of the immortality of the soul. Indeed, although St. Thomas, as a creative thinker, was superior to the Arab Aristotelians, their anti-Christian interpretations were undoubtedly a fairer representation of Aristotle's meaning than the Thomist expositions. Thus, Aquinas's doctrine of the soul, although it steered him past the Scylla of explicit dualism, brought him dangerously near the Charybdis of heterodoxy. However, he reconciled his account of the soul with the immortality of man by recourse to the doctrine of reincarnation. He said that the soul, although not corruptible *per se*, or even *per accidens*, by reason of its substantial unity with the body, needs the body for its complete being, and hence after death the soul is, as it were, in an incomplete, unnatural state, from which it is only retrieved, at the resurrection, by reunion with the body. Recurring to the simile of the curve, one might diagrammatise the three states thus:

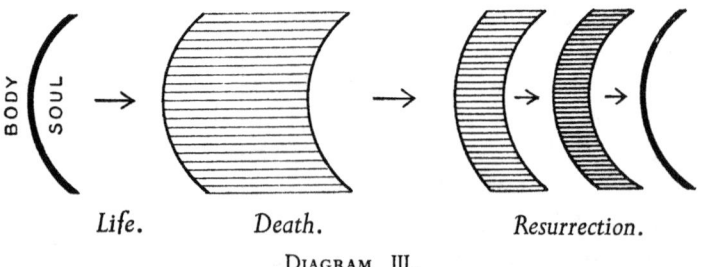

Life.   Death.   Resurrection.
DIAGRAM III.

Aquinas's theory illustrates, perhaps more clearly than any doctrine of Aristotle himself, the materialism latent in Aristotle's interpretation of the Platonic concept of the immaterial Real.

The First Renaissance of Platonism

The popular thought of the Middle Ages was based on a different interpretation of Plato's thought, which, although like that of Aquinas a misinterpretation, was much nearer the spirit of Platonism. The aspect of Plato's teaching which captured the general imagination in mediaeval times, as it has captivated the Stoics and the fathers, was the doctrine of the world-soul. This doctrine, which gave birth to the idea of the Logos, reappeared in the Middle Ages in a new form, less subtle than Philo's concept of the Logos, although by no means so crude as the materialistic interpretation of the Stoics. The mediaeval doctrine (which may be called the *biological* form of Plato's theory, to distinguish it from the Stoic and patristic modifications) was that the cosmos is a vast organism of which God is the immaterial soul. God, although immaterial, is bound to the matter of the cosmos, to the stars and other heavenly bodies, as man is bound to his body of flesh and blood, so that man, in the most literal sense of the word, in the biological sense, is a microcosm of the universe. The most extraordinary cosmologies were worked out, in which the various parts of the heavens were equated to different parts of the human body. In spite of the invective which Aquinas bestows on this view, it continued to flourish in his lifetime and persisted for long after. Even in the seventeenth century similar theories were widely current. Kepler, for example, believed that the earth was a vast organism, and that one day the gills by which it breathed would be found on the floor of the sea.

"*Clearly, if all the events of Nature are to be expressible as syllables of one and the same language, the letters which compose the syllables cannot be colours or sounds or odours. . . .*"

A. E. TAYLOR

CHAPTER XI

The Second Renaissance of Platonism: The Italian Renaissance

MEDIAEVAL culture grew out of the Carolingian revival of learning, a Platonic Renaissance. Yet the Italian Renaissance, which was a conscious repudiation of the mediaeval outlook, was also, on its philosophical and scientific side, a Renaissance of Platonism. The truth of this paradox lies in the width and diversity of Plato's philosophy, which were such that mediaeval and Renaissance thought, superficially so antithetic, nevertheless sprang from the common ground of Europe's Platonic inheritance. The diverse elements of Greek thought which came together in Plato's philosophy, a *summa*, as it were, of Greek culture, formed a unity too grand and complex to be assimilated by any subsequent culture, so that much of the development of European thought is an analysis of Platonism back into its pre-Platonic elements, a reversal of Plato's original synthesis of the discoveries of earlier thinkers. Very broadly speaking, two great streams of thought were confluent in the philosophy of Plato, the one Pythagorean, the other Socratic. And these are the two streams into which Platonism subsequently divided, for while mediaeval European culture was predominantly Socratic, the scientific learning of the Mohammedans drew its inspiration from the Pythagorean tradition. The mediaeval Christian mind ignored the latter because it could understand only the former. Socrates might well have acquiesced in the opinion that, "To discuss the

The Second Renaissance of Platonism

nature and position of the Earth does not help us in the hope of the life to come." At least he would have completely sympathised with the mediaeval viewpoint, so concisely expressed in St. Ambrose's aphorism, a viewpoint from which Nature is a thin backcloth for the solid drama of human life. But to Plato, and to the Pythagoreans, the outlook of St. Ambrose would have been incomprehensible. Plato's world of Forms was the objective truth of *this* world, both in its moral and its mathematical aspects. The mediaeval mind distorted it into a supernatural world, which was regarded, not as the ground of objective truth, transcending the merely personal outlook, but as the source of personal salvation. There were other reasons for the neglect in Christendom of the Pythagorean aspect of Plato's teaching. Of these not the least was the mere fact that it had been so enthusiastically taken up by Mohammedans and Jews. Arabic translations of Euclid, Ptolemy, Hippocrates and others, not only carried the Ionian-Pythagorean tradition into the Mohammedan world, but resulted in important advances in chemical and mathematical investigation. Hence mathematics and chemistry became associated in the Christian mind with pagan culture, and hence, by a negligibly small extension, with black magic and other immoral pursuits. It is significant that Roger Bacon, a prophet of the Renaissance born three centuries before his time, stresses the fundamental importance of the study of Arabic science. The neo-Aristotelian culture which dominated the dying mediaeval culture of Bacon's time was, however, even more than the Socratic culture which it replaced, unsympathetic to the scientific outlook. This was partly due to a defect in Aristotle's philosophy, partly the fault of the schoolmen. Had the schoolmen acquired some of Aristotle's belief in observation, instead of regarding his observations as infallible, Bacon's views might have fallen on more fertile ground. But, quite apart from the exaggerated *a priori* bias which was the chief limitation of scholasticism, a rebirth of science would have

The Idea of the Soul in Western Philosophy and Science

been impossible in any culture dominated by the Aristotelian outlook. A whole community of Aristotles, spending its whole time in the observation of Nature, would never have produced modern science, or anything in the faintest degree resembling it. For Aristotle did not have Plato's understanding of mathematics, or share his faith in its possibilities. In this, as in so many other matters, Aristotle accepted the common-sense viewpoint. He believed, as any common-sense philosopher of his time would have believed, that any further advances in mathematics, although they might be of theoretical interest, could have no influence on the scientific study of Nature. The history of science has shown that Plato's faith was right and Aristotle's common sense hopelessly at fault. How enchanted would Plato have been, could he have foreseen, for example, the use of such intellectual playthings as 'imaginary' numbers in such an entirely practical sphere as that of electrical engineering; and how bewildered Aristotle would have been. It is often asserted by modern writers that the primary feature of the Renaissance of science was the observation of natural phenomena, as opposed to the *a priori* approach of the schoolmen. Emphatically, it was nothing of the kind. Modern science originated in the reappearance in Europe of the Pythagorean-Platonic belief in the significance of Number. In the scientific sphere, the renaissance of that belief was *the* Renaissance. *Pari passu* with the growth of mathematical discovery, more and more observations were needed to feed the mathematical machine, and observation therefore became an increasingly necessary and important part of the technique of science. But, to begin with, the number of observations was small, and the number of experiments smaller, compared with the immense amount of mathematical investigation performed by the pioneers of science. (Even Galileo, for example, attacked Aristotle's theory of falling bodies on purely logical grounds before he performed his famous experiments.)[1]

---

[1] Galileo's 'logical' proof that heavy bodies do not fall more rapidly than lighter ones may be summarised as follows. Consider a body made of four equal sections, *a*, *b*,

The Second Renaissance of Platonism

It is significant that the first successful applications of mathematical technique were made in the realm of astronomy, the branch of science of which Plato had most practical knowledge, and the one which he considered to be the most amenable to mathematical study. It was not a coincidence that this should have been so, for these applications grew directly out of the Pythagorean-Platonic revival in the Italian universities of the fifteenth and sixteenth centuries.

The fall of Constantinople, which brought to Europe the Aristotelian corpus, from which grew the last brief flowering of scholasticism, also brought the Platonic learning which inspired the new culture and overthrew scholasticism. Except for the *Timaeus*, Plato had been known only through Augustine and other Christian interpreters. Now that the principal dialogues became known in the original, their Pythagorean content, which had been ignored by the fathers, was eagerly studied by Italian scholars, prominent among whom was the famous Nicholas of Cusa. The works of the Ionian physicists were also studied in the Italian universities, notably by Telesio and Berigard. A Pythagorean philosophy was expounded by Pico de Mirandola, and his pupil, Maria da Novara, Professor of Astronomy at Bologna, and teacher of Copernicus, criticised Ptolemy's system, not on empirical grounds (in any case it fitted the facts quite well) but for quite different reasons. He criticised it because it was too complex and unwieldy to satisfy the Pythagorean doctrine of mathematical order or 'harmony.' Studying under Novara, Copernicus learnt Greek and read the works of the Pythagorean astronomers. The astronomical system for which he is remembered was in effect a rejection of the Aristotelian geocentric system, which had been perpetuated by the Alexandrian scientist Ptolemy, and

---

c and *d*. Let one section, *d*, be detached. If heavy bodies fall more rapidly than light ones, then the remaining part (*a b c*) will fall more rapidly than *d*. Hence if *d* is now rejoined to *a b c* it will retard its fall: that is, the heavy body *a b c d* will fall less rapidly than the lighter one *a b c*. Hence the original proposition, that heavy bodies fall more rapidly than light ones, is shown to be self-contradictory.

The Idea of the Soul in Western Philosophy and Science

a return to the Pythagorean-Platonic view that the earth is a sphere which moves around the sun.[1] What were the advantages of Copernicus's rehabilitation, in mathematical dress, of the Pythagorean theory? It explained no facts which Ptolemy's system did not account for; and in many ways it seemed to contradict empirical evidence, with which Ptolemy's system agreed. If, as Copernicus maintained, the Earth swept out twice yearly a vast arc, subtending a chord 186,000,000 miles long, there should be an annual parallax of the fixed stars. That is to say, the apparent relative positions of the stars should change (as the apparent relative positions of a group of trees change as the observer alters his position in the field). To-day we know that the parallax does occur, although, owing to the enormous distances of the stars, it is so minute that it can only be observed, for some of the nearer stars, with telescopes and a refined photographic technique. But neither Copernicus nor his contemporaries knew this. Also, since Copernicus lived a century before the foundation of modern dynamics by Galileo, it was thought that if Copernicus's theory were correct, a body thrown up vertically should fall on a spot west of the point of projection. From the purely empirical point of view, then, Copernicus's system was actually inferior to that of Ptolemy, given the state of empirical knowledge of the time. But the new system had one advantage over Ptolemy's. Mathematically, it was simpler. Ptolemy's system merely satisfied the facts of observation; that of Copernicus satisfied, in addition, the Pythagorean doctrine of mathematical harmony. In modern language, it was a more 'economical' description of the facts than Ptolemy's. It was a prototype of a new way of looking at the universe, not entirely novel, because a hint of it had appeared long before in Greece,

---

[1] The early Pythagoreans did not identify their 'central-fire' with the sun. This was done later by Herakleides of Pontos and Aristarchos of Samos (see Burnet, *Early Greek Philosophy*, 151). However, the essential point is that the Pythagoreans regarded the earth, not as a fixed frame of reference, but as a planet moving in space with other planets. The heliocentric hypothesis is a special form of this view.

The Second Renaissance of Platonism

but it was new in modern Europe, and it was the beginning of the outlook, unknown in mediaeval times, which dominates our pattern of culture to-day. Its fruitfulness and significance lies in this, that it was an organic synthesis of the empirical and the *a priori* tendencies of the human mind. To-day it is a fashionable commonplace to talk of the sterility of pure *a priorism*; it is often forgotten that one-sided empiricism is just as barren. Long before the efflorescence of Greek culture the Egyptians and Babylonians had accumulated an immense amount of empirical knowledge, knowledge of geometrical, astronomical, chemical and physical fact. Yet for the purpose of understanding natural principles and predicting natural phenomena, all this knowledge was as useless as the interminable conceptual argument of the schoolmen.[1] And it was not merely accidental that this fertile marriage of the *a priori* and the empirical grew out of a Platonic renaissance; it was a union on which Plato would have bestowed his enthusiastic blessing. To-day he is so often represented as an armchair thinker who held all perceptual knowledge to be valueless. Nothing could be more superficial or unfair than this view, usually based on a misinterpretation of one sentence in the *Timaeus*. Apart from the fact that there are numerous passages in the dialogues in which he insists on the necessity of extensive and accurate observation, the whole argument of his theory of Forms is explicitly against such a view. For the essential point of the theory is, not that observation is valueless, but that only mathematical abstractions from phenomena are significant for the scientist. We have seen that this conception was suggested to Plato by the Pythagorean school of

[1] The Babylonians, for example, could not really predict eclipses, in spite of their diligence in astronomical observation, because they hardly advanced beyond pure empiricism. They found that eclipses occurred at regular intervals in a cycle of 223 lunar months. But from this they could not tell whether or not an eclipse would be visible at Babylon, because, being ignorant of the cause of eclipses, they could not take into account the geocentric parallax. If an eclipse did not occur (i.e. was not visible at Babylon) at the expected time, this was considered a good omen. See Burnet, *Early Greek Philosophy*, i, 4.

philosophy. It is, for example, the numerical abstractions from the phenomena of vibrating strings which are scientifically important, not the qualitative nature of the sound heard. Only a mathematical investigation of the former will enable one to *predict* the behaviour of other vibrating strings. This, of course, is the fundamental point on which the outlook of Copernicus, of modern physicists and of Plato finds itself in contradiction with the teaching of Aristotle. Qualities, for Aristotle, were the important things; for him the greenness of the trees, the bitterness or sweetness of foods, the fragrance of the rose, the consonance or dissonance of sounds, were qualities existing, independently of human perception, 'out there' in the external world. These, for him and for the schoolmen, were the abstractions in terms of which the unification of natural phenomena must be sought. But for Plato the Aristotelian qualities were mere appearances which 'rolled about between Being and not-Being,' their *esse* being solely in the act of perception. Hence in Plato's thought the Pythagorean doctrine of number receives support from epistemological considerations which were presumably unknown to the early Pythagoreans. If the true ground of knowledge cannot be found in the deceitful world of qualities, it must be sought in quantities. Already, before Plato, the atomists had shown how qualities such as greenness could be considered as secondary aspects of quantities such as the size, shape and motions of atoms, although, of course, the idea was not successfully applied to the study of Nature until quite recent times.

Once Aristotle's geocentric universe had been disposed of, the way was made clear for the abandonment of his qualitative physics. The re-creation of physics on a Pythagorean basis was the work of Copernicus's great successors, Kepler and Galileo. Like Copernicus, they worked in a neo-Platonic cultural environment, and both, moreover, were anxious to acknowledge their debt to Plato and the Pythagoreans. Kepler's famous laws were inspired, as Kepler is at great pains to

The Second Renaissance of Platonism

declare, by the same mystical faith in number which inspired the Pythagorean philosophy and Plato's mathematical Forms. It is not, as Dampier-Whetham suggests, "one of the ironies of history that a return to the mystical doctrine of numbers should have led Copernicus and Kepler to formulate a system, which, through Galileo and Newton, takes us in direct descent to the mechanical philosophy of the eighteenth century."[1] Nothing, on the contrary, could have been more natural. Of course, their deeply emotional attitude towards number often led the early Pythagoreans into speculative methods which are now known to be invalid as a means of natural investigation. Because, for example, ten was considered to be the 'perfect' number, they thought that there must be ten heavenly bodies. They therefore (very properly, granting their premises) invented a counter-earth ($\dot{\alpha}\nu\tau\iota\chi\theta\omega\nu$) to make the nine observed bodies, namely the fixed stars, the sun, the five planets, the earth and the moon, agree with the theoretical number. The prediction, in the nineteenth century, of the existence of the planet Neptune, in order to account for the irregularities of the orbit of Uranus, was a manifestation, indeed a lineal descendant, of the same scientific faith that led the Pythagoreans to postulate the existence of an $\dot{\alpha}\nu\tau\iota\chi\theta\omega\nu$. By the nineteenth century, however, more was known about the technique of using the *a priori* desire to find mathematical symmetry in the universe. Certain manifestations of that desire, such as the discovery of the laws regulating the vibration of strings, lead to fruitful results, others, based on grounds such as the perfection of the number ten, are not confirmed by observation. It is easy to understand, however, that in their pioneer enthusiasm the Pythagoreans should have failed to distinguish between the scientific and the fanciful applications of their philosophical theory. The tensor calculus, to choose from contemporary physics an example of a sophisticated use of mathematical technique, has this essential quality

[1] Dampier-Whetham, *A History of Science*.

in common with the naïvest Pythagorean fancies, that it is an attempt to satisfy an emotional desire, the desire to express the relations of a complex perceptual manifold in terse and symmetrical mathematical symbolism. It is now customary, while stressing the fanciful aspects of Pythagoreanism, to forget that this emotional desire is the motive power of science.

Kepler's mathematical investigations were a curious transition from the mystical neo-Pythagoreanism of the Renaissance to the semi-positivistic Pythagoreanism of modern physics. For example, Kepler thought that, as the planets were impelled by an Aristotelian unmoved Mover, an unchanging *primum mobile*, all planets should move with unvarying speed around their elliptical orbits. Observation showed that this was not so. Determined, however, to find something which showed a linear variation with time, Kepler manipulated the results of his observations until he discovered the so-called second law that "the area swept out in any orbit by the straight line joining the centres of the sun and a planet, are proportional to the times."[1] Thus his metaphysical principle was vindicated, the regularity which he had looked for in the linear path being attached instead to the areas swept out by it. The discovery which gave him the greatest joy, and which he regarded as of much greater importance than the laws for which he is famous, was one of the more extravagant issues of his Pythagorean outlook. This was his discovery that the spheres containing the orbits of the planets can be inscribed and circumscribed around Plato's five regular solids. Referring to this discovery he writes:

"The intense pleasure I have received from this discovery can never be told in words. I regretted no more the time wasted; I tired of no labour; I shunned no toil of reckoning, days and nights spent in calculation, until I could see whether my hypothesis would agree with the orbits of Copernicus, or whether my joy was to vanish into air."[2]

[1] Quoted from Dampier-Whetham, *History of Science*, chapter iii.
[2] Oliver Lodge, *Pioneers of Science*. Quoted from Burt, *Metaphysical Foundations of Modern Science*.

The Second Renaissance of Platonism

Galileo's chief contribution to science was also a return to a Platonic principle. Plato believed that once a body were set in motion it would continue to move unless impeded by some external resistance to its motion. The schoolmen, following Aristotle, thought that motion required the continual application of force to sustain it. By his experiments with inclined planes, Galileo proved Plato's assumption to be the correct one. Further, he saw that it is not necessary to postulate a force to keep the planets in motion, but that what did require explanation was the curvature of the planetary paths. If left to themselves, the planets should move for ever of their own accord, but in straight lines. The required explanation of the curved paths was found, not by Galileo, but by Newton. Once Newton had synthesised the theories of Galileo and Kepler into a new whole, the pattern of modern science was determined. The gravitational theory combines Galileo's law of motion with Kepler's mathematical description of the orbits of the planets, gravitational attraction being brought in to explain the deviation of the planetary paths from straight lines. One would expect such a gravitational force to obey an inverse square law, since one may conceive the attractive force to be dissipated over the surface of a sphere of increasing radius as it spreads out into space from the centre of attraction. Proceeding on this assumption of an inverse square law, Newton was able to arrive at a mathematical deduction of the laws which Kepler had derived from the observations of Tycho Brahe.

In spite of its important place in Newtonian theory, Galileo's law of motion is less important in the history of thought than his revival of the theories of the Greek atomists. Although the schoolmen knew of these theories, which Plato reproduces in the *Timaeus*, they were not deeply interested in them, and when they became acquainted with Aristotle's metaphysics and physics, they followed him in his rejection of the atomic theory. This is just what one might have expected, for like

Aristotle the schoolmen always adopted the common-sense view about physical matters, however transcendental their metaphysical views. It is common sense that the earth goes round the sun, one can see that it does, with one's own eyes, just as easily as one can see that matter is continuous, not atomic.

Although the original atomic theory was not due to the Pythagoreans, its revival by Galileo was the direct outcome of the contemporary revival of Pythagorean Platonism. It was Kepler who laid the foundation on which Galileo built his epistemology. Kepler believed, not only that the task of science was the discovery of mathematical harmonies, but that the hidden mathematical harmony of nature is the *cause* of natural phenomena. Things are as they are, not out of arbitrary caprice, but because of mathematical necessity. Kepler was aware that this view brought him into conflict with Aristotle. For if mathematical harmony is the all-pervading cause of things, it follows that the qualities revealed by sense perception are less real than the quantitative relations discovered by mathematical reasoning. Greenness, for example, is an unique qualitative fact, redness or a bitter taste another. The qualitative differences between these are absolute and irreducible. Since it is impossible to find a common perceptual ground for the plurality of unique qualities given in perception, a philosophy, such as Aristotle's, which does not question the independent reality of such qualities, must assume that only the individual is real. But quantity, unlike quality, is continuous, and if the real cause of phenomena is quantitative, or mathematical harmony, then there *are* no irreducible facts; all material phenomena must be organically connected parts of a vast mathematical continuum, and given the requisite mathematical skill, it must be possible to deduce any part of nature from other parts. On this view the irreducible qualitative facts given in sensation must be in some sense illusory, and only the universal is real. Reasoning of this kind led Kepler to his

The Second Renaissance of Platonism

belief that the real world is inherently quantitative, in spite of the evidence of the senses to the contrary. Kepler's philosophical speculations did not go further than this suggestive but very vague identification of the Platonic Forms with the world of mathematical conceptions. His belief in the inferior ontological status of perceptions was simply an attempt to give some sort of metaphysical expression to his conviction that only mathematical truth is universal and certain. But he did not attempt to describe the relation between percepts and mathematical concepts; nor could he say in what way the former were less real than the latter. In spite of his doubts about their reality he does not seem to have doubted that percepts, whatever they might be, are really 'out there' in some kind of independent external world. Although, therefore, Kepler seems to have been groping towards epistemological arguments such as those of Plato in the *Theaetetus*, or those of the Greek atomists, there is no evidence that he ever succeeded in formulating such arguments.

It was along these lines, however, that Galileo extended Kepler's views. In place of Kepler's obscure distinction between the perceptual and the real world, Galileo makes a clear and simply definable separation between objective qualities. The former are primary, the latter secondary: to the latter class belong all qualitative perceptual distinctions, whether of colour, taste, smell, sound or heat. These are secondary, because they exist, not in the thing observed, but only in the mind of the observer, and when he ceases to observe they cease to exist; they are purely mental, having no being apart from minds. The 'real' world, that is to say the world as it exists independently of being perceived, is colourless, odourless and silent; it is a world having only such purely mathematical attributes as extension, shape, motion and weight,[1] and these, the real or primary qualities, are translated by the

---

[1] Galileo seems to have been in some doubt whether weight should be called primary or secondary.

sense organs into the secondary or mental qualities. Hence the uncertain and illusory nature of the perceptual world arises from the arbitrary and varying transformations which the real world undergoes in its passage through the organs of perception. As will be seen from the following citation, Galileo's reasons for this view are in principle identical with those which Plato, in the *Theaetetus*, imputes to Protagoras:

> "I think that by an illustration I can explain my meaning more clearly. I pass a hand, first over a marble statue, then over a living man. Concerning all the effects which come from the hand, as regards the hand itself, they are the same whether on the one or on the other object, that is, these primary accidents, namely motion and touch (for we call them by no other names) but the animate body which suffers that operation feels various affections according to the different parts touched, and if the sole of the foot, the kneecap, or the armpit be touched, it perceives besides the common sense of touch, another affection, to which we have given a particular name, calling it tickling. Now this affection is all ours, and does not belong to the hand at all. And it seems to me that they would greatly err who would say that the hand, besides motion and touch, possessed in itself another faculty from those, namely the tickling faculty; so that tickling would be an accident that exists in it. A piece of paper, or a feather, lightly rubbed on whatever part of our body you wish, performs, as regards itself, everywhere the same operation, that is, movement and touch; but in us, if touched between the eyes, on the nose, and under the nostrils, it excites an almost intolerable tickling, though elsewhere it can hardly be felt at all. Now this tickling is all in us, and not in the feather, and if the animate and sensitive body be removed, it is nothing more than a mere name. Of precisely a similar and not greater existence do I believe those various qualities to be possessed, which are attributed to natural bodies, such as tastes, odours, colours and others." [1]

It is clear that, like Plato, Galileo regarded the perceptual world as a derivative world, which, in the sense that it derives its being from a more ultimate world, may be said to "roll about between Being and non-Being."

How is the perceptual world related to the real world? How does the qualitative, subjective world derive its being

[1] Opere. iv. 333 ff. Quoted from Burt, loc. cit.

The Second Renaissance of Platonism

from the quantitative, objective world, and in what does the quantitative nature of the real world consist? Kepler had not even envisaged the possibility of an answer to these questions; Galileo, on the other hand, put forward a solution which transformed the emotional, intuitive Pythagoreanism of Copernicus and Kepler into an hypothesis so simple, clear and fruitful that it still dominates the scientific outlook. Briefly, Galileo's view was that the objective world consists of material quanta, or atoms, and that the qualitative differences of the perceptual world are a mental translation of the quantitative changes of the atomic world. Heat, for example, does not exist independently of perception; it is simply a subjective way of experiencing the average velocity of a swarm of atoms. The velocity of the atoms is real, and exists whether it is perceived or not; the sensation of heat, caused by the bombardment of atoms, is subjective, different in different observers, even when they are observing the same object, and has no existence apart from their experience. Similarly with the other senses. Taste, in its almost infinite qualitative variety, is but the mental counterpart of the shape and velocity of the atoms in the substances tasted. These epistemological consequences of the atomic theory have less scientific than philosophical importance. Considered purely as a physical hypothesis, the utility of the atomic theory lies in the fact that it translates qualitative alterations into purely quantitative changes of pattern. For example, the perceptual differences between ice, water and steam are not susceptible of mathematical treatment. But the atomic theory reduces these differences to changes in the spatial relationships of water molecules, which are less closely packed in steam than in liquid water. Such configurational differences, unlike the immediate perceptual differences with which they are associated, can be expressed in mathematical symbols. The application of this simple principle to chemical phenomena, in the nineteenth century, was one of the greatest achievements of human thought.

The Idea of the Soul in Western Philosophy and Science

As we have pointed out, Galileo's atomism was an adaptation of the Greek atomism which was being revived by his contemporaries. And neither the physical nor the epistemological deductions which he made from the atomic theory were original, for both had been quite clearly formulated by Democritus and his school, if not, indeed, by Leucippus. What was new, however, and of supreme importance, was Galileo's synthesis of Pythagorean philosophy and of Greek atomic theory. The Democritan form of the atomic theory was in itself of little use as a scientific tool, because it did not suggest a technique by which its *a priori* concepts could be related to the perceptual world. On the other hand, the Aristotelian method, the mere observation, undirected by conceptual principles, of secondary qualities, was even more useless for scientific purposes. As soon as the quantitative consequences of the atomic theory were understood, it became a scientific hypothesis, that is, an hypothesis suggesting measurements. It was Galileo's intuition of the mathematical possibilities of Democritus's theory which made science, as we know it, possible.

Nevertheless, the epistemological implications of Galileo's neo-Pythagorean atomism, and not the mathematical physics to which it also gave rise, were the most important philosophical outcome of the Pythagorean Renaissance. To follow out these implications to their logical conclusion, thus crystallising into an explicit philosophical system the neo-Pythagorean thought of the Renaissance, was the work of Galileo's great contemporary, Descartes.

"*Qu'on me donne l'etendue et le mouvement et je vais refaire le monde.*"

DESCARTES

CHAPTER XII

The Para-Physical Psyche:
The Neo-Pythagorean Philosophy of Descartes

THE development of European thought in the sixteenth and seventeenth centuries was in many ways strikingly analogous to the development of Ionian thought in the ancient world. In both periods the outstanding thinkers were nature philosophers. Each period was dominated by one fundamental idea, the early one by the idea of Physis, the later epoch by the Pythagorean concept of Number, an immaterial, mathematical Physis. And because of the preponderant interest in external Nature, the concept of the soul is all but absent from Renaissance, as from Ionian speculation. Yet each period gave rise to a metaphysical doctrine of the soul which was to dominate thought for centuries afterwards.

Descartes' philosophy, which was partly an expression of, partly a reaction from, the outlook of his predecessors, stands in much the same relation to the modern world as that of Socrates to the ancient world. Cartesianism has moulded the modern outlook, in part directly and in part through Kant, just as the Socratic aspect of Platonism was the dominant element in mediaeval culture.

Cogito, ergo sum. I think, therefore I am. This, the most celebrated of Descartes' utterances, may be regarded as a protest against the neglect, in the philosophy of his time, of man and the problem of the soul. Galileo had shown that perceptions are 'mental' events, at any rate in the sense that they do not belong merely (i.e. absolutely) to the surface of physical objects. But the 'subjectivity' of percepts does not in any way detract from their reality, still less from that of the mental world in which they have their being. Let us say, with Galileo, that the redness of the rose is 'not really out there,' that it is a creation of my Psyche, having no place in the physical world. The redness, as such, is just an irreducible fact of experience, and if it does not exist in the physical world, its reality must be rooted elsewhere, and the physical world is so much the poorer. In the sense that they do not exist apart from me, all my perceptions may be deceitful, but the mere fact that I am thus deceived is a self-evident guarantee of *my* reality! Merely in order to be deceived, I must really exist. Galileo's arguments may indeed lead me to doubt the existence of the physical world, but it is impossible to doubt the existence of the mental, or psychical world which I call "I." In the very act of trying to doubt it, I should be forced to admit its reality. For if I doubt, at least I cannot deny the reality of my doubting. Though the whole physical world may crumble before my scepticism, at least there remains . . . my scepticism! *Quod si fallor, sum.* Descartes' arguments remind us, inevitably, of Augustine's famous epigram, which may well have suggested the Cartesian *cogito, ergo sum.* Augustine's phrase was intended as a refutation of the superficial scepticism of the Academy, and no doubt that of Descartes stood in much the same relation to the sceptical implications of Galileo's epistemology.[1] The Psyche, which in Galileo's mathematical universe was in danger of extinction, is reinstated by the Cartesian formula as an ultimate fact.

But, although his philosophy ostensibly begins with it, Descartes was not primarily interested in the self. It is true that from the notion of the self he deduces the existence and veracity of God, and from the veracity of God the existence of an external world. But the arguments by which he does

[1] Although Descartes does not explicitly present it in this light.

The Para-Physical Psyche

this seem curiously artificial, and indeed incredible,[1] for the simple reason that he was innately convinced of that which he purports to arrive at by rational argument, namely, the existence of an external world in so far as it is clearly and distinctly apprehensible.

In so far as it is clearly and distinctly apprehensible. In this innocent-looking qualification lies the whole crux of the Cartesian philosophy. For, to Descartes, clearly and distinctly meant *mathematically* apprehensible. Before and above all, Descartes was a Pythagorean. And his Pythagoreanism, like that of Copernicus, Galileo, Kepler and for that matter Pythagoras, was not so much the result of a chain of reasoning, as the emotional attitude which inspired his reasonings. Copernicus and Kepler, indeed, hardly attempted to discover reasons for their Pythagorean outlook: Galileo had the genius to discover very good ones in a reinterpretation of the atomism of Democritus, and Descartes embodied them in a metaphysical system. His philosophy was a formal metaphysical expression of the Pythagorean tradition of the previous century, as well as the medium through which that tradition became dominant in modern culture. It is therefore peculiarly apposite (almost too much so, as though Nature were imitating Art) that his whole career should have been haunted and directed by a vision, an ecstasy such as the ancient Pythagoreans were wont to experience, in which the identity of natural law and mathematical truth was revealed to him. It was from this Pythagorean vision on St. Martin's eve, this vision which to the end of his life was his most vivid memory, that his whole philosophy came into being.

Although Descartes was a more acute metaphysician than any of his great contemporaries, his philosophical outlook, like theirs, rested almost entirely on an unquestioned faith in

---

[1] This is not to say that the ontological arguments of St. Anselm and Campanella (of which the Cartesian arguments are restatements) are in themselves incredible, but simply that Descartes' adaptations of these arguments, torn from their scholastic setting and transplanted into his anti-scholastic philosophy, carry no conviction.

the reality and primacy of mathematical truth. Could he have been more critical, more self-conscious even, of that faith, he would no doubt have anticipated Berkeley's discovery of the 'subjective' nature, not merely of the secondary qualities, but also of the so-called primary ones. As it was, he merely repeated,[1] Galileo's arguments for the subjectivity of the secondary qualities, and accepted, as uncritically as Galileo, the objective reality of the primary qualities. And this for the same reason as Galileo, namely, that these are the raw material of the mathematician. The primary qualities, for Descartes, constitute the essence of materiality. Motion and extension alone are 'really out there,' while the redness of the rose and all the other secondary qualities are mere subjective additions, added by the Psyche in the act of perception. However much the secondary qualities of an object may change, however different they may appear to different observers, they are always modes of extension. We can quite readily conceive of the material world deprived of colours, tastes, odours and sounds. Deprived of all these it would still be a spatial world, and, since spatiality is the very essence of matter, a material world. But it is impossible to conceive of an unextended body. As Kant later expressed it, we can 'imagine away' every secondary quality of a material body, but we cannot imagine away the space which it occupies.[2]

Descartes' identification of matter and extension leads to some curious consequences, of which the most important is that there is no such thing as 'empty space.' What we think of as 'empty' space is simply a region of the spatial manifold displaying different properties from those other regions which we call material. This view, as others have pointed out,[3] has

---

[1] Presumably without having seen *Il Saggiatore*.

[2] Thus Kant founded the *a priori* nature of the primary qualities on the very grounds which, to Descartes, seemed to prove their objectivity!

[3] See, for example, A. E. Taylor in *Contemporary British Philosophy*: What gives the generalised theory of relativity at once its fascination for the physicist by instinct and the repellent character it has for the average non-scientific man is that it seems

The Para-Physical Psyche

affinities with the picture of the universe given by relativity mechanics. It was in order to leave matter with nothing but geometrical qualities that Descartes was led to construct his extraordinary cosmology. The chief feature of this cosmology is its explanation of weight, and of planetary movement, by the idea of 'vortices' in space. All motion, terrestrial and celestial, is impressed on matter by the vortices, in which it passively swims. By this hypothesis Descartes was able to dispense with 'occult' notions such as the force, or attraction, of Galileo, and the 'active powers' by which Kepler explained celestial motion. Thus matter, in the Cartesian system, is deprived of every shred of intrinsic activity. The only attributes left to it are extension, and the passive ability to be moved from without. Motion was impressed on it in the beginning by God's creation of the vortices. But, once God has thus impressed this primary motion on the material world, there is no further necessity for divine action.[1] The primary motion is simply partitioned out and transferred (without increase or diminution in total amount) from body to body, according to laws deducible from the mathematical nature of extension.

But what of the Psyche, on the reality of which the whole Cartesian system is based? What of life; what place has it in this grandiose scheme? What of the secondary qualities, and of emotions and thoughts? These cannot be reduced to extension. Still less can they be dismissed as unreal. Even if I only 'think' I see colours, at any rate I really think I see them. The secondary qualities are as real as anything else, even if they are not really out there. And if the reality of these things cannot be reduced to extension, it must be of an altogether different kind from that of matter. As the being of matter is in extension, that of mind is in thinking (hence *cogito*) by

---

to eliminate the ultimate 'irrational' stuff, 'first matter' from scientific theory. It achieves what the greatest of all rationalists among modern philosophers, Descartes, dreamed of three hundred years ago, the identification of 'matter' with 'extension.'

[1] Except in so far as the gross quantity of motion is maintained by His 'general concourse.'

which Descartes seems to have meant what we should denote by the wider term, cognisance, including not thinking only, but also volition, perception and imagination. The thinking mind and extended matter are in every respect the opposite of one another. Matter, the *res extensa*, is dead and infinitely divisible. Mind, the *res cogitans*, is living, and being unextended, indivisible. The Psyche has no spatial extension, the external world no life.

Now this notion of dead matter, which to the modern mind seems almost self-evident, was one of Descartes' more revolutionary inventions. Far from being an obvious or naïve conception, it is a highly metaphysical view to which we have grown so accustomed, owing to the profound effect of Cartesianism on modern culture, that we find some difficulty in conceiving of any other. Thales was expressing a much more obvious and natural view when he said that the magnet and amber have souls (i.e. life) because of their attractive power. We have seen that Descartes, in his desire to deprive matter of every trace of activity or life, constructed a mechanistic cosmology in which even the gravitational property of matter is impressed on it from without. A matter which retained weight, or attractive force, as an intrinsic property, would not be quite dead, and therefore not completely distinct from the spiritual or living part of the universe, the *res cogitans*.

Far from allowing a soul to the magnet, or amber, Descartes would not even concede one to animals. That is to say, he extended his mechanistic, neo-Pythagorean view of the universe to the animal body. In this he was, as it were, extrapolating the previous development of Renaissance thought. The schoolmen had followed the ancients in believing the matter of the heavenly bodies to be different from, because more divine and perfect than, terrestrial matter. And such a view was natural enough. To uncritical sense perception there seems to be little community between the behaviour of the heavenly bodies and that of mere terrestrial matter, between

The Para-Physical Psyche

the mathematical perfection of the planet's path and the idle fluttering of foliage in the wind. And the behaviour of living things must have seemed even more unpredictable, more capricious than the wind that bloweth where it listeth. But Galileo's researches had laid the foundations of a science of terrestrial, or 'local,' motion employing the same mathematical technique which Kepler had applied to the study of planetary motions. And in Newton's laws the identification of celestial and terrestrial mechanics became complete. Descartes' physiology was a logical extension of this evolution of ideas. If the mathematical 'harmony' of celestial mechanics can be extended to include terrestrial matter, why should it not be extended one stage further, to *living* matter? Why should the laws of mechanics cease to apply at the surface of the living body? Like the rest of Nature, the living body is a material structure, and therefore, like the rest of Nature, must be simply a mathematical machine, wholly explicable and wholly predictable in terms of mathematical concepts such as impact and motion. There is no need, in such a machine, for a soul to animate it or for an *entelecheia* to provide a final cause for its activities. Such concepts, it seemed to Descartes, are as superfluous as the mediaeval concept of spirits which guided the planets in their courses. True, the motions of the various parts of the body, like the momentum of the planets, must be derived ultimately from the primordial motion impressed by God on the vortices. But if God had ceased to exist, after setting the machinery of the world in motion, it would have gone on moving, and animals, which are just specially complicated parts of the great cosmic machine, would have come into being and gone on living without divine aid.[1] The swallows appear in the spring for the same kind of reason that explains the regular striking of a clock, or the regular reappearance of a planet. The flight of the lamb from the wolf is a purely automatic process, initiated by the rays of light

[1] This, as Descartes saw, implies an evolutionary view of life.

reflected from the wolf and falling on the optic nerve of the lamb. Descartes even attempted to describe the working parts of the animal body, as one would describe the levers and wheels of a man-made machine.

He became acquainted with, and eagerly adopted, the theory of the circulation of the blood propounded by his contemporary, Harvey. This discovery, together with his own numerous and painstaking dissections, formed the basis of his theory of animal mechanism. He believed that certain particles of the circulating blood are converted by the warmth of the heart into a fluid, more subtle than the blood, which he called 'animal spirits.' The animal spirits, leaving the circulatory system, run up into the cavities, or ventricles, of the brain. Connected to these cavities are the nerves, which Descartes took to be hollow tubes. These nerves are of two kinds (see Diagram IV). Afferent nerves, a, a_1, bring in impulses from the sense organs, S, to the ventricles. These afferent impulses generate in the ventricles an 'agitation' which causes animal spirits to flow along the outgoing, or efferent nerves, e, e_1, thus setting into motion the muscles, or other effector organs, E. From S to E there is an unbroken chain of mechanical cause and effect, obeying just the same mathematical laws which govern the motions of the planets and of non-living terrestrial matter. The series of events, from S to E, is purely physical; there is no reference to the Psyche, or to any psychological concepts such as sensation or volition. This *omission* is the most brilliant and significant stroke in the Cartesian system, one which only a thinker of superlative courage and insight could have made.

But how is man related to this mechanistic scheme? How can the philosophy which bases itself on the position that 'I think, therefore I am,' lead to a psychology which omits all reference to the Psyche?

I think, that is, I am conscious, therefore I am. Descartes' problem is this—how is consciousness related to the mechanis-

The Para-Physical Psyche

tic scheme, of which even living matter is an integral part? Descartes very neatly disposed of the problem, in so far as the lower animals are concerned, simply by denying that they are conscious. An animal, he said, is merely a complex auto-

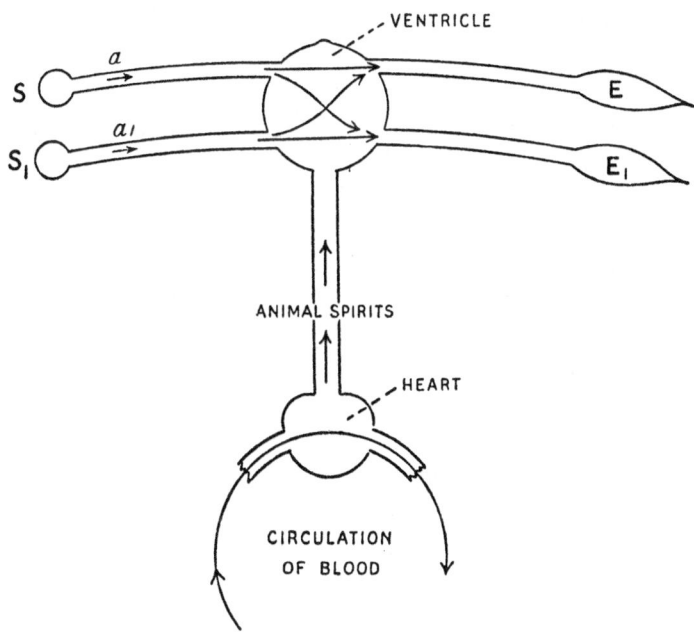

DIAGRAM IV.—THE ANIMAL ORGANISM.

S, S_1 = Sense Organs. a, a_1 = Afferent impulses.
E, E_1 = Effector Organs. e, e_1 = Efferent impulses.

maton without sensations, volitions, thoughts, in short, without a Psyche. Although it is a specially complex and highly organised part of the material world, an animal is purely material; it moves as blindly as a planet or a clock.

So that the problem, for Descartes, is narrowed down to the human organism. We have seen that in the statement, *cogito, ergo sum*, Descartes was emphasising the ultimate, irreducible nature of consciousness. From Galileo's demonstration of the 'subjectivity' of percepts, it is not a very big step to doubt the existence of an external world altogether. But since even the most thorough-going subjectivist cannot doubt the existence of his sensations (though he may refuse to refer them to an external cause), consciousness is a fact more ultimate and certain even than the existence of an external world; it is the one fact that cannot be doubted, since doubting is itself just a special instance of consciousness. But if consciousness cannot be explained away, still less can it be fitted into the mechanistic scheme, the *res extensa*. The redness of the rose, the philosopher's scepticism, these are utterly separate from extension and motion; their reality is not spatial, but psychical. So much, we have seen, follows directly from the Galilean-Cartesian theory of perception embodied in the doctrine of 'primary' and 'secondary' qualities. The *res cogitans* and the *res extensa* are mutually exclusive.

And there we have the solution of Descartes' problem. Man is a dual being, a mechanism in the extended realm, a soul in the realm of consciousness. Like the living matter of the animal body, the human body is an integral fragment of the great mechanistic scheme. In the human body, as in that of the animal, there is an unbroken chain of physical cause and effect from receptor to effector. Like the lower animals, man is an automaton. But he is a *conscious* automaton—not a mere machine, like the animal, but a machine with a Psyche. Or rather, a machine *and* a Psyche. For the Psyche and the machine do not touch at any point. The Psyche does not do anything to the machine (since the physical sequence from receptor to effector is unbroken), nor, conversely, does the machine act on the Psyche. The spiritual Psyche and its spatial machine are like two clocks, adjusted to move in exact unison, but never interacting.

And however odd this notion may seem, it follows with undeniable logic from Descartes' neo-Pythagorean assumptions. If material and psychical being are different in essence,

The Para-Physical Psyche

the essence of the one being in extension, that of the other in thought (i.e. cognition), then any interaction of mind on matter or vice versa, is absolutely precluded. For if they interacted in any way, events in the one could only be understood by reference to events in the other, and thus the supposedly different essences would turn out to be mere aspects of one essence. Hence in order to keep the external world purely a world of extension, to keep it, in other words, a purely mathematical world, Descartes had to deny, not the reality of the Psyche, for that was impossible, but the possibility of interaction between the physical and the psychical world. The idea, derived from introspection, that mind and body interact, must be illusory.

If light, reflected from the rose, falls on my retina, I perceive redness. But the physical event (i.e. the photo-chemical change in my retina) does not cause the psychical event (the sensation of redness). I perceive redness because my Psyche is 'wound up' as it were, to experience redness just when the afferent impulse from the rose reaches my brain. This clock strikes the hour at the same moment as that other one, not *because* the other strikes, but because the two mechanisms were designed to move in unison. "How red the rose," I say; but that does not mean that the physical rose, the extended entity 'out there' has in any way affected my Psyche. The afferent impulse from the rose, falling on my retina, causes an efferent impulse which moves my vocal chords and facial muscles in such and such a way, producing the sounds "How red the rose." But all that is purely mechanistic, entirely in the *res extensa*, having nothing to do with my Psyche. Between my volition and the vocal movements there is no causal connection; my Psyche was simply 'wound up' to make such and such an act of volition just when my vocal apparatus moved in such and such a way.

While denying the existence of a causal bond between mind and body, Descartes hesitated to deny all psycho-physical interconnection. What, then, is the relationship if not a causal one? Descartes' answer was that corporeal events may be the 'occasions' of mental events, and vice versa. Unfortunately, it is an answer to which no very precise meaning may be attached. By saying that corporeal and mental events could be the occasions of each other, he evidently meant to indicate some connection closer than mere temporal simultaneity, yet less close than a causal connection. But it is difficult to imagine the nature of such a bond, and Descartes himself does not enlighten us by a precise definition. Indeed, one suspects that he is unconsciously trying to affirm and deny interaction in the same breath, thus satisfying the demands both of common sense and of the Cartesian metaphysics.

In his more consistent passages, however, it is clear that Descartes has in mind a parallelism, without interconnection of any kind, between machine and Psyche. Moreover, the Psyche, being an unextended essence, cannot be in one part of the body rather than another, or indeed *in a place* of any kind. But Descartes maintained that the Psyche is 'present to' the body in one part of the brain, namely, the pineal body. There the Psyche, which is not extended, 'acts into' the world of extension. The meaning of 'present to' is as difficult to imagine as that of the term 'occasion' in its Cartesian usage, and no doubt the ambiguity of both terms springs from the same ambiguity in Descartes' thought. We have already seen that Descartes was aware of the fundamental relationship of the nervous system to bodily movement and sensation. And this particular part of the nervous system, the pineal, was selected as the *point d'appui* of the soul because of its position above certain cavities, through which, Descartes believed, the animal spirits flow into the ventricles of the brain. Secondly, the pineal, unlike most cerebral structures, is not reduplicated on the right and left sides of the brain. Only in such an unpaired organ could the Psyche, being extensionless, come into relationship with the extended universe. The process may

The Para-Physical Psyche

be symbolised thus: (Diagram V). As in the animal, the sequence of events, S A B′ E, from sense organ to effector organ, is a chain of physical causation, uninterrupted by intervention from the Psyche. But the Psyche is 'present to' the pineal body. This relationship we have endeavoured to show by symbolising the Psyche, or *res cogitans*, as an area, enclosed by a dotted line, around the pineal. (It must, of course, be

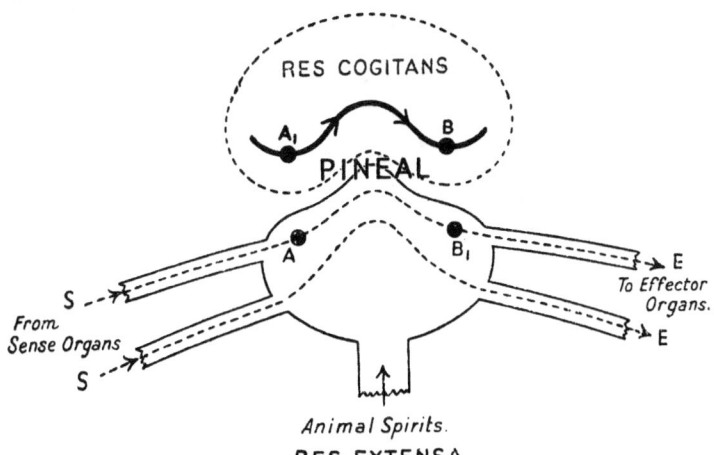

DIAGRAM V. THE HUMAN ORGANISM.

kept in mind that the *res cogitans* does not occupy space.) The motion of the animal spirits, entering the ventricle at A, is the 'occasion' of the sensation A′ in the *res cogitans*. Similarly an act of volition, B, in the *res cogitans* is the 'occasion' of the efferent impulses leaving the ventricle at B′. But between A and A, or between B and B, there is no causal bond. The psychical sequence A′ B, is merely parallel to the physical sequence A B′.

Thus far Descartes' psychology, even if incredible, is wholly consistent with itself. But he deviated considerably from the strict doctrine of psycho-physical parallelism, or 'occasionalism' which we have outlined. He always denies, as he must to avoid flagrant inconsistency, any psycho-physical

The Idea of the Soul in Western Philosophy and Science

causation. But he also asserts that psychical events may 'direct'[1] physical events, in the following way. Suppose that an efferent impulse, entering the ventricle at P (Diagram VI), could with an equal expenditure of energy cause an efferent impulse to leave either at Q or at R. Of course the efferent impulse Q Q' would result in a different action from the impulse R R', because it would stimulate different effectors. Descartes sup-

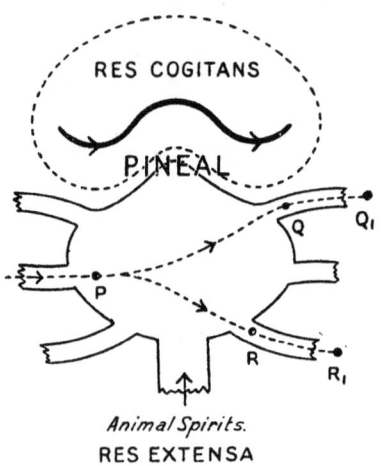

DIAGRAM VI. THE HUMAN ORGANISM.

poses that the Psyche, 'acting into' the pineal body, may determine which of the two possible paths the physical impulse shall follow. Thus, in directing the impulse into one channel or the other, the Psyche, without interrupting the physical sequence of cause and effect, and without putting energy into it, would nevertheless control its outcome.

Unfortunately, even this kind of relationship between mind and body is quite inconsistent with the Cartesian metaphysical dualism. For if it be really possible for the (physical) event P to cause either Q or R, this can only mean that P, independently of the Psyche, *has a choice* of Q or R. For whether the Psyche

[1] Thus the driver of an automobile is not the cause of its motion, but he nevertheless directs it.

The Para-Physical Psyche

is there or not, P cannot cause both Q and R. Hence, if the Psyche does not choose for it, it must itself make a choice between the two possibilities lying before it. This implies that the sequence P ⟶ Q or R is not purely physical, in the Cartesian sense of the word. And if such open possibilities exist in that part of the *res extensa* which we call the human body, they can, on Descartes' own showing, occur anywhere else in the spatial realm, and the material world would then cease to be a mathematical mechanism of the Pythagorean type. If, on the other hand, the event P left to itself (i.e. uninfluenced by the Psyche) could cause Q only, and not R, then the Psyche, in determining that it shall cause R, is imposing a physical force, in the direction QR, on the flow of animal spirits.[1]

Hence the result of any sort of 'direction' of the body by the Psyche is either to make the Psyche physical or the body psychical, in either event destroying the mind-matter dualism which is the basis of Descartes' metaphysics. We have seen how, in order to make the *res extensa* a wholly 'dead,' unspiritual world, Descartes had to conceive even of gravitational motion as impressed from without on an entirely inert matter (by the vortices). The directive interaction between spirit and matter is of course a surreptitious reintroduction into the material world of the spiritual force which Descartes so carefully expurgated in his physical theory.

* * * * *

Descartes' philosophical successors and adherents were quick to seize on the inconsistencies of his psychological theory, and to remove them from the Cartesian canon. If even the 'directive' action of the Psyche be disallowed, how are we to explain the parallelism which is all that Descartes' system will logically support? If there be no psycho-physical interaction, how can there be even a psycho-physical parallelism? If there is a psycho-physical parallelism, and on this

[1] See Appendix, p. 164.

point it is really impossible to doubt our intuition, how can it be maintained that there is no psycho-physical interaction? There are hints, in Descartes' own writings, of a metaphysical way out of the dilemma, although he did not himself follow them up consistently. Had he done so, he would have formulated a philosophy of 'Occasionalism' similar to that of Malebranche, the greatest of the Cartesian thinkers. In so far as it can be briefly summarised, the Occasionalist doctrine is simply that neither mind nor matter is substantial. God is the only true substance; mind and matter are each modes of the divine substance. Hence neither the physical sequence of events in the body, nor the psychical sequence in the mind is really a causal sequence. Each is but a temporal succession of effects, of which the single cause is the will of God.

* * * * *

The academic philosophies to which Descartes' thought gave rise, however, are of small importance compared with the extraordinary orientation it has imparted to all intellectual activity in modern Europe. That its effects were so far-reaching was due, less to its purely philosophical merits than to the overwhelming success of the mechanistic method which it advocated for scientific investigation. And it was not unnatural that modern thought, influenced more deeply by the scientific outlook than by any other factor, and profoundly impressed by the practical success of Cartesian mechanism, should have accepted, more or less uncritically, the metaphysic with which that method was associated. If we may invert a popular metaphor, modern culture has taken in, not only Descartes' mechanistic baby, but the metaphysical bath water with which he surrounded it.

It is, then, in the Cartesian metaphysic that the peculiar individuality of the contemporary pattern of culture has its roots. Yet the novelty of Descartes' thought springs, not from fundamental principles, but rather from the fact that it is the

The Para-Physical Psyche

clearest expression of a concept which is latent in all philosophies, perhaps even in the myths which preceded philosophy. It is the ancient tendency to divide Being into two great classes, which, finding in Cartesianism so perfect an expression, differentiates it so sharply from all previous thought.

We have referred to this tendency as it appears in the thought of even the most primitive cultures. Even before he can analyse his own speech, primitive man expresses, in holophrastic form, his unconscious realisation that the whole of his experience can be analysed into two classes, on the one hand the existence of external objects and on the other hand the existence of those objects as visual and memory images in consciousness. Of course, this conception carries with it no more than the faintest intuition of epistemological problems. Not that the idea of an essential difference between object and percept was formulated by primitive man; such a notion could hardly have been made comprehensible to him. For him the mental image is simply a reflection of the object. Except that the image is conceived as somehow 'thinner,' less palpable, than the object, the two are only numerically different. But the distinction between object and percept, however vaguely conceived, is of supreme importance to the mind of primitive man. The duality of the world is for him its most general characteristic, and his language expresses this duality by dividing Being into two kinds, namely, objects and souls. Primitively the soul is simply the percept or image, depending on an observer for its existence, as distinct from the object of perception, conceived to have an independent life. And, if only because of the technical inadequacy of primitive language, the two kinds of entity, intuitively distinguished, are not explicitly separated. On the contrary, objects and souls are conceived as everywhere in mutual compenetration, meeting and fusing in the metabolism of a living world. Indeed, for primitive man the most important feature of the universe is its impregnation, as it were, by soul. Just because

The Idea of the Soul in Western Philosophy and Science

the world is alive it can be influenced by sympathetic magic; the 'object' can be controlled by manipulating its 'soul.' Primitive myth is an emotional, as magic is a practical, expression of this fundamental intuition of duality, for the mythical world of gods and heroes represents a world not merely chronologically, but in some sense ontologically prior to the phenomenal world. Because they realised that the ontological priority of the 'real' world is not adequately symbolised by putting it in a remote region of space and time, the Ionians substituted Physis for the gods and heroes. Physis which is not in remote parts of, but everywhere pervading the spatio-temporal world. The change from the mythological to the philosophical point of view is epitomised by Thales' saying, "All things are full of gods." Nor could one find a more concise expression of the fact that, for Ionian cosmology as for the primitive cults of the soul, the universe was a living universe; the immanent Physis is alive. The history of Ionian thought is the development of the idea that the distinction between Physis and the phenomenal world is a distinction between reality and appearance. And although the idea attained its full expression in the philosophy of Parmenides, it was left to Plato to follow out its full implications. Through Platonism the hylozoic universe of the Ionians was transmitted to the Christian world. The Christ Logos, like the Fire Logos of the Stoics and the Platonic world-soul from which both derived, was a living principle permeating the material world. Because the physicists of Ionia had seen all things as full of gods, the mediaeval Christians were enabled to see God in all things. Nor was the Aristotelian universe a dead universe. It is true that matter as conceived by Aristotle was not living matter as that of the Ionians had been. But it was matter pervaded by living Entelechy, by 'final' as distinct from mere mechanical causation.

Like the Aristotelian Entelechy, like the Fire Logos and the Christ Logos and the Forms of the Thomist hierarchy,

The Para-Physical Psyche

Descartes' *res cogitans* is a modification of the Platonic immaterial Real, the lineal descendant, through Thomism[1] and St. Augustine's neo-Platonism, of Plato's "Real existence, colourless, non-spatial, and intangible, visible only to the intelligence which sits at the helm of the soul." The *res cogitans* and the mediaeval concept of the Spirit have St. Augustine as their common ancestor. Both concepts, like Augustine's Platonism, are Socratic, in that they are derived from Platonism in its Socratic aspect. We have seen, also, how the other half of the Cartesian metaphysic grew out of the revival of the mathematical aspect of Platonism, the aspect which had been ignored by the fathers and the schoolmen.

But Descartes was unable to repeat the Platonic synthesis of teleological and mathematical truth. His *res extensa* was the product of Renaissance, or Pythagorean Platonism, his *res cogitans* that of the Socratic Platonism of an earlier age. The Cartesian universe is . . . two universes, each representing a half of Plato's universe, severed by history and rounded off by Descartes into a self-subsistent whole.

The universe of extended entities, on the one hand, of colourless and soulless quanta moving silently in an eternal and minutely predestined mathematical dance; on the other hand, a capricious qualitative world of scents and sounds and colours, a world of fluent and illusory phantoms, subjective appearances haunting certain delicate, labile and infinitesimally small bits of matter called living organisms. The Psyche, the Logos which will not go into a spatio-temporal Schema, yet cannot be explained away, is stuffed into the unilluminable recesses of the pineal gland. With it, into this fantastic biological limbo, go all the action and passion of the human soul, and with them, Beauty, Justice, and other essences which in Plato's philosophy occupied a very different realm. Copernicus' astronomy removed man from the centre of the universe; Descartes' philosophy all but pushed him quite outside it.

[1] Thomism was an important part of Descartes' curriculum at La Flèche.

APPENDIX TO CHAPTER XII

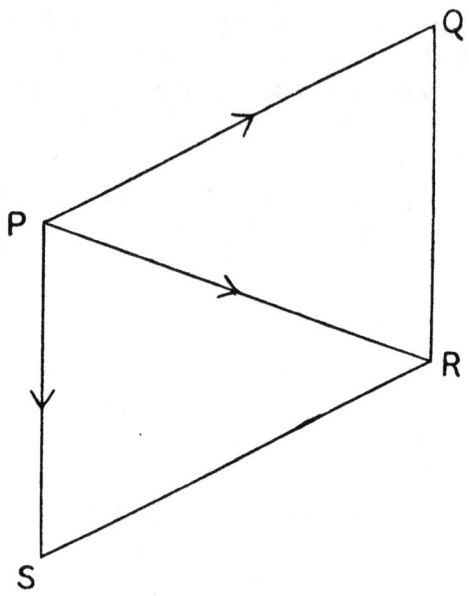

DIAGRAM VII.—Let PQ represent the 'undirected' path of the animal spirits, that is, the path which would be taken if there were no directive action by the Psyche. And let PR represent the path actually followed by the animal spirits, as the result of the directive action of the Psyche. By constructing a parallelogram of forces PQRS, it can be seen that the Psyche is exerting a force in the direction PS (or QR) on the flow of animal spirits.

> "*Que diable allait-il faire dans cette galère?*"
>
> MOLIÈRE

CHAPTER XIII

The Cartesian Traditions

PHILOSOPHY, science and the man in the street have each, in different ways, come to terms with Descartes' philosophy.

Although 'vitalistic' theories are older than Cartesianism, it is nevertheless true that, in modern times, vitalism has arisen as a compromise between Cartesianism and commonsense thought. The modern common-sense conceptions of God and the material world are in origin and essence Cartesian, although Descartes, could he be aware of them, might well hasten to disclaim parental responsibility. It is to Cartesianism that we owe the prevalent 'common sense' view of the physical world as a self-subsistent mechanism, created by God, but thereafter independent of divine causation and intervention.[1] And common sense has accepted, not entirely, but with important reservations, the Cartesian view of the Psyche. To mediaeval common sense the immaterial Real was a divine Logos, an universal spirit which moves the whole of matter, and of which the individual soul is a microcosm. The contemporary common-sense view is Cartesian, in that it conceives the Psyche to be restricted to organic beings, little islands of life in an infinite sea of soulless mechanism. Too often, indeed, the Psyche is thought of, quite literally, as a little speck of *material*, surrounded by an expanse, inconceivably large, of matter of quite a different character. Thus common thought, combining incompatibles in the inimitable

---

[1] Although Descartes himself often leans towards the (more profound) mediaeval view, for which creation is not an act in time but an *eternal* relation between Creator and creature.

The Idea of the Soul in Western Philosophy and Science

manner of common thought, unites in one protean concept the primitive view of the soul as some kind of thin matter, a 'breath' or vapour, and the sophisticated Cartesian idea of a *res cogitans*. Hence the uncomfortable and, unfortunately, widespread suspicion, engendered in avid minds by a diet of popular astronomy, that the importance of the soul is somehow commensurate with the insignificant dimensions of the human brain in relation to the immensity of the light-year. But even common sense has found itself quite unable to digest Descartes' psycho-physical parallelism. And, with much less reason, it has found the Cartesian extension of mechanism to the human body equally difficult of acceptance. To the ordinary man (and in such matters the testimony of the ordinary man is by no means to be discounted) it is just obvious that the mind acts on the body, and that in so acting it is a free and autonomous entity, unconstrained by mechanistic, or any other extrinsic laws. Accordingly the human (if not the animal) body, is conceived to be, at least in part, immune from the otherwise universal dominion of mechanism. This freedom and immunity is conceived to be conferred by the Psyche, which is thought of as some kind of 'vital' or anti-mechanistic principle which in the human organism modifies the purely mechanical behaviour of 'dead' matter. So that in popular, as distinct from philosophical thought, the immaterial Real has become a sort of unsubstantial, though really material, 'vital' principle related to the brain in much the same way as an operator to a telephone exchange. Dionysos is now indeed, a *fallen* god, a poor wage slave, operating single-handed in its osseous prison a machine of almost unbelievable complexity. Such a view, in so far as it admits of precise philosophical statement at all, is incapable of withstanding the slightest critical analysis. Yet Descartes himself must bear some, at least, of the responsibility for this view, for it will readily be seen that his account of the 'directive' action of the Psyche contains the germ of what we have called the common-sense or vitalistic view.

The Cartesian Traditions

While common sense quite calmly accepted what it believed to be the consequences of Descartes' dualism, rejecting on the other hand Cartesian mechanism, philosophical thought has generally speaking taken the opposite course of accepting the mechanism but repudiating, or at least mitigating, the dualism. Except in the systems of the English empiricists, the Cartesian concept of mechanism has indeed been a dominant influence in all serious philosophy since Descartes. Spinoza's treatment of the concept of substance has its origin in the Cartesian doctrine of occasionalism which was perfected by Malebranche. By means of his new concept of substance, Spinoza was able to reconcile Cartesian mechanism with his concept of an immanent Deity, thus avoiding the dualistic implications of Cartesianism in its original form. And the fundamental features of Leibniz's monadology, as of Spinoza's pantheism, are its complete rejection of Descartes' qualitative dualism and an equally thoroughgoing acceptance of Cartesian mechanism, now incorporated into a qualitatively monistic but substantially pluralistic universe. Finally, Kant's *Critique*, the most impressive if not quite the happiest product of modern philosophy, attempted to deduce, from purely *a priori* considerations, the Pythagorean presuppositions of Renaissance and Cartesian thought. It purported to demonstrate that mathematical truth and Cartesian mechanism are necessities of thought, and that, from its intrinsic nature, the spatio-temporal world could not be other than a mathematical machine in the Cartesian sense. In respect of scope and generality Kant's philosophy therefore stands in much the same relation to Descartes' philosophy as the latter to the thought of Galileo, Kepler, Copernicus and others. His thought is in fact a rational justification of the semi-mystical beliefs of Renaissance neo-Platonism.

The scientist, without bothering overmuch about the philosophical implications of mechanism, has tested it out in fact by accepting it as a working hypothesis. In physics the success of the mathematical approach is too well known to call for much comment. As we have already pointed out, relativity mechanics has reduced physical method to pure geometry to an extent which Descartes, given the limited mathematical and observational techniques of his time, could only envisage in inspired prophecy. In the biological sphere the application of the mechanistic method promises to give results as startling, and from the philosophical point of view, as significant as those of the new physics. As a speculative idea, biological mechanism is as old as Anaxagoras, and as a mature philosophical concept as old as Descartes, but as an experimental method, comparatively new. A philosophical concept is one thing, a successful experimental technique quite another. The concept of biological evolution, like most of our fundamental ideas, as old as classical Greece, was negligible as a cultural influence until brought to the touchstone of detailed observation. Although the evolutionary concept was familiar to Descartes, to the Renaissance philosophers and for that matter to St. Thomas Aquinas, it had to wait for Darwin before it could become a force in our pattern of culture. *Mutatis mutandis*, the same is true of Greek atomism, and of Zeno the Eleatic's conceptions of the relativity of space and time. For all the refinement and maturity of his metaphysics, Descartes himself postulated mechanism more as a matter of faith than of pure reasoning. It is true that Kant purports to provide us with what amounts to an *a priori* proof of the necessity of Cartesian mechanism. But the discovery, in the nineteenth century, of non-Euclidean geometry, has on the smallest estimate, thrown doubt on some of the deductions of the *Critique*. Therefore, it is at least open to suspicion that Kant's deduction of mechanism may be susceptible to objections of a like kind.

In the last resort, then, the validity of biological mechanism can only be established by biological experiment. And it is perhaps one of the most significant cultural events of the present day that the abstract conception of mechanism is

The Cartesian Traditions

'coming alive' in the hands of the experimentalist. It is no mere accident that the outstanding feature of Descartes' philosophy, the first both in time and importance of modern philosophies, should be the concept of biological mechanism. Nor is it a mere accident that Plato should put his discussion of biological mechanism at the most dramatic point of the most dramatic of his dialogues. For it is precisely the idea of biological mechanism, or 'behaviourism,' as it is now usually called, which Socrates is made to discuss, in the *Phaedo*, as he sits awaiting his execution at Athens.[1] This prominence of the behaviouristic concept just at the two crucial points in the history of Western thought, far from being fortuitous, is due rather to its supreme importance. Two and a half millennia ago, Socrates was no doubt justified in dismissing as 'infantile' the behaviourism which he attributed to Anaxagoras. Moreover, it is understandable that behaviouristic views should have played no part in the Socratic culture of the Middle Ages; they could not, because the means for their experimental verification were not available. But to-day, owing to the growth of the Pythagorean culture which we have inherited from Descartes, biological mechanism is no longer infantile. It is growing up, with extraordinary rapidity, into a system of concepts as revolutionary as those which have already emerged from the use of the Pythagorean method in the realm of inorganic Nature. These concepts must give an entirely new orientation to the central problem of philosophy, epitomised by the words Physis and Psyche. Indeed, we shall now endeavour to show that the Socratic problem of the relationship between mind and matter appears in a changed light because the 'infantile' notions of Anaxagoras have grown into a mature science. Because it presents the issue between Anaxagoras and Socrates with such vivid and deliberate dramatic intensity, as though foreshadowing its importance for modern thought, Plato's 'behaviouristic' passage in the *Phaedo* may indeed be regarded as prophetic.

[1] See page 71.

> "*The second difficulty was created by the fact that the Aristotelian viewpoint still prevails to some extent in biology, namely, that an animal moves only for a purpose, either to seek food or to seek its mate or to undertake something else connected with the preservation of the individual or the race. The Aristotelians had explained the processes in the inanimate world in the same teleological way. Science began when Galileo overthrew the Aristotelian mode of thought and introduced the method of quantitative experiments which leads to mathematical laws free from the metaphysical conception of purpose and reduces the reactions of animals to quantitative laws. This has been attempted by the tropism theory of animal conduct.*"
>
> JACQUES LOEB

CHAPTER XIV

The Neo-Pythagorean Method in Biology

ANY attempt at verbal description of biological mechanism is almost comparable, in foolhardiness, to a description of the beauty of a picture which the reader cannot see. The former can only be fully understood in the biological laboratory, as the latter may only be appreciated in the picture gallery. To handle living matter under experimental conditions, to remove, say, the heart from a living animal and incorporate it in an artificial circulatory system, to keep it beating and alive under such conditions and to be able to accelerate its beat or retard it, even to stop or start it at will, as easily as one controls an internal combustion engine . . . such commonplace laboratory manipulations carry with them an immediacy of imaginative appeal which is hardly translatable into verbal description.

In everyday life the animal organism presents itself to us as an entity of an unique kind, incapable of resolution into simpler entities, still less of synthesis from such. Hence the

The Neo-Pythagorean Method

vitalistic assumptions of common-sense thought. The methods and results of the experimental biologist, however, present the organism in a wholly different light, as an arrangement of parts which is indeed complex, but, like any other material configuration, susceptible to the ordinary technique of the physicist or chemist. To the biologist the living organism is much as, say, a wireless set to the physicist. Like the wireless set, the organism is a machine which can be taken to pieces and put together again. But whereas the physicist starts by considering very simple groups of events, from which he may synthesise such a complex organism as a wireless set, the biologist must take the complex organism as a going concern. He is in fact rather in the position of the 'untutored savage' faced by a chronometer, and hence his difficulties are altogether of a different kind from those which confront the chemist or physicist. His mastery over living matter, although already striking, is still quite limited. He can, it is true, manufacture two-headed or ten-legged frogs, cyclopean fishes and frogs with eyes in their backs; with relative ease he can perform such teratological feats as the grafting of a half animal of one species on to a half animal of another, or the production of tadpoles as big as frogs and frogs no larger than flies; he can change cocks into hens and grow fragments of chick heart, *in vitro*, conserving their youth and vitality long after their natural owner would have grown up and died of old age.

But he cannot yet, and may not for some time be able to, create a living organism out of the carbon, hydrogen, oxygen and the few other elements which enter into the make up of living matter. He might indeed be compared with a savage, who, having acquired a number of chronometers, has learnt how to take them to pieces and refit them, and even how to arrange the cog-wheels and other parts into new clocks of his own design, although he is still without the technical resources which would enable him to make cog-wheels and springs out of mineral ores. Nevertheless, the number of

The Idea of the Soul in Western Philosophy and Science

'organic' compounds which can be synthesised from their inorganic elements is growing daily. When Wöhler synthesised urea, previously unobtainable except from living organisms, he had destroyed one of the stock arguments of the vitalist. "When, in 1828, Wöhler prepared the ammonia salt of his acid he was astonished to find that the salt . . . did not appear to exhibit the character of an ammonia salt at all, but turned out to be identical with urea, a substance which heretofore had been known only as one of the organic compounds of urine. Prior to this discovery a wide and impassable gulf had in the minds of chemists separated the mineral from the organic kingdom. Inorganic bodies had all appeared to be derivable from their elements by a succession of acts of binary combination. . . . Organic substances, on the other hand, were supposed to be things of an entirely different order; in them the few elements which they all consist of were assumed to be united with one another, each with each, in a mysterious manner, which could be brought about only by the agency of 'vital force.' Vital force, it was now seen, had nothing to do with the formation of urea at any rate. The gulf was bridged over. . . ."[1]

The more recent and elaborate syntheses, by Fischer, of the complex polypeptides, has carried the science of chemistry into the very heart of living structure. Already we are, as it were, beginning to learn how to make some of the simpler kinds of cog-wheel.

But such feats being still in their infancy, the most striking result of the mechanistic method is the biologist's power to predict the behaviour of the organism as a whole. Long before our hypothetical savage could find out how to make a clock for himself, he would learn to predict the behaviour of clocks.

In broad principle the theory propounded by Descartes as a means of predicting animal behaviour was a remarkably accurate prevision, in spite of the fact that it was erroneous

---

[1] "Wohler," *Encyclopaedia Britannica*, ninth edition.

The Neo-Pythagorean Method

in every conceivable point of detail. That is to say, it is now an established experimental fact that afferent impulses, flowing in from the sense organs, cause impulses to flow out along the efferent nerves to the muscles and other effectors. But Descartes was mistaken in taking the nerves to be hollow structures. In fact the nervous impulse, although it is a material process, as Descartes thought, does not consist of a flow of material

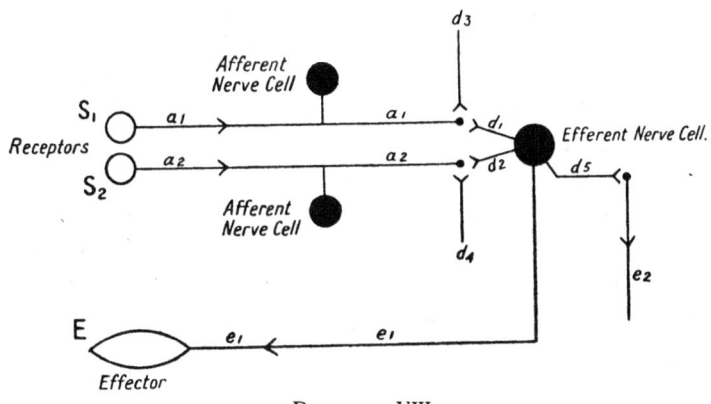

DIAGRAM VIII.

down the nerve. It may best be compared, not with the flow of liquid in a tube, but with the progress of a flame along a fuse, or of a wave down a stretched rope. In either instance, nothing material is transported; what travels is a material process, in the nerve a metabolic process. So that, whereas Descartes thought the nervous system was like an hydraulic system, we now know that it is more nearly comparable with a telephone exchange. The units of the biological 'exchange,' that is, of the central nervous system, are of two kinds, namely, the afferent and efferent nerve cells or *neurones*. The diagram (VIII) shows one efferent and two afferent nerve cells: the long conducting threads (a_1 and a_2) of the afferent nerve cells bring impulses from the sense organs (S) into the central nervous system, where they flow into the short conducting threads (d_1, d_2, etc.) of the efferent nerve cells. From the efferent neurones they flow back, through the long efferent threads (*e*) to the effector organ E. The lamb, Descartes asserted, flees from the wolf because the afferent impulses from the lamb's eye, passing down the optic nerve, are reflected back to the muscles of its legs, thus causing them to make running movements. In the diagram, S_1 or S_2 would represent the lamb's eye, a_1 or a_2 its optic nerve, and E the muscles of its legs. The impulse from the retina of the eye, set up there by the image of the wolf, flows into the central nervous system, whence it is reflected back, as it were, to the muscles, so that the flight of the lamb is a 'reflex' action and the nervous impulse which causes it a reflex 'arc.' Of course the pattern of reflex arcs in the central nervous system is immensely complex. Through connections such as d_3 and d_4 the afferent impulses may flow into other efferent paths, and through still other connections such as d_5 and e_2 the efferent neurones at different levels within the central nervous system are interconnected. Hence, as in a telephone exchange, any incoming or afferent impulse may be deflected into any required outgoing or efferent path.

We have seen how Socrates imputes to Anaxagoras a desire to schematise the actions of the human organism solely in terms of effector organs such as 'bones and sinews,'[1] thereby reducing the activity of the living being to a purely perceptual and mathematical pattern such as Pythagoras had revealed in musical phenomena. To-day the experimental biologist, the modern Anaxagoras, is discovering the physical schematisation of the Psyche, not in the effector organs themselves, but in the pattern of reflex arcs, the labyrinth of Cartesian units of action and passion which mediates the behaviour of a frog, or Socrates, or of any other living being.

The stock examples of reflex action are the contraction of the pupil of the eye in strong illumination, and the watering of the mouth caused by the smell or sight of food. In the first

[1] Vide ante, p. 71.

The Neo-Pythagorean Method

instance the receptor (S) is the retina of the eye and the effector (E) the iris muscle; in the second instance the receptor is the retina or the olfactory epithelium, the effector being the salivary gland. Not only simple reflexes of this kind, but even the most elaborately co-ordinated actions, may take place in the absence of conscious effort, or indeed in the entire absence of consciousness. Thus a headless frog, if a drop of acid be put on its back, will bring the extremity of its hind limb to the exact spot and wipe away the irritant. And there is the notorious behaviour of the decapitated hen, which if permitted will run around the farmyard.

The first comprehensive attempt at a Cartesian explanation of animal behaviour, without reference to psychological concepts, was made by Jacques Loeb.[1] His theory of animal tropism was in fact the first experimental verification of the bio-mechanistic concept discussed by Socrates in the *Phaedo* and formulated in detail by Descartes. A tropism is the "turning of an organism, or part of one, in a particular direction in response to some special external stimulus."[2] The definition reminds one of Descartes' explanation of the flight of the lamb from the wolf; and this must have been, in effect, the first instance of a theory of reflex tropism, for it is not a specific mechanistic theory of behaviour, but rather the general concept of 'behaviourism,' which is attributed to Anaxagoras in the *Phaedo*. Loeb, however, demonstrated the existence of reflex tropisms, not in mammals (where, as we shall see later, a simple theory of reflex tropism is in any case inapplicable) but in much simpler forms of animal life. For example, it is well known that certain insects 'like' the light; that is to say, they will turn themselves until they face any bright light in their vicinity, and creep towards it. In Loeb's terminology, they are *positively phototropic*. His mechanistic theory of phototropism is based on the fact that if the right eye of an

[1] J. Loeb, *Forced Movements, Tropisms and Animal Conduct*.
[2] *Oxford English Dictionary*.

The Idea of the Soul in Western Philosophy and Science

insect be more strongly illuminated than the left eye, the legs of the right side are more acutely flexed than those of the left side. Therefore when the animal moves forwards, it will be carried along a curve to the right, owing to the fact that the legs of the left side, being more extended than those of the right side, have a greater locomotory effect than the oppo-

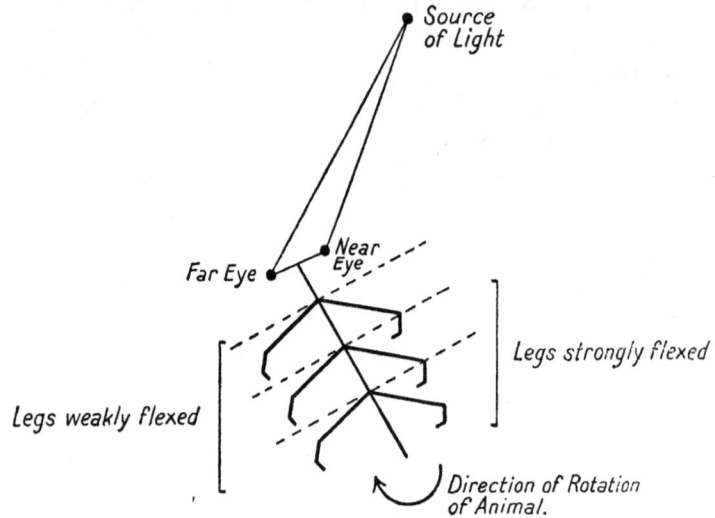

DIAGRAM IXA.

site members. Now, if such an insect be illuminated from a source of light lying to its right (as in Diagram IXA), its 'near' eye, receiving the light less obliquely than the 'far' eye, will be more strongly illuminated. Therefore the legs of the right side will be more acutely flexed than the opposite ones, and the animal will rotate towards its right side, as described above. That is, it will rotate until it faces the light. Then the eyes will be symmetrically illuminated, the legs symmetrically flexed, and the animal will go straight towards the light.[1]

Loeb's theory of heliotropism has this striking advantage over any attempt to account for the behaviour of the insect

[1] For a more formal explanation, see the Appendix to this chapter (Diagram IXB).

The Neo-Pythagorean Method

in terms of its supposed sensations and desires. The content of the insect's consciousness (or for that matter of the consciousness of a fellow human) cannot be observed. Nor does there seem to be any possibility of our ever observing such, so that an explanation of this type is in terms of entities which seem to be *in principle* unobservable. But a mechanistic theory, such as Loeb's, is entirely in terms of physical entities, which in principle, if not always in fact, are susceptible of observation and measurement. On the basis of such observations and measurements we can predict the behaviour of the insect in experimentally devised conditions. If our observations coincide with these predictions, the theory may be accepted as a hypothesis which will suggest still further predictions and observations, in the light of which the theoretical basis may be made increasingly precise and comprehensive.

For example, it follows from Loeb's theory that an insect with one eye removed, or covered, should, in a uniformly illuminated environment, make 'circus' movements with the normal eye toward the centre of the circular path. This prediction is found to be verified by experiment. And if a normal animal be exposed to two sources of illumination it should move between them at an angle depending on the positions and relative intensities of the lights. For known conditions this angle can easily be calculated, and it is found to agree with the observed angle.[1]

Of the tropisms investigated by Loeb and contemporary workers, one of the most remarkable is geotropism, the orientation of the animal with respect to the gravitational field. It is quite obvious, without any special knowledge of

[1] A most odd and interesting outcome of Loeb's theory was the Heliotropic Machine of J. H. Hammond. This machine, the idea of which was suggested to its inventor by the theory of animal heliotropism, consists of a box on wheels, provided with selenium cells and a steering gear. The selenium cells, representing the eyes of the insect, control the steering gear through relays, thus reproducing the effect of the light-controlled 'tone' of the leg muscles of the insect. Such a contrivance can be stopped and started by an external source of light and will follow a moving light even though the latter be made to follow a devious path.

The Idea of the Soul in Western Philosophy and Science

biology, that our eyes are light receptors; to know this we have but to close our eyes. But that we have 'geo-receptors' is by no means so apparent. We cannot normally see our

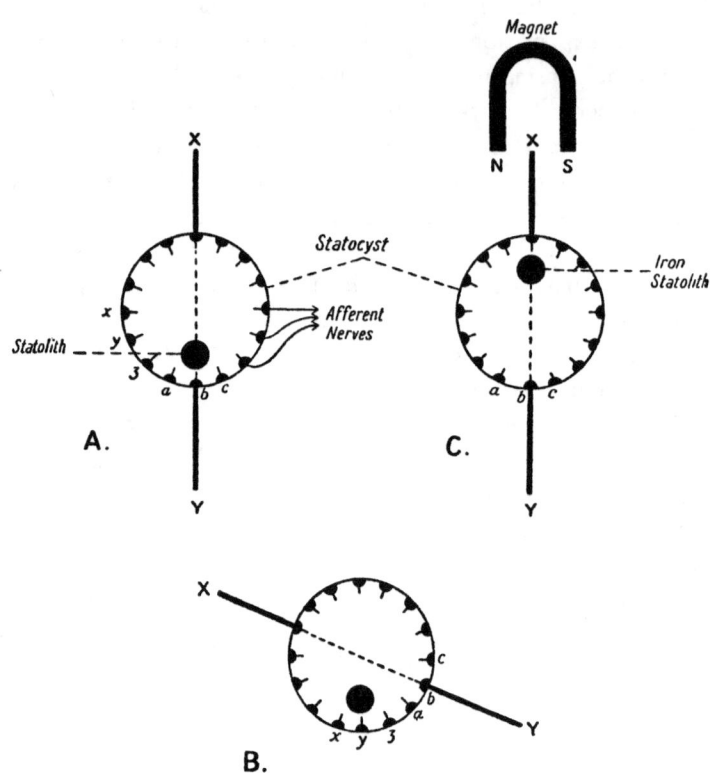

DIAGRAM X.
A. Upright Animal.   B. Tilted Animal.
C. Animal with Iron Statolith pulled up by a Magnet.

geo-receptors, nor can we shut out our sensations of gravitation, as we can those of light. Hence it does not even occur to us to ask how it is we know, even in the dark or when our eyes are closed, whether we are 'right side up' or 'up side down.' For this reason the receptors which give us this information were not discovered until quite recent times. In

The Neo-Pythagorean Method

Crustacea and other invertebrates the receptor for geotropic reflexes is the statocyst. This consists (Diagram X) simply of a hollow sphere, lined on its inner surface with numerous nerve endings, and enclosing a small solid particle or *statolith*. If the animal be swimming normally (right side up) the statolith presses on the lower nerve endings (a, b and c). But if the animal becomes tilted the statolith will press on different nerve endings (x, y and z). So that for every given degree of tilt of the animal, there is a different position of the statolith, and hence a different nervous impulse from the statocyst. The various afferent impulses from the statocyst are reflected back to the leg muscles, which by their swimming movements correct the tilt of the animal. Although more complex, our own geo-receptors in the internal ear are in principle identical with those of the crustacean. If deprived of the internal ear by disease, we can no longer tell, without the help of our eyes, whether we are vertical, horizontal or upside down. In dealing with the geotropic reflexes of the crustacean, however, there is no need to refer to the supposed content of the animal's consciousness. Its behaviour can be completely described in terms of the simple fact that changes in the position of the statolith bring about reflex changes in the swimming movements so as to restore the animal to an upright position. Deprived of its statocysts, the creature swims upside down, sidewise or in any other orientation, indifferently. Such an animal is 'geo-blind,' as an animal deprived of its eyes is light blind. With the statocyst of one side removed, the animal swims in spirals. This is analogous with the circus movements of a unilaterally blinded animal.

Usually, the statolith is secreted by the tissues of the animal. But sometimes the lith is a sand grain placed in the cyst by the animal. This fact was ingeniously used by Kreidl for experimental purposes, in this way. The sand grains fall out at every moult and are then replaced by the animal. Kreidl took a moulting animal and put it in a dish with iron filings instead of sand, so that the animal provided itself with iron liths. By bringing a magnet near such an animal the statolith can be attracted to the upper part of the statocyst, although the animal is still swimming right side up (Diagram Xc). The lith is now in the position which it would normally occupy if the animal were upside down. Now the normal swimming reflex comes into operation to bring the lith back to the nerve endings a, b, c, so that the animal swims upside down as long as the magnet is held above it. By means of the magnet the space perceived by the animal has been turned through two right angles. If two magnets are used the animal orients itself to the resultant magnetic field, behaving in a manner analogous with that of a heliotropic animal exposed to two lights.

The theory of reflex tropisms, of which we have given a bare outline, has proved itself to be an extraordinarily fruitful means for the mechanistic description of animal behaviour. Although modern work has necessitated numerous modifications of Loeb's original theories, it has revealed no inadequacy in the type of Cartesian method which he advocated.[1]

Obviously, however, the concept of reflex tropism goes only a very small way towards a complete mechanistic theory of animal behaviour. Anaxagoras, far from being able to produce a physical schematisation of the actions of Socrates in terms of such a concept, would need far more than this even for the description of the behaviour of a dog. It is possible that the behaviour of certain invertebrates, particularly insects, may indeed be very largely explained in terms of quite simple reflex tropisms. But this is certainly not true of even the least highly organised vertebrates. For even superficial observation shows that the behaviour of the higher vertebrates is, in principle, different from anything which could be schematised in terms of tropisms, however numerous or complex.

It is matter of common experience, for example, that a dog 'knows its master.' That is to say, it is an objective fact that

[1] See *Die Mechanik der Orientierung der Tiere in Raum*, Biological Reviews, 1931.

The Neo-Pythagorean Method

the dog's behaviour on seeing its master is quite different from its behaviour towards strangers. The fact that the animal is capable of such a distinction implies that it is capable of *learning from experience*. When we say that it knows its master, or its feeding dish, we clearly mean that it has learned to correlate certain features of its experience. It is obvious that no amount of analysis can resolve an activity of this kind into simple reflex behaviour of the 'slot-machine' type.

Long before any mechanistic theory of learning could be attempted it was well known that associative memory is bound up with the 'higher' centres of the brain, namely, the cerebral hemispheres. A frog deprived of its forebrain is simply a reflex automaton. It shows no spontaneous activity, although it responds readily to various stimuli. A given stimulus, however, evokes the same response always, so that the behaviour of the 'spinal' animal, although immensely more complex, is not in principle different from that of a slot machine. But in the intact animal, a given stimulus evokes sometimes one response, sometimes quite another response. It is a 'purposeful' organism with a definite, if, by human standards, limited capacity to profit by experience. Whereas the behaviour of the spinal animal is entirely predictable, that of the complete organism seems to offer no foothold for scientific prediction.

And, although the vitalistic position was somewhat damaged by early biochemical and behaviouristic studies, as long as 'purposeful' behaviour remained impervious to mechanistic explanation, vitalists could still point to this as a 'vital' activity different in kind from anything which could be observed in the purely physico-chemical realm. To the obvious objection that the higher activities of the organism were dependent on the cerebral hemispheres the vitalist could give the obvious reply that the brain was merely the instrument of vital force, so that the disappearance of purposeful activity caused by the loss of the higher centres did not disprove the existence of vital force. (Any more than the absence of a piano could be held to prove the non-existence of a pianist!) In effect this is what Socrates says in his discussion of behaviourism in the *Phaedo*:

"For, heavens above, these bones and sinews of mine would long ago have arrived in Megara or Boetia, propelled there by the conception of that which is best, had it not seemed to me more just and honourable to submit than to run away. Of course it is perfectly true to say that I could not put my desires into action without my bones and sinews and such like. But to say that it is in these things, and not in my reason, that the causes of my actions are to be found, would be the most utter contradiction in terms. . . ."

Clearly, the only effective reply to Socrates' position would be an extension of the Cartesian method to include purposeful behaviour. This was provided by Pavlov's discovery of the conditioned reflex.

The Neo-Pythagorean Method

APPENDIX TO CHAPTER XIV

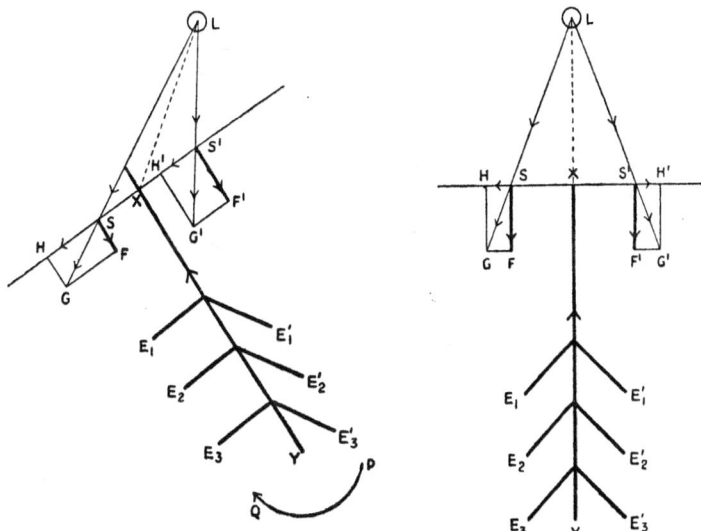

DIAGRAM IXB.—HELIOTROPISM.

Thus, in Diagram IXB, above, let L represent the source of light, S' and S the right and left eyes respectively. The axis of bilateral symmetry makes an angle LXY with the light rays LX. Let $SG = S'G'$ represent the intensity of illumination. (Assuming that LS is equal to LS', which is approximately true unless the source of light is very near the animal.) Now let SFGH and S'F'G'H' be parallelograms of intensity, resolving the intensity of illumination into components parallel and normal to the retinae. Then the normal components SF and S'F' represent the relative rates of photochemical change in S and S' respectively. Since the angle S'G'F' is greater than the angle SGF, then S'F' is greater than SF. And since S'F' is greater than SF, then the limbs of the right side (E'_1, E'_2 and E'_3) will be more strongly flexed than the limbs (E_1, E_2 and E_3) of the opposite side. Hence the animal will be caused to rotate in the direction of the arrow PQ. This will bring the long axis into the line LX. Then $SF = S'F'$, so that the limbs will be symmetrically flexed and the animal will be carried along its axis of bilateral symmetry towards the source of light, L.

> "Natural philosophy should never ask, what is in the mind and what is in Nature. To do so is a confession that it has failed to express relations between things perceptively known."
>
> WHITEHEAD

CHAPTER XV

The Physical Schema of the Animal Psyche: The Conditioned Reflex

THE simple reflexes and tropisms of the kind we have described are called by Pavlov 'unconditioned' reflexes. Such reflexes are transmitted by heredity and are found in every normal individual of the species. As is implied by the word 'unconditioned,' they are not influenced by the history of the individual; like the colour of the eyes, or any other inherited characteristic, they are fixed by causes outside the experience of the organism itself.

But in addition to this inherited equipment of unconditioned reflexes, each individual shows certain reactions and activities peculiar to itself, reactions acquired by it during its individual existence. For example, A's dog may react in a certain way to the words "Going out?", while to B's dog these words may be meaningless, although he may show a similar reaction to the words "Coming for a walk?" Such acquired reactions, conditioned by the unique experience of the individual, are called by Pavlov *conditioned* reflexes. Pavlov's contribution to the study of behaviour has consisted in the synthesis and analysis of conditioned reflexes under experimental conditions.

A conditioned reflex always arises through the modification or 'conditioning' of another reflex, which may itself be either conditioned or unconditioned. Let us consider the simpler instance, where a conditioned reflex is built up on the basis of an unconditioned response. For example, a hungry dog

Physical Schema of Animal Psyche

salivates when it is shown meat. Here the (visual) stimulus is the sight of the meat, and the response the activity of the salivary glands. Both stimulus and response are unconditioned. Now, suppose that every time the dog is shown meat an electric bell is sounded within the animal's hearing. Ordinarily, of course, the sound of the bell has no effect on the dog's salivary glands. But after the meat and the bell have been presented simultaneously on several occasions, it is found that the bell alone will stimulate the salivary glands to activity. The originally neutral sound stimulus is now said to be a conditioned stimulus in virtue of the new effect which it has acquired.

In the above example the conditioned stimulus is auditory and the unconditioned stimulus visual. The conditioned stimulus may, of course, stimulate the same sense organ as the unconditioned one. If a white triangle were presented to the dog, in place of the sound of the bell, the animal would become conditioned to salivate on being shown the white triangle without the meat. Conditioned reflexes may in fact be built up with any combination of effectors and receptors. In Pavlov's work, however, the effector used was almost always the salivary gland, since this effector lends itself so well to exact quantitative observation, owing to the ease with which the secretion may be collected and measured. Although Pavlov's method has been developed to give results of the utmost complexity and precision, the simple basic principle remains unaltered, namely, that *the simultaneous presentation of an unconditioned and a neutral stimulus results in a modification of the organism such that the neutral stimulus becomes effective or conditioned*. By means of this simple principle the psychological phenomena which we call 'learning by experience' can be translated into physico-chemical terms of an exact quantitative nature. Instead of saying that the dog 'learns to recognise' its feeding dish we may say, omitting all reference to the dog's mind, that it has become conditioned to the visual stimulus

The Idea of the Soul in Western Philosophy and Science

of the dish. And if the conditioning is built up under laboratory conditions it can be expressed in precise quantitative terms.

It would be out of place here to attempt a detailed exposition of Pavlov's methods. Nevertheless, it will be useful to give a general idea of his experimental procedure, in order that the reader may have concrete examples of the way in which the phenomena of 'learning by experience' may be translated into purely mechanistic description.

For example, the study of conditioned reflexes may be used to estimate an animal's powers of perceptual discrimination, without reference to psychological concepts. A dog has been conditioned to salivate, say, on being shown a white circle. If it is now shown a long white oval, this also stimulates a salivary secretion, almost as effectively as the circle. Now, suppose that it is repeatedly shown that oval *without* the unconditioned stimulus (e.g. meat) and the circle *with* the unconditioned stimulus. Under such conditions the secretion induced by the oval becomes progressively less. But the circle, which is tested by being shown once in every ten trials (say) without the meat, retains its full effect on the salivary glands. After a succession of trials the effect of the oval can be reduced to zero, leaving the effect of the circle, however, at full strength. In 'mechanistic' terms the visual conditioned stimulus has been made more specific: in 'psychological' terms, the dog has 'learned to discriminate' between the significance of the oval and that of the circle. The latter signifies that food is imminent, the former does not. Suppose now that the experiment be repeated, the animal being shown a slightly broader (i.e. more circular) oval, instead of the elongated one. At first the broader oval will stimulate the salivary gland, although to a lesser extent than the circle. By a repetition of the procedure already described, however, the effect of the second oval can also be experimentally extinguished. The conditioned stimulus is still more specific; the animal has learned a still finer power of perceptual discrimination. The procedure may again be

Physical Schema of Animal Psyche

repeated, this time with a still broader oval, leading to a still greater increase in the specificity of the conditioned stimulus. But as the ovals more and more nearly approach the circular form, a point is reached when no further increase in specificity is attainable.[1] In this way it is possible to arrive at an exact estimation of the animal's powers of form discrimination solely in terms of the percepts *of the experimenter*.

Similar methods may be used to test the discrimination of any of the sense receptors. If, for example, the dog be conditioned to respond to a sound of 800 vibrations per second, it is found that sounds over a range of about 600 to 1,000 vibrations will act in the same way as the conditioned stimulus. But if these accessory stimuli are presented without reinforcement from the unconditioned stimulus, while the stimulus of 800 vibrations per second is constantly reinforced, the range of effective stimulation can be made progressively narrower, just as in the instance of the circle and the ellipses. This method of narrowing the irradiation of the conditioned stimulus is called differential inhibition. By the use of differential inhibition it can be shown that while the form vision of the dog is much less acute than that of the human being, its discrimination of sounds is much finer, intervals of an eighth of a tone being readily discriminated. By the same method it can be shown that colour discrimination is absent; dogs are colour blind.

The relative strength of the stimuli does not markedly affect the progress of differential inhibition. That is to say, the animal may be conditioned to respond to a weak stimulus, while a strong stimulus of different quality is ignored. For example, the animal might be trained to respond to a very soft note of 500 vibrations per second, but to ignore much louder notes of 400 or 600 vibrations per second. Now, if it were not for

---

[1] If the experimenter persistently tries to increase the specificity of a stimulus beyond too fine a limit, a catastrophic destruction of all the animal's conditioned reflexes results, from which it takes weeks to recover. Such a condition is exactly comparable with the 'nervous breakdown' induced in a human being by mental overstrain.

The Idea of the Soul in Western Philosophy and Science

Pavlov's work it would be impossible to account for such behaviour except by reference to the psychological concept of 'voluntary choice.' The vibration of 500 vibrations per second, we should have to say, has acquired a certain significance or meaning for the dog, and it is to this non-material significance or meaning (rather than to the physical vibration *qua* vibration) that the dog is reacting. This would be equivalent to saying that the animal's behaviour is controlled by the concept of food, just as Socrates said his actions were controlled, not by his bones and sinews, but by the 'concept of that which is best.' But it is now possible, for the behaviour of the dog at any rate, to substitute for the 'Socratic,' or psychological, explanation a purely physical or Pythagorean mode of description. Pavlov's concept of differential inhibition within a complex system of reflex arcs provides us with a simple mechanistic counterpart for the introspective notion of voluntary choice.

So far we have described only the synthesis of conditioned reflexes by the simultaneous presentation of the conditioned and unconditioned stimuli. The presentation need not, however, be simultaneous. The conditioned stimulus may begin before the unconditioned stimulus is presented. (It is not possible, however, to condition a stimulus presented after the unconditioned stimulus.) If the stimuli overlap in time, that is if the conditioned stimulus be continued up to and after the beginning of the unconditioned stimulus, a *delayed* reflex is formed. If they do not overlap, the conditioned stimulus stopping before the beginning of the unconditioned stimulus, a *trace* reflex is formed. There are certain interesting differences, into which we cannot enter here, between the properties of delayed and trace reflexes. In either instance, however, the resulting conditioned reflex has a 'latent period' equivalent to the time which was allowed to elapse between the presentation of the conditioned and unconditioned stimuli. If, say, ten seconds elapsed between the presentations in the

Physical Schema of Animal Psyche

training period, then when the conditioned stimulus is presented alone there is a delay of ten seconds before the response begins. Experimental analysis shows that this delay is not passive, but the result of an active inhibitory process in the nervous system during the latent period. For very long trace reflexes (e.g. with a latent period of half an hour) the internal inhibition may be so strong that it spreads over the whole cerebral cortex, resulting in an extinction, not only of the trace reflex, but of all other conditioned reflexes. The inhibition may even spread to the lower centres, so that the animal falls into a deep sleep for the duration of the latent period.

If, during the synthesis of a reflex, an accidental stimulus accompanies the conditioned stimulus, the effect of the latter is diminished or extinguished. This effect, which may result from an accidental noise, or even from a change of illumination caused by a cloud obscuring the sun, is called external inhibition, to distinguish it from the internal inhibition which we have already described.[1] The term indicates that the cause of inhibition does not arise within the nervous system, but rather from the external 'competition' of two stimuli.

Suppose that by differential inhibition an animal has been trained to respond to a narrow range of vibrations in the neighbourhood of 500 vibrations per second, and to ignore other sounds. Further, suppose that the presentation of a differentially inhibited stimulus of say 400 vibrations is accompanied by some extraneous stimulus such as a flash of light. It is then found that the animal responds to the inhibited stimulus; the flash of light has, as it were, released the internal inhibition. That is to say, external inhibition inhibits internal inhibition. It is clear that a mechanistic basis for the psychological concept of 'attention' may be found in the external inhibition of internally inhibited conditioned reflexes.

[1] To eliminate undesired external inhibition the animal is kept in a separate room from the observer, in order to exclude the inhibitory effect of his movements. All the stimuli are presented by means of mechanical controls from the observation room, and the animal is observed through a periscope.

The Idea of the Soul in Western Philosophy and Science

So far we have confined ourselves to 'first order' conditioned reflexes. But it is possible, on the basis of first order reflexes, to build up second order reflexes. The animal is conditioned to respond, for example, to a white circle. To synthesise a secondary reflex, this stimulus is presented and withdrawn. Fifteen seconds, say, after the withdrawal, a new stimulus is presented, the sound of a metronome for instance. (Simultaneous presentation would result in external inhibition.) After several repetitions of this sequence the metronome alone will evoke the response previously associated with the white circle.[1] This is a conditioned excitatory reflex of the second order. Conditioned inhibitory reflexes of the second order may be synthesised in the same way. On the basis of a secondary reflex a third order reflex, either excitatory or inhibitory, may be built up. In dogs it is not possible to build up higher reflexes than this.

We have necessarily restricted ourselves to the briefest indication of the methods and results of Pavlov and his school. Yet it is apparent, in the light of Pavlov's discoveries, that certain kinds of behaviour which are obviously 'purposeful' may be translated into a purely physical schematisation in terms of primary, secondary and tertiary reflexes, either simultaneous or of the trace or delayed type, mutually interrelated through internal, external and differential inhibitions of the first, second or third order. Socrates, perhaps, like many of our contemporaries who have been brought up in a purely 'humanistic' culture of the mediaeval or Socratic type, would have been appalled by these rather complex technicalities, even more than by the 'infantile' behaviouristic notions of Anaxagoras. But their formal, quasi-mathematical beauty would have delighted the Pythagoreans, above all Plato, the greatest of the Pythagorean thinkers. For Pavlov's theory discovers in living beings that which for Plato was fully revealed only in

---

[1] This and other examples are taken from *Conditioned Reflexes*, by Pavlov. English translation by Anrep.

musical phenomena and in the paths of the heavenly bodies, namely, the mathematical 'harmony' which he desired to find, although the science of his day was unequal to this task, everywhere in the material world, even in such common things as 'hair, mud and dirt.'[1] And although the spatio-temporal configurations or 'harmonies' in terms of which Pavlov describes the pattern of animal behaviour are of considerable apparent complexity, they nevertheless, like Kepler's laws, satisfy the Pythagorean canon of mathematical simplicity. For the formal principle embodied in all Pavlov's descriptions, the principle given in the definition of the conditioned reflex, is really one of extreme simplicity. And as the Renaissance thinkers took the Pythagorean faith into new realms by seeking mathematical harmonies in all terrestrial things, so the experimental biologist of to-day is taking it into new realms by endeavouring, in the light of Pavlov's principle, to schematise the behaviour of the higher animals, including man himself, solely in terms of 'relations between things perceptively known.'

[1] *Parmenides*, 135e.

"The soul has worn out its welcome."

WILLIAM JAMES

CHAPTER XVI

The Physical Schema of the Human Psyche: Behaviourism

So far we have treated animal behaviour as though it were a series of more or less discrete conditioned responses. This is of course an abstraction from the facts. The behaviour of an organism is a complex continuum, not a series of highly simplified and unrelated situations contrived by an experimenter. Whereas we have described the behaviour of the organism as if it were a discontinuous series of instantaneous photographs, like a lantern show, it is in fact comparable with a continuous story moving on a cinema screen, a succession of events which, although diverse, are integrated into an unified pattern.

The necessity of this abstraction arises from the nature of the material which Nature presents to the biologist. Since the biologist must deal with the complex wholes which we call organisms, his first task must be analytical. The abstractions which result from his analysis are, however, justified if he remembers that they are abstractions, and if, in addition, he can use his abstractions to resynthesise, conceptually, the concrete complexity of the whole organism. The savage must take his chronometer to pieces in order to understand the mechanism as a whole. In so doing he is not likely to confuse a cogwheel with a whole chronometer, any more than the experimental zoologist is likely to confuse a conditioned reflex with the whole history of the organism.

In order to arrive at a concrete picture of animal behaviour, it must be considered as an integrated pattern. And if it can

Physical Schema of Human Psyche

be shown that the elements of that pattern are conditioned reflexes, the abstractions made in the interests of mechanistic description will have been justified.

Just as the simplest type of conditioned reflex arises from the unconditioned activity of a single effector organ, so the unconditioned or fortuitous activity of groups of effectors may be conditioned to give integrated patterns of conditioned reflexes.

This may be shown by experiments of the following kind. Suppose a hungry rat be put in a cage which can be opened by a simple latch. Food, visible to the rat, is put outside the cage. Stimulated by the food, the rat runs around the cage in a random fashion: the undirected activity of its leg muscles corresponds to the unconditioned activity of the salivary gland in Pavlov's experiments with dogs. The latch being of fairly simple construction, the rat will eventually release it accidentally, thus gaining access to the food. If this experiment be repeated a number of times the rat will get out of the cage more and more quickly until it learns to go through the necessary movements in the minimum time, that is, with complete elimination of unnecessary movements. The original unintegrated behaviour pattern (running at random around the cage) has become an integrated pattern. Certain elements of the unintegrated pattern have become positively conditioned reactions, others, those eliminated, have suffered differential inhibition. The completely integrated set of movements may be analysed as follows:[1] (1) Running to the door. (2) Lifting the latch. (3) Pulling back the door. (4) Running to the food.

The integration of the pattern lies in the fact that the response (1) is also a stimulus for response (2), and this, in turn, a stimulus for the third response, and so on until the pattern is completed. But how, it will be asked, can a response (such as running to the door) be called a stimulus? Are not

[1] See *Behaviourism*, J. B. Watson, p. 24.

response and stimulus, by definition, different? The answer to this is that stimuli come to the organism, not only from the outside world, but also from its own body. This may be illustrated from our own experience. It is quite simple, even with one's eyes closed, to bring the tip of one's finger to the end of the nose, or to grasp, say the first finger of the left hand between the fingers of the right hand. A little reflection will show that these feats are much more remarkable than they may at first sight appear. Further reflection will show that, in order to perform them, we must have very accurate information, independent of vision, about the relative positions of our limbs. Without looking at it we know quite well whether a finger is bent or straight, and to what degree. The sense organs which give us this information are the so-called *kinaesthetic* receptors or muscle spindles. These are simply little sense organs embedded in our muscles. Their function is to respond to variations in the tension of the muscles, just as our eyes respond to variations in illumination. If these kinaesthetic receptors are damaged, as in the disease called *locomotor ataxy*, the patient has no direct source of kinaesthetic information, so that he can only walk with even moderate success by carefully watching the movements of his legs. To return to our rats. It is now clear that the initial response of the rat, namely, running, is also a stimulus, a kinaesthetic stimulus which serves in turn as a basis for the next part of the reflex pattern. It is possible to verify the truth of this assumption by experimental methods. Rats can readily be taught to 'run' a maze. The maze customarily used in the laboratory is quite complicated, being in fact a miniature replica of the Hampton Court maze (Diagram XI).

Food is put in the centre of the maze and the rat outside. At the first trial, of course, the rat takes a considerable time to reach the centre of the maze, since it gets there by random activity. But in subsequent trials the time of running the maze becomes progressively less, until the rat can run to the centre

Physical Schema of Human Psyche

without taking a single wrong turning. If one of the passages of the maze then be made longer, the rat tries to turn where the opening was previously situated, proving that it is the kinaesthetic sense which has been conditioned. This is confirmed by the fact that blindfolding the rat does not decrease its proficiency. The significance of experiments of this kind is that they show how a mechanistic description may be applied,

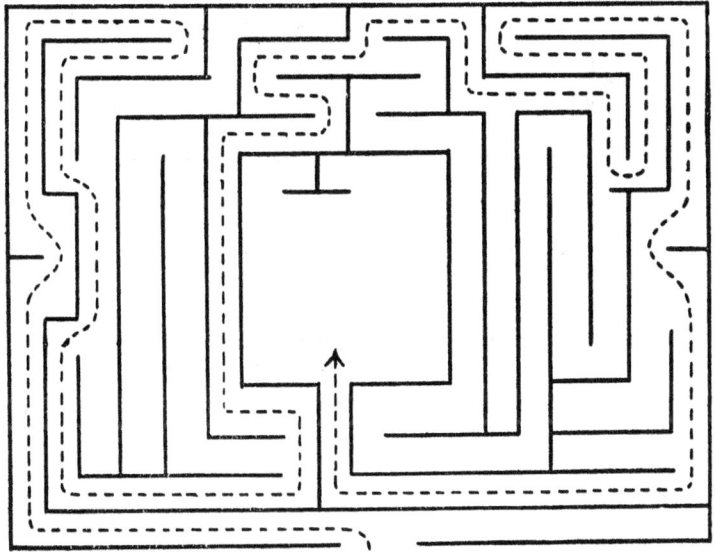

DIAGRAM XI.—THE HAMPTON COURT MAZE.

not only to the very simple reactions described in the preceding chapter, but also to feats of learning of the most complicated nature. Instead of saying that the rat 'learns' to run the maze the mechanist will say that its behaviour has been modified by the integration of a pattern of conditioned kinaesthetic responses.

By recording the time taken for successive trials during the learning period it is possible to construct a 'learning curve,' of the type shown in Diagram XII. From this it may be seen that the learning, at first very rapid, becomes slower as the

The Idea of the Soul in Western Philosophy and Science

animal's performance approaches perfection. If an animal which has learnt a maze be kept away from it for some time, say six months, it will run it in practically the minimum time on its first retrial. This simple experiment gives the mechanist a mechanistic counterpart for the concept of memory. Instead of saying that the rat remembers the maze, he will say that such

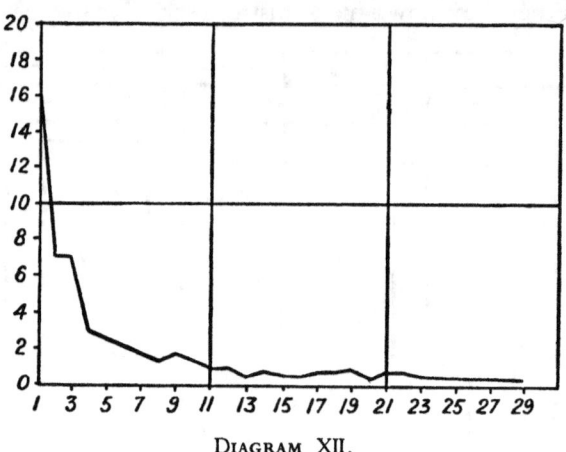

DIAGRAM XII.

On the vertical axis is shown the number of minutes taken to reach the food; on the horizontal axis the number of trials given. On the first trial 16 minutes were required, on the third trial 7 minutes, and so on until the thirteenth trial, when the rat took only 20 seconds to run the maze. (From *Behaviourism*, J. B. Watson, p. 169.)

and such a pattern of conditioned kinaesthetic responses has been retained to the extent of, say, 92 per cent. Any pattern of conditioned responses is called by the behaviourist a 'habit,' so that, briefly, memory may be described as the retention of habit.

The behaviourist in fact maintains that all animal and human behaviour may be described and explained in terms of response patterns or habits. In animals these patterns are of two kinds only. There are muscular habits, of the type shown in running a maze. (In human beings the most important muscular responses are of course manual.) And there are emotional

Physical Schema of Human Psyche

responses and habits. In the human being there are, in addition, verbal habits.

Emotional responses are a special class of a more general type of response which may be called *visceral*. All responses of this type are internal or 'implicit.' For example, we see a child in front of a pastry shop,[1] and we may think, because the child is doing or saying nothing, that the stimulus (the pastry) is calling forth no response. But if the child is hungry its viscera will be the scene of very numerous and important responses. The stomach will be performing the rhythmical contractions which are felt subjectively as hunger; the salivary glands will be pouring out their secretion; and the ductless or endocrine glands will also be active, causing vaso-motor changes which bring about a redistribution of blood throughout the body.

Emotions, like alimentary and sexual appetites, are accompanied by visceral changes such as we have described. Doctors are familiar with the difficulty of measuring the pulse rate of a nervous patient, since the contact with the doctor's hand, or the mere presence of the doctor in the room, may cause the pulse to beat with abnormal rapidity. Similarly, if a man merely hears a name which for him has some special emotional significance, the name of his lover for instance, there will be marked visceral changes (in his blood pressure, in the electrical conductivity of his protoplasm, etc.), which can readily be observed and expressed in numerical terms. Words which have no emotional significance are of course without such visceral effects.

Emotional responses can be conditioned, inhibited, irradiated or differentiated in just the same way as the salivary responses of the dog or the muscular responses of the rat. For example, the first time a man speaks in public he usually undergoes an emotional experience known as nervousness. In behaviouristic language there is, among other visceral re-

[1] This and other examples are taken from Watson's book, *Behaviourism*.

sponses, a disturbance of the vaso-motor apparatus. If the speaker's normal blood pressure is 140, it may run up to 150 during his first address. But if he subsequently becomes accustomed to public speaking his nervousness wears off. The repeated stimulus of facing an audience brings about a differential conditioned response of the vaso-motor apparatus. We have seen how a dog, trained to salivate on hearing a note of 500 vibrations per second, at first responds to a wide range of notes, but ceases to do so if these are not reinforced by the unconditioned stimulus. In the same way the vaso-motor responses of the speaker (provided his addresses are not accompanied by fear-producing stimuli from the audience!) undergo differential inhibition.

But what is the unconditioned response for such an emotional reaction as fear? Even very young children show the fear response in numerous situations. Nearly all children, for example, show a marked fear response to rats or other small furry animals. Watson's description of the response is as follows: " . . . a start, a respiratory pause followed by more rapid breathing with marked vaso-motor changes, sudden closures of the eyes, clutching of the hands, puckering of the lips. . . ." If, however, infants are closely observed from the moment of birth, it is found that only two stimuli will call forth the fear response. These are (1) sudden loud or discordant noises and (2) sudden loss of support. The fear response evoked by a furry animal is therefore a conditioned response. Such conditioned emotional responses can be built up experimentally. On first seeing a furry animal, a rabbit say, a baby's first reaction is almost invariably to grasp it; often it tries to put the animal in its mouth. There is, therefore, no unconditioned emotional response to this stimulus, but simply a 'manipulatory' response. If, however, the presentation of the animal be accompanied by a discordant noise, the sight of the animal, without the noise, becomes a conditioned fear stimulus. Moreover, the irradiation of the conditioned

Physical Schema of Human Psyche

stimulus may be very wide, so that not only rabbits, but anything furry in appearance, even a piece of cotton wool, will now serve as a conditioned fear stimulus. The fear of rabbits may persist even after the child has reached maturity, although the irradiated conditioned stimuli at first associated with this reaction may quite soon become extinguished by differential inhibition. But before this happens, any of the numerous conditioned stimuli within the range of irradiation may serve as an unconditioned stimulus for a secondary fear stimulus. This in turn will be associated with numerous irradiated stimuli, any of which may give rise to a tertiary conditioned stimulus. As there is apparently no limit, in human beings, to the formation of conditioned reflexes of higher orders, this process may proceed indefinitely.

The newly born infant shows only two other types of unconditioned emotional response, the rage response and the love response. Like the fear response, these are called forth only by a very limited number of unconditioned stimuli; the rage response, for example, being originally evoked by one stimulus only, namely the hampering of bodily movements. But, like the fear response, the rage and love responses can be conditioned by other stimuli. Since the unconditioned love response, caused by the stimulation of the erogenous zones, is usually brought about by the mother, the child rapidly becomes conditioned to show the love response at the mere sight of the mother.

Because of the extraordinary rapidity with which these responses undergo conditioning, even very young children have an emotional life of great complexity. In mechanistic terms, the visceral reactions become rapidly integrated into complex patterns of conditioned stimuli. A complete knowledge of the conditioning of these patterns, patterns of alimentary, vaso-motor and endocrine activity, would enable one to give a complete description of the emotional life of an individual, animal or human, without reference to the psychical pattern, which is in any case inaccessible to everyone but the individual in question. From knowledge of this kind the future configuration of the visceral, that is the emotional pattern, is predictable by the same methods which are applied to any other physico-chemical process. Owing, however, to the inaccessible nature of most of the visceral reactions, the 'mechanisation' of the emotions must, in spite of the technical virtuosity of the biophysicists and biochemists, proceed more slowly than the mechanisation of overt muscular behaviour. Nevertheless, in spite of the technical difficulties involved, the mechanistic description of emotional behaviour takes its departure, like most scientific descriptions, from observations of quite a commonplace nature. In Watson's picturesque phrasing, "The 'cold sweat' of fear, the 'bursting heart,' the 'bowed head' in apathy and grief, the 'exuberance of youth,' the 'palpitating heart' of the swain or maiden are more than mere literary expressions; they are bits of genuine observation." And, even with the very limited amount of experimental work which can be done on the human subject, mechanistic analysis has proved so fruitful a means of controlling and predicting emotional behaviour that there is little reason to doubt that human and animal emotions can be described in the same mechanistic terms which are applicable to the learning of a maze by a rat. Those who wish to pursue this aspect of the subject are referred to Watson's book on Behaviourism and to Aldous Huxley's well-known behaviouristic romance.

Verbal behaviour, which in animals is of little or no importance, is the most significant activity of the human organism. If a non-human intelligence, some being from another world, say, could visit the earth, it would be by our language habits (since he could know nothing of our thoughts) that he would distinguish us from the rest of the animal creation. Our manual skill differs only in degree from that of the apes, but language is a specifically human activity by which we have made for ourselves a new world which no ape can hope to enter.

Physical Schema of Human Psyche

We have seen that emotional behaviour is built up from a very few unconditioned responses. The same is true of verbal, or as Watson calls it, *laryngeal* behaviour. The larynx is of course the main effector for verbal behaviour, just as the 'voluntary' muscles are the manual effectors and the viscera the emotional effectors. Verbal behaviour, then, starts with the unlearned laryngeal responses of the baby. One may venture the assertion that the young of our species is notorious for these. Sounds like 'a,' 'u' and 'nah' appear on the first day, soon to be followed by more complex sounds such as 'ahgoo.'[1]

While the development of verbal behaviour is slow and complex, the principle involved is the same very simple one which underlies kinaesthetic and emotional conditioning. Indeed, verbal behaviour may be regarded as a special instance of kinaesthetic conditioning, since the control of the vocal membranes is effected by muscles. The basis of verbal behaviour is that auditory stimuli become conditioned stimuli for perceived objects. Just as the dog can be conditioned to respond to a white circle in the same way as it responds to meat, so the child becomes conditioned in such a way that the auditory stimulus 'mama' evokes the same response as the visual perception of the mother. To revert for a moment to introspective language, the sound 'mama' acquires a *meaning* for the child, in the same sense that the white circle comes to 'mean' meat for the dog. For the mechanist, however, the concept of the conditioned reflex, which has reference only to percepts, replaces the subjective concept of 'meaning.'

So far we have talked as if the rôle of the child were simply to respond to verbal stimulation, as a dog responds, by salivation or in some other way, to a given conditioned stimulus. But of course the child also learns to reproduce the verbal stimulus for itself. It learns, for example, to say 'mama' when it sees its mother. This kind of learning is comparable

[1] Watson, op. cit., p. 183.

The Idea of the Soul in Western Philosophy and Science

with the conditioned activity of an animal which learns to thread a maze or escape from a problem box. Let us suppose that in order to get out of the box the rat has to perform four actions, a—b—c—d. The four appropriate actions and many inappropriate ones will be contained in the random activity of the rat, and the conditioning, as we have explained, consists in the inhibition of the unsuitable responses. If we denote the latter by the letters p, q, r and s, we may symbolise the conditioning process as follows (Diagram XIII):

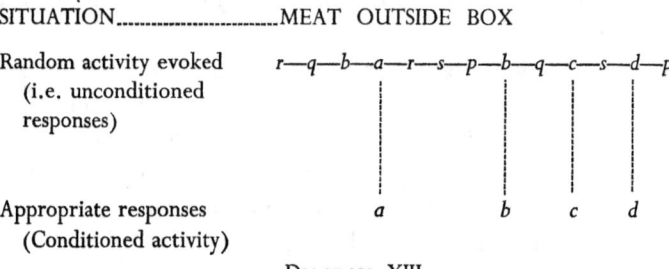

SITUATION............................MEAT OUTSIDE BOX

Random activity evoked r—q—b—a—r—s—p—b—q—c—s—d—p
  (i.e. unconditioned
  responses)

Appropriate responses a b c d
  (Conditioned activity)

DIAGRAM XIII.

The chief difference between this and the conditioning of a baby to say 'mama' when it sees its mother is that the response a—b—c—d is an integrated pattern of locomotory reflexes, while the sequence 'mama' is a pattern of conditioned laryngeal reflexes. In both instances the effectors are muscles. So that, on analogy with Diagram XIII we can make a diagram for laryngeal conditioning (Diagram XIV).

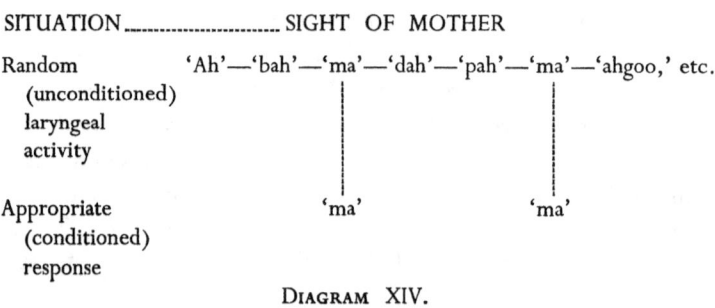

SITUATION.......................... SIGHT OF MOTHER

Random   'Ah'—'bah'—'ma'—'dah'—'pah'—'ma'—'ahgoo,' etc.
  (unconditioned)
  laryngeal
  activity

Appropriate   'ma'   'ma'
  (conditioned)
  response

DIAGRAM XIV.

Physical Schema of Human Psyche

When the rat reaches the meat, the latter ceases to stimulate muscular activity. When the baby succeeds in saying 'mama,' the sight of the mother ceases to stimulate laryngeal activity. In each instance the conditioned pattern is attained when the presented situation is transformed into a new situation. For the rat the new situation is simply a change in its spatial relations with the meat. But for the laryngeal conditioning the matter is more complex. The stimulus is not simply the sight of the mother. First, the auditory stimulus 'mama' becomes a conditioned stimulus for the visual appearance of the mother, as a white circle, say, becomes a conditioned stimulus for meat. Then the visual stimulus (sight of mother) conditions laryngeal activity in virtue of the fact that it has become a substitute stimulus for the auditory stimulus 'mama.' The laryngeal activity ceases when it reproduces the auditory stimulus.

In the above example of laryngeal conditioning the unconditioned stimulus (sight of mother) is an abstraction from experience of the simplest possible kind, of the kind, namely, which corresponds in language to the noun. And the noun itself 'mama' is a verbal pattern of a very simple nature. It is with such patterns, of course, that verbal conditioning must begin. Watson[1] gives, for example, the complete vocabulary of a child of nineteen months. Out of a total of fifty-two words, thirty-six words of this vocabulary are nouns. Of these the greater part are single-syllable words, and of the remainder the majority are either abbreviations of two-syllable words or repetitions of a single syllable. Thus, for 'lady,' the child substituted 'la-la,' for 'please,' 'blea' and 'No-no' for 'Nora.' In principle, primitive language progresses little beyond this stage; it is much more elaborate, of course, than any baby talk, but nevertheless an elaboration at the baby talk level, not an emergence to a higher level. Such language, as we have seen, has nouns for objects and holophrases for situations, but

[1] Op. cit., p. 183.

no parts of speech as we understand them. There is, as it were, a one-to-one correspondence between speech and language, each noun denoting an object, each holophrase a situation, complex but unique. A holophrase such as *mamilapinatapai*[1] is the verbal counterpart of the performance of a rat in a maze. The holophrase, a laryngeal pattern of conditioned reflexes, like the kinaesthetic pattern of the rat, is a single complex, *indivisible* response to an elaborate and unique situation. Holophrastic language, then, consists of little more than a set of substitute stimuli, or symbols, for the various objects of perceptual and social experience. Between the symbols themselves there is no interplay and only implicit connection: the 'vertical' connection between percept and word is the all-important one.

The development of language consists in the bringing to light of these implicit connections, so that the symbols themselves become connected by symbolical connections. The Waicuri,[2] for example, cannot analyse the holophrases '*bedare*,' '*edare*,' etc., into their separate elements, so that for them each holophrase of this series is unique. Nevertheless, they are implicitly connected by the common element '*are*.' When such implicit connections become consciously understood, the symbols cease to be mere static reproductions of bits of past experience; they come to constitute an entirely new world of experience, which, in virtue of its acquired internal relations, can develop independently of the perceptual world. The 'horizontal' connections between the symbols themselves are now of primary importance. Originally photographic, the symbols are now, to use a mathematical term, operators. Hence language becomes a technique for the manipulation of relations in entire independence of the perceptual world. It becomes, in fact, a system of relations. Failure to realise this will inevitably result in a misuse of language, a fact which may be illustrated from the works of almost any philosopher.

[1] Ante, p. 19.   [2] Ante, p. 20.

Physical Schema of Human Psyche

Perhaps one of the most flagrant offenders, in this respect, is the English philosopher, Green, who so far mistakes language for something else that he sees Nature itself as nothing but a system of relations present to a consciousness.[1]

The verbal behaviour of a child learning English, or any other highly evolved language, is a compromise between the language of its adult teachers and the holophrastic word forms of its remote ancestors. Consider the following instance of verbal conditioning, given by Watson. "When B, whose word conditioning we have just considered, had 52 words at his command, we noticed the first putting together of two words. This occurred on August 13th. . . . For a month prior to that date we had been setting a verbal pattern of two words for some time, such as 'hello, mama,' 'hello, dada,' without results. On this day his mother said 'Say good-bye to daddy.' She set the verbal pattern 'good-bye da.' He repeated after her 'bye'—then hesitated and five seconds later came the word 'da.' This brought on him a shower of petting, verbal commendation and the like. Later in the day he said with the same long interval between the sounds 'bye-bow wow.' On August 15th, two days later, we got him to say 'hello—mama,' 'hello—Rose,' 'ta-ta—Rose,' 'ta-ta—mama,' ('ta-ta' means 'thank you'). In each case the two-word stimulus had to be given before the response could be called out. . . . On August 24th he put two words together without any verbal stimulus from the parents, for example he pointed to his father's shoe and said 'shoe—da,' and pointing to his mother's shoe 'shoe—ma.' Then the next four days he used all the above two-word responses at one time or another without any pattern being set, and some additional ones for which a two-word pattern had never been set, such as the following: 'tee-tee bow-wow' (dog urinates), 'bébé go-go' (when a little

---

[1] Philosophical positivists, on the other hand, who dismiss as meaningless all verbal manipulation not directly related to percepts, fall into an error which is the converse of that committed by idealistic philosophers.

neighbour took his cart). . . . From this time on development in the two-word stage took place rapidly. The three-word stage was somewhat slow in coming as was talking in sentences corresponding to the ordinary adult social patterns. No new facts, however, seemed to come to light during these stages."[1]

The phrase "bébé go-go" is quite clearly an attempt to express by a holophrase a concept for which the child has not yet acquired the adult verbal equipment. And the forms "shoe——da," "shoe——ma" should be compared with such holophrases as "edare," "bedare," etc. Of course, the child's language does not now recapitulate the holophrastic language of its ancestors. As these examples show, however, the child tends to form holophrases whenever its technical equipment is inadequate to its need for expression. Since, in a normal child, the former follows closely behind the latter, the 'holophrastic' stage is ill-defined and evanescent, a brief vestige of an ancestral habit.

After the two-word stage the verbal patterns become more complex by the same sort of process whereby a rat 'learns' a maze. Laryngeal responses become conditioned kinaesthetic stimuli for further laryngeal responses, so that elaborate patterns of conditioned laryngeal behaviour are rapidly synthesised. 'Memory' in human beings is largely the retention of verbal habits, analogous with the retention of kinaesthetic habits by a rat which has learnt a maze. When, for instance, a friend's name is mentioned, it serves as a conditioned stimulus for the verbal organisation which association with him has integrated into our behaviour pattern. And, of course, visceral or manual habits may also be recalled by a verbal stimulus. If A has acquired an emotional reaction towards B, say that he fears B, then the mere mention of B's name will be a conditioned stimulus for the visceral behaviour which he experiences as fear.

[1] Op. cit., p. 184.

Physical Schema of Human Psyche

We have reproduced, without comment, the behaviourist view that our verbal habits constitute the real distinction between human behaviour and that of the other animals. It is hardly necessary to point out that this is not the common view. Man is, if only *soi-disant*, *sapiens*, the thinking animal, superior to the brutes because he alone possesses the faculty of thought. With this the behaviourist would agree, adding, however, that thinking and talking are really the same thing. Or rather, thinking is simply talking to oneself; thought consists of sub-vocal laryngeal patterns. This has not been proved by direct experimental evidence, but Watson brings forward a number of highly interesting observations in support of it.

His main line of evidence comes from watching the behaviour of children. He points out that a child "talks incessantly when alone." Here he is surely understating the evidence for his views. Most normal adults sometimes talk to themselves *when alone*, especially if absorbed in some interesting and difficult problem. The difference between the normal child and the normal adult is that the child talks to itself regardless of whether it is alone or not. Anyone who has watched a child playing in a room full of adults or in a street among passers-by, must have been struck by the complete unself-consciousness with which it gives verbal expression to its thoughts and feelings. And even in company, adults do not always think entirely 'to themselves.' Many people (and not by any means illiterate persons only) move their lips when reading. Such people, whose thinking has not become entirely sub-vocal, have remained at a stage through which the child normally passes in learning to read. It is indeed possible that the habit of sub-vocal reading is, historically, comparatively recent, as the following quotation would seem to show:

"But when he was reading, he drew his eyes along over the leaves, and his heart searched into its sense, but his voice and tongue were silent. Oft-times when we were present . . . we still saw him reading to himself and never otherwise: so that having sat long in silence (for who durst be so bold as to interrupt him, so intentive to his study?) we were fain to depart."[1]

The above passage is a description, from the *Confessions of St. Augustine*, of 'The Employments and Studies of St. Ambrose.' The writer goes on to discuss the significance of this strange habit of reading 'to oneself':

> "We conjectured, that . . . he was wary perchance too, lest some hearer being struck into suspense, and eager upon it, if the author he read should deliver anything obscurely, he should be put to it to expound it, or to discuss some of the harder questions; so that spending away his time about this work, he could not turn over so many volumes as he desired: although peradventure the preserving of his voice (which a little speaking used to weaken) might be a just reason for his reading to himself."

It is possible that, in prehistoric times, sub-vocal thinking was as rare as sub-vocal reading seems to have been in the time of St. Augustine. Indeed it would seem very probable that thought arose in the history of the race, as it now arises in the history of the individual, through the replacement of explicit by implicit verbal behaviour.

Deaf and dumb people, who cannot acquire laryngeal habits, can replace them, to some degree, by manual habits. On the behaviourist theory of thinking we should expect such persons to think by means of implicit manual movements. Watson states that he has found considerable evidence that this is so, and cites the example of Laura Bridgman, a deaf, dumb and blind patient who was taught a finger language. "Even in her dreams Laura talked to herself by using the finger language with great rapidity."[2]

Being afflicted with blindness, poor Laura was beyond the reach of the usual social restraints which convert the explicit speech of the child into implicit speech, which we call thinking. Since she can only know the movements of her hands by kinaesthesis, thought and speech must be, for her, absolutely identical.

---

[1] St. Augustine's *Confessions*. English translation by William Watts.
[2] Watson, op. cit., p. 193.

Physical Schema of Human Psyche

For the majority of us, however, the two are very different. There are innumerable situations in which it is biologically advantageous that our speech should remain implicit. We refrain from thinking aloud for the same reason that tigers and deer refrain from walking noisily in each other's proximity. Each reader will be able to fill in the analogy from his own experience of living.

So far we have discussed visceral, verbal and manual habits as though they were three quite separate activities of the organism. But, of course, in any concrete instance of learning

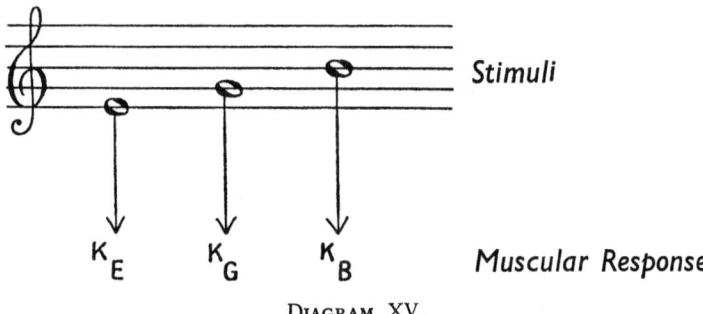

DIAGRAM XV.
(From Watson, *Behaviourism*, modified.)

or remembering, all three types of activity are concurrent. Corresponding to the kinaesthetic learning of the rat in the maze, there is a parallel visceral (i.e. emotional) conditioning, and, in human beings, verbal conditioning as well. So that for a complete representation of learning we should need three learning curves instead of the single curve of kinaesthetic conditioning by which we represented the learning of a maze by a rat. The most obvious aspect of learning to ride a horse, for example, is the synthesis of integrated patterns of muscular reflexes; but the visceral conditioning involved is just as real and necessary a part of the training, since it would not be possible to learn to ride unless our original fear responses (e.g. on first cantering or jumping) suffered differential inhibition. And both the muscular and visceral responses are

The Idea of the Soul in Western Philosophy and Science

here subordinate to the (sub-vocal) verbal responses stimulated in us by the verbal behaviour of the instructor.

The interdependence of the three types of activity is very clearly shown in Watson's discussion of the processes involved in learning to play a tune on a keyboard.[1] For simplicity let us imagine that the tune consists of a single series of notes. Here we have a series of stimuli, the notes, and a series of (kinaesthetic) responses, consisting in pressing the appropriate keys (Diagram XV).

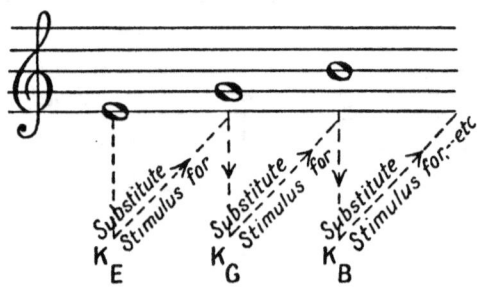

DIAGRAM XVI.

(From Watson, *Behaviourism*, modified.)

But, after we have practised the tune sufficiently, we come to know it 'by heart'; that is to say, the initial note on the score is sufficient to call forth the total response. The muscular responses K_E, K_G, etc., are now also stimuli: K_E has become a substitute (kinaesthetic) stimulus for K_G; K_G in turn is a substitute kinaesthetic stimulus for K_B, and so on until the completion of the tune. As with the learning of the maze by the rat, the sequence of separate responses has become an integrated pattern of mutually conditioned responses and stimuli (Diagram XVI).

In addition to the overt manual response, however, each note has a visceral response (V_E, V_G, etc., Diagram XVII) and a laryngeal response (L_E, L_G, etc.), and these can become

[1] See Watson, op. cit., pp. 202 et seq.

Physical Schema of Human Psyche

substitute stimuli as easily as the kinaesthetic responses. Not only so, but a visceral substitute stimulus may evoke, not the manual response directly, but a verbal (sub-vocal) substitute

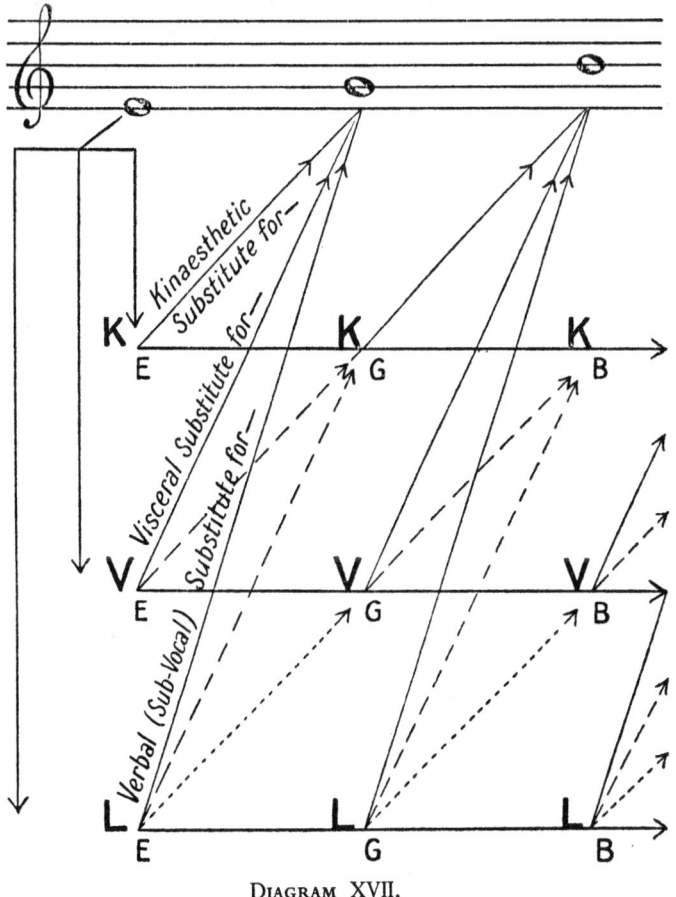

DIAGRAM XVII.
(From Watson, *Behaviourism*, modified.)

stimulus, which in turn evokes the manual response. Or the kinaesthetic substitute stimulus for the first note may evoke the visceral substitute stimulus for the second, which may evoke the verbal substitute stimulus for the third, which in turn may evoke the visceral substitute stimulus for the fourth . . . and so on to almost any degree of complexity, as shown by the dotted lines in Diagram XVII.

The inter-related kinaesthetic, sub-vocal and visceral patterns of conditioned substitute stimuli together comprise the complex unity which we call the "thought" of the piece of music. It should be noted that although in many other types of learning (e.g. in learning a proposition of Euclid) the verbal conditioning is predominant, it plays a very subordinate part in the example we have given, of keyboard conditioning. Owing to the preponderantly emotional appeal of music, the visceral response patterns play a part only subordinate in importance to the kinaesthetic patterns. In fact, we may say that it is literally and scientifically, as well as metaphorically, true that we learn a piece of music "by heart." In such types of learning, where manual and visceral responses predominate, we are "thinking without words"; if the verbal organisation predominates, we are thinking in words. In animals, thinking is of the former type only. Human thinking is never, of course, purely verbal, or purely kinaesthetic or visceral. *It is always the whole organism that thinks*, although sometimes one part of it, sometimes another, plays a dominant rôle in the process.

In our presentation of behaviourism we have deliberately refrained from critical comment, believing that a clearer picture of the behaviourist doctrine will emerge if exposition and criticism are not intermingled. Of course, mechanism, and Watson's theory in particular, since it concerns human beings, has aroused numerous adverse criticisms, some intelligent, others less so. We shall discuss these in a later section.

It should now be obvious, however, that if Watson's theory, or one similar, wins acceptance, then Descartes' dream of extending mechanism to the living organism has been realised in principle, although not yet completely in experimental fact. (For that matter, mechanism has not been completely realised in the inorganic realm in experimental fact, otherwise the work

Physical Schema of Human Psyche

of physics and chemistry would be finished.) Behaviourism, so far the last word of the neo-Pythagorean method in biology, has done for Cartesianism what Newton's laws did for the neo-Pythagorean speculations of the Renaissance philosophers.

We have already expressed the opinion that Descartes' omission of the Psyche, in his scientific account of organic activity, was the most significant and brilliant of his metaphysical inventions. And it should be clearly kept in mind that it was Descartes, not Anaxagoras or any other, who first discovered the possibility of this omission and considered its metaphysical implications, for the modern concept of the soul, which came down to Descartes through Plato and the Christian philosophers, from Socrates, had no part in the nature philosophy of Anaxagoras. Indeed, the whole significance of Plato's discussion of human behaviour in the *Phaedo* is that it is Socrates, the vitalist, not Anaxagoras, the mechanist, who really conceives the idea which we now call 'behaviourism,' although Socrates is made to father it on Anaxagoras by saying that his metaphysical system would lead to a behaviouristic philosophy if carried to its logical consequences. But Anaxagoras' mechanistic theories of 'air, ether and water' are only behaviouristic when considered in the light of the Socratic teleology and the Socratic concept of the Psyche. For before Socrates the concept of the spiritual or non-material real was unknown. So that even if he had foreseen the results of modern experimental biology, Anaxagoras would still have been unable, from ignorance of the Socratic concept of spiritual reality, to understand the Cartesian philosophy, which is a Socratic theory of the soul, reconsidered and revised in the light of a theory of biological mechanism. The basic concept of Descartes' theory of biological mechanism, of course, is simply that animal (and human) action and passion is susceptible of a purely perceptual schematisation, a schematisation in terms of the physics and chemistry of the body. Modern behaviourism is an attempt at a detailed experimental justi-

The Idea of the Soul in Western Philosophy and Science

fication of this philosophical concept. Socrates, discussing this idea of the perceptual schematisation of behaviour, concluded that it would leave no room for an immaterial, or spiritual Psyche. Descartes, analysing the issue more narrowly, showed that even the most uncompromising behaviourist cannot really dismiss the Socratic idea of the Psyche as an obsolete concept which has 'worn out its welcome.' The concept of spiritual reality must be modified, indeed, but not abandoned, if it can be shown that psychical activity may be perceptually schematised. In effect, when Descartes said 'I think'—that is, understand and perceive—'therefore I am,' he was saying, 'I think, therefore I am in some sense a spirit, a Psyche in the Socratic significance of the term.' But since even my thinking may be perceptually described, the relationship between matter and spirit cannot be as Socrates conceived it to be. The Psyche, Descartes concluded, is not supra-physical, but para-physical. The theory of the para-physical Psyche is not, however, the only means whereby the Socratic concept of the soul may be reconciled with biological mechanism. After considering certain other aspects of the neo-Pythagorean method in biology, we shall suggest an alternative modification of the Socratic theory.

"*Ein jedes jedes kann.*"

DRIESCH

CHAPTER XVII

The Drieschian Entelechy

WE have already pointed out that both mechanism and vitalism, in their modern forms, find their origin in the philosophy of Descartes, and that while Cartesian mechanism has been incorporated into several major philosophical systems, and almost universally accepted by biologists, vitalism has tended to sink to the status of a vaguely defined popular belief, based on a naïve and imperfect understanding of the philosophical issues involved. This, like other generalisations of its kind, is subject to exceptions. The vitalistic beliefs of Driesch, J. S. Haldane and others may well be erroneous, but they certainly cannot be dismissed as naïve. In particular, the vitalism of Driesch, a thinker whose achievements in either science or philosophy would entitle him to a position of eminence in the intellectual world, must demand our careful attention.

For Socrates the purposive or teleological character of the universe was most clearly manifested in human behaviour, above all, of course, in the ethical aspect of human behaviour. In the physical workings of teleology, in the 'bones and sinews' through which human purposes effected, he was not interested; he was content to find the Psyche by introspection. Aristotle, although so profoundly affected by the Socratic-Platonic concept of spiritual teleology, was, like the pre-Socratics, interested less in the problems of the human spirit than in man's physical environment. It was therefore in physical processes, not in things introspectively known, but in things perceptually known, that he sought teleology. Lacking the requisite technique, Aristotle could not hope to emulate the modern behaviourist by investigating the perceptually knowable aspect of conscious behaviour; but, even in his day, the processes of organic development, the ontogenetic changes whereby the egg grows into an embryo and the embryo into an adult, could be readily, if not very minutely observed. A modern philosopher has said that Aristotle dissected fishes with Plato's thoughts in his head. Perhaps the essence of Aristotle's thought might be more truly epitomised by saying that he watched ontogeny with Plato's thoughts in his head, for it is the image of ontogenetic change, the analogy of the divine sculptor sculpturing living form, which haunts and pervades his metaphysics. Because he was by temper a naturalist and a physicist, and by education a Platonist, he saw the problem of Being in the light of this most elaborately co-ordinated (and therefore most strikingly teleological) of all natural processes of Becoming, that through which the physical environment is moulded and integrated into an organic pattern. To-day the ontogenetic process, of which Aristotle could only observe the most general features, has been subjected to an intensive and fruitful analysis, not merely from the morphological, but also from the experimental, the neo-Pythagorean, point of view. Moreover, the most ambitious of all vitalistic philosophies, the neo-Aristotelian philosophy of Driesch, is based mainly on the results of this analysis, although Driesch, like Aristotle, conceives of Entelechy as the directing force, not only of ontogeny, but also of conscious behaviour. Having at his disposal a more minute and accurate knowledge of ontogeny that Aristotle could hope to attain, Driesch has been able, by relating the abstract notion of Entelechy to concrete physical processes, to create a new concept of Entelechy. Comparing his idea of Entelechy with that of Aristotle, Driesch likens the latter with a mould which he has filled with new contents.

Although their discovery has involved the invention of a special and elaborate experimental technique, the scientific

The Drieschian Entelechy

data out of which Driesch has elaborated his new generalisations are in principle of the simplest nature.

The eggs of most animal forms develop, in their initial stages, in conformity with the following very simple pattern. Starting from a single cell or *blastomere*, the egg repeatedly divides itself into symmetrical halves, so that the embryo passes successively through two-, four-, eight-, sixteen- and thirty-two-cell stages . . . and so on, the size of the individual cells decreasing in inverse proportion as the cells become more numerous. In the early stages of development

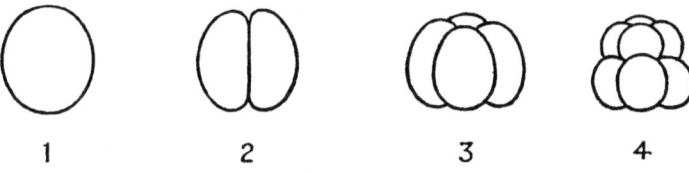

DIAGRAM XVIII.—CLEAVAGE OF THE EGG.

1–4.—One, two, four and eight-cell stages of the segmenting embryo.

the several blastomeres are quite indistinguishable from each other, but as division continues this homogeneity gives place to heterogeneity. That is to say, as the cells become more numerous they also become specialised in different ways to form the various tissues of the body . . . brain, kidney and so on.

Mere observation tells us nothing, of course, of the nature of the developmental processes. But these may be analysed by interfering with normal development in various ways, either directly by operating on the embryo, or indirectly by changing its environment. The pioneer in this field of experiment was the German biologist, Roux. His work has given rise to the modern science of experimental embryology, now the most important and fundamental branch of biological enquiry.

It is possible, for example, to separate the halves of a two-blastomere embryo, and these will then develop in isolation

The Idea of the Soul in Western Philosophy and Science

from each other. This was done by Driesch in 1891, on the egg of the sea-urchin, Echinus. The result of this experiment, since confirmed by many other workers, was extraordinary. Each half of the egg gives rise, not, as might be expected, to a half-embryo, but to a *complete* embryo of small size. This

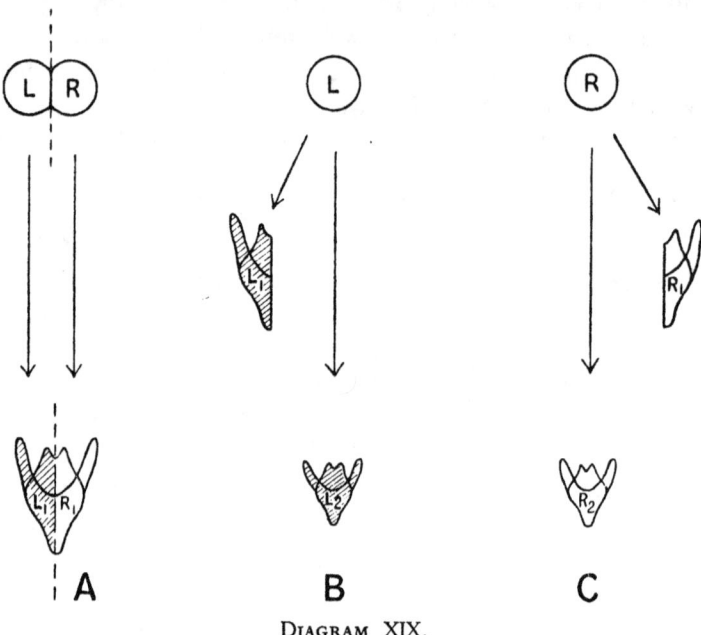

DIAGRAM XIX.

DEVELOPMENT OF ECHINUS FROM SINGLE BLASTOMERE.

is shown in Diagram XIX, where L represents the left-hand blastomere of the two-cell stage. Normally, L develops into the left-hand half L_1 of the embryo, and R into the right-hand half R_1 (XIX A). But if L be separated from R, it gives the perfect, although small, embryo L_2, not the half-embryo L_1 (XIX B). And similarly, R by itself gives the complete embryo R_2, not the half-embryo R_1 which it would ordinarily form (XIX C).

Further, if a four-cell embryo be separated into two halves,

The Drieschian Entelechy

each consisting of two cells, each half will 'regulate' to give a complete embryo, differing only in size from the normal embryo. Moreover, it does not matter *which* two blastomeres are taken from the four-blastomere stage; any half will give a complete embryo. Nor is this all. Even a single cell, removed

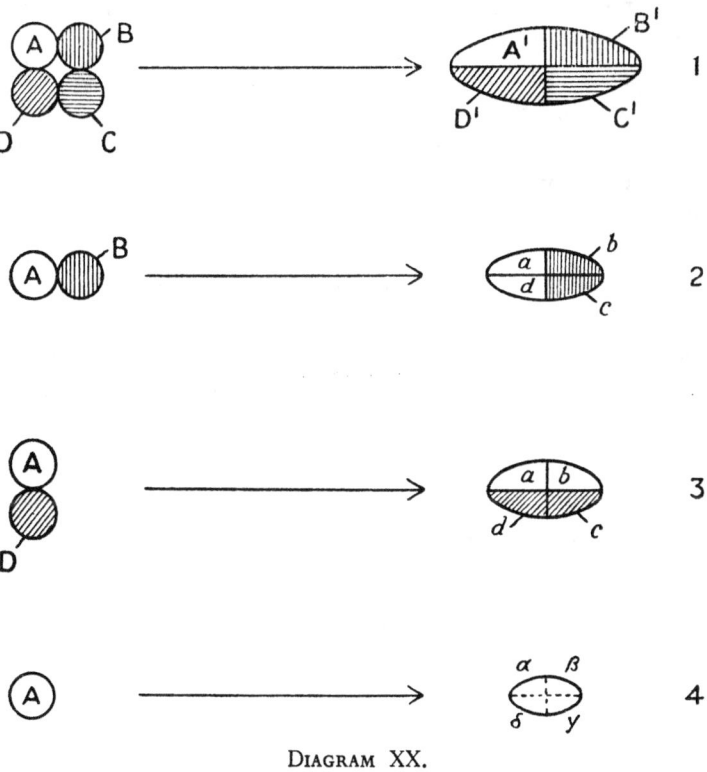

DIAGRAM XX.

from the other three cells of the four-blastomere embryo, will 'regulate' to form a complete embryo. These facts may be conveniently summarised in diagrammatic form. For simplicity, let us represent a perfect embryo by an ellipse, e.g. the ellipse A'B'C'D' in Diagram XX (1). If ABCD be the four-cell stage, then A gives rise to A', B to B', and so on. Now consider what happens when two cells, A and B say, are removed from the others, so that they develop into a complete embryo, instead of a half-embryo A'B'. The cell A, which normally gives rise to one of the quarters A', of the large embryo, now gives rise (Diagram XX (2)) to (ad) which is a half of the small embryo ($abcd$). The size of (ad) is of course the same as that of A, but it will be readily seen that it must contain quite different organs.

Suppose that AB is the left side of the animal, and BC the anterior end; then AD is the posterior end and DC the left side. It follows that in (1) A gives rise to the organs of the *left posterior* part of the embryo, whereas in (2) the same cell develops into the right *and* left posterior parts. The two cells AD will also give a complete embryo (3), if separated from the rest of the egg. Here again, A gives a half-embryo (ab), but this time it is the *anterior* and *posterior* organs of the left side; in other words, the whole of the organs of the left side, which are formed from A. And if A be allowed to develop in complete isolation (4), it gives the whole *organism*, $\alpha\beta\gamma\delta$. So that A is capable of forming at least four entirely different sets of organs:

(1) A develops into the organs of the *left posterior quarter* of the embryo.
(2) A develops into the organs of the *posterior half* of the embryo.
(3) A develops into the organs of the *left half* of the embryo.
(4) A develops into the organs of the *whole* embryo.

The really remarkable nature of these facts will be apparent if it is remembered that the embryo, which we have figured as a simple ellipse, is really, of course, a complex organism, having a nervous system, sense organs, locomotory organs, excretory organs and so on. So that a part of A which in (1) develops into nervous tissue, might in (2) form, say, parts of the kidney, digestive tract and body wall, while in (3) the same region of A might give rise to a sense organ and part of the nervous system, whereas yet another set of organs would be the result in (4). But in all four instances the net result is a whole organism. Moreover, the embryo may be deformed

The Drieschian Entelechy

or divided in numerous other ways, yet still give a perfect embryo. There are, of course, limits to the amount of regulation which is possible. For example, a single blastomere from the eight-cell stage of Echinus will not give a whole embryo, but two cells, separated from the other six, will develop normally, and if the two rings of four cells, of which the eight-cell stage is composed, be compressed into a flat ring of eight cells, the deformed embryo will nevertheless give a perfect larva. And, even up to a very advanced stage, a half-embryo will reorganise itself to form a complete animal.

In all such instances the fixed end result, irrespective of the size or origin of the blastomeres from which it develops, is the whole organism. The history of any given part of the embryo is not, however, fixed; it adapts itself in such a way as to collaborate with the other parts in the production of a whole organism. And in order that this may be possible, the nature of the egg must be such that *any* part of it has the potentiality of giving rise to *any* organ, part of an organ, or group of organs in the embryo, although in each given instance of development, only one of this infinite number of potentialities is realised. This is the fundamental fact which Driesch has summarised in his well-known phrase *Ein jedes jedes kann*. The pun is, unfortunately, untranslatable, but the sense may perhaps be approximately rendered, "Each can do all."

Thus, in Diagram XXI, let A, B and C be any three regions of the egg, and let A', B' and C' be three regions of the embryo, such that in normal development A gives rise to A', B to B' and C to C'. In Driesch's terminology, A' is the *prospective value* of A, B' of B and so on. The prospective value of any region of the embryo is simply . . . what it develops into in any given instance of development, . . . in this instance, normal development. In the above diagram, prospective values are indicated by solid lines. But each region has also a *prospective potency*, which may be defined as . . . the sum of the various things it *can* turn into, in different circumstances, as need arises. The prospective potency of any given region, although not unlimited, is so wide that it is impossible to set definite limits to it. Prospective potencies are shown in the diagram as broken lines. That is to say, although A normally develops into A', it *can* develop into B', or C', or perhaps even into B' and C'. Similarly, B *can* develop into A' or C', and C into A' or B'. Moreover, if development is experimentally interfered with, each region 'chooses' just the one prospective value, out of its innumerable prospective potencies,

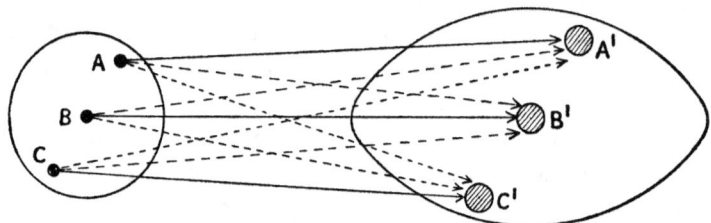

DIAGRAM XXI.—"EIN JEDES JEDES KANN."
Solid lines = *Prospective Values* (in normal development).
Broken lines = *Prospective Potencies*.

which will lead to the formation of a perfect organism from the mutilated egg. Stated in the most general possible terms, Driesch's argument is that no machine, no merely mechanical arrangement of parts, however elaborately constituted, could do this.

For let us suppose that the development of the egg is the result of interaction within a complex mechanical arrangement of parts, comparable with a man-made machine.

Now we know that any portion of the egg, above a certain limit of size, can also make a complete, although miniature, embryo. Let us represent such a portion by the circle A (Diagram XXII). Then we must suppose that this portion, A, contains a complex arrangement of parts, a machine, which is the exact duplicate in miniature of the whole egg. Now, let us draw a region B, of the same size as A, and partially over-

The Drieschian Entelechy

lapping it. Since B, too, can form a whole embryo, it also must contain a duplicate of our hypothetical machine. And so on for similar regions such as C, D, etc. We can, in fact, draw an infinite number of such overlapping regions within the egg, and each must contain the same complex mechanical arrangement of parts. Further, it is obvious that two circles (the regions would actually be spheres of course) can be overlapped so that any region of one corresponds to any region of

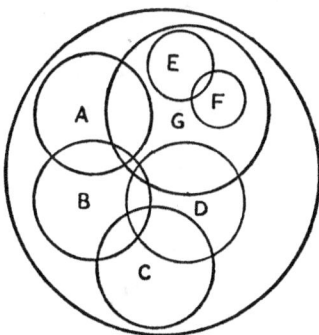

DIAGRAM XXII.

the same size in the other. Hence any part of our machine must be the same as any other part of it of the same size. And since larger regions, such as G, and smaller regions, such as E and F, can also form a perfect organism, it follows that every part of our machine is exactly the same as every other part of it. But this is logically self-contradictory. There cannot possibly be a heterogeneous system of material particles, such that any part of it is exactly similar to any other part of it, for such a system is by definition homogeneous! And if it *is* homogeneous it cannot, of course, be a machine, since any machine depends for its working on the differences (in size, shape, etc.) between its various parts.

Therefore we are forced to conclude that the *end* of development, the perfect organism, cannot be caused by, or at any rate cannot be wholly caused by the natural processes in the embryo which precede its formation. Rather, these processes must in some way be determined by the end in which they culminate. Other lines of argument point to the same conclusion. If the development of the egg were a strictly mechanical, or physico-chemical process, the same cause would always have the same ontogenetic effect. But we have seen that the same cause, for example the blastomere A in our earlier discussion, can produce quite different effects in order that the development may always culminate in a perfect embryo. Here again it is the end which seems to determine the means, just as a human purpose determines the material means by which it is realised. If a man desires to build a house, it is the idea of the house which determines the material process of building. For example, two builders might, independently of one another, each build a house from the same design. Different numbers of labourers may be employed on the two sites, or one builder might elect to put up the various wings in a different order from that chosen by the other. In either instance the physical processes involved in the realisation of the idea of the house would be different. Or again, if a part of one of the houses were to suffer accidental destruction during the building, it would be 'regenerated' by the builder to conform to the architect's plan. In short, the 'ontogenies' of the two houses, considered merely as material configurations, may be as different as one likes. Yet each process culminates in the same end. In the same way, the perfect organism may supervene from an indefinite diversity of material histories in the embryo, according to the degree and nature of the regulation which the latter is called upon to perform. Therefore, for the organism as for the house, the end must be an autonomous entity which determines the means. And since the adult organism, considered solely as a material arrangement of parts, cannot cause the processes which preceded it in time, the end which controls these processes cannot be a material thing. It is a non-spatial, immaterial entity, a final cause which, as it

The Drieschian Entelechy

were, draws material processes into itself. But such an entity, which contains its end, or 'telos' in itself, is as Driesch maintains, none other than Aristotle's ἐντελέχεια. It is a remarkable fact that Aristotle, knowing nothing of the modern science of experimental embryology, should have intuitively foreseen one of the most striking results of that science, namely, the demonstration of the 'telos-having' nature of the forces which guide ontogeny. Later, we shall contend that Driesch is mistaken in supposing that Entelechy cannot be perceptually schematised. But of the existence of Entelechy, in the restricted sense defined by the words τέλος and ἔχειν, there can be no possible doubt.

In what way does the Entelechy determine the ontogenetic processes? We have seen that the essence of regulation is that if the egg be deformed or disturbed in any way, each region chooses just the one prospective value, from its range of prospective potencies, which will enable it to collaborate with the rest of the egg in the formation of a perfect embryo. It is this 'selective' action which Driesch attributes to his Entelechy. The latter might be compared with a sphere (Diagram XXIII) enclosing a source of light and pierced by a small hole which lets through only one narrow ray. The light which does not emerge is comparable with the unrealised prospective potencies of a given region of the egg, the ray which escapes is then the realised prospective potency, that is, the prospective value in a given ontogeny. By turning in this or that direction, the sphere (i.e. the Entelechy) can release any required 'prospective value.' The Entelechy must be imagined as exercising this selection in every region of the egg, in such a way that the combined prospective values result in the genesis of a perfect organism.

The 'selective' action of Driesch's Entelechy should be compared with the 'directive' action of Descartes' *res cogitans*. No doubt the latter played some part in suggesting Driesch's hypothesis. Like Descartes, Driesch is anxious to maintain

The Idea of the Soul in Western Philosophy and Science

that his Entelechy does not add to, or subtract from the total energy of the organism. This, it may be pointed out, is the least concession which even the most extreme vitalist must now make to mechanism, on account of the indisputable experimental evidence that the law of conservation of energy holds as rigidly in the living organism as in the inorganic world. And, again following Descartes, Driesch maintains that his

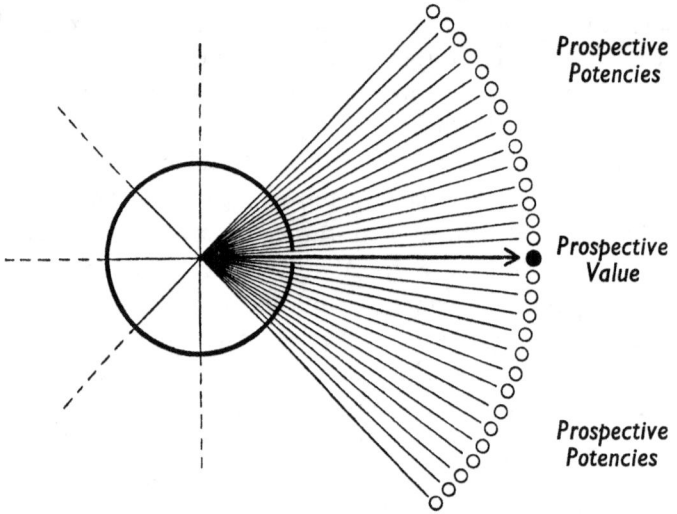

DIAGRAM XXIII.—THE SELECTIVE ACTION OF ENTELECHY.

vitalistic agency acts, not 'in,' but 'into' space, as the *res cogitans* 'acts into' the pineal gland.[1]

We have seen that Descartes, in the vitalistic mood which was really so antithetic to the main trend of his thought, was scarcely successful in his attempt to postulate a directive agency which would be without action on the energy exchange within the organism. In reconciling the corresponding aspects of his Entelechy, Driesch has been more successful than Descartes. To show how Entelechy can 'select,' without creating or destroying energy, he has recourse to Clerk Maxwell's well-known

[1] H. Driesch, *The Problem of Individuality*, p. 73.

The Drieschian Entelechy

thermodynamical fantasy of the molecular 'demon.' The second law of thermodynamics states that energy cannot pass from a system of low temperature into one of higher temperature, but only in the reverse direction. Maxwell's fantasy, or parable, was designed to show that by the selective activity of a 'psychical' being, this law could be transcended without affecting the gross energy relations of the combined systems. Imagine a container, divided into two halves by a compartment in which there is a small aperture, which can be opened or closed by a door. Further, suppose that one compartment, A, contains a gas at a higher temperature than that in the compartment B, on the other side of the partition. Finally, we have to imagine a little demon, in compartment B, standing at the door. Ordinarily he keeps the door closed, but whenever he sees a molecule of more than average velocity approaching the door, he opens it and lets the molecule through. By this means he increases the average velocity of the molecules in A at the expense of those in B, so that the hot compartment, A, becomes hotter at the expense of the cooler one. Yet the demon would not have added to, or subtracted from, the total energy of the system AB. It is in some such way as this that Driesch conceives his Entelechy to work.

Like Maxwell's demon, the Entelechy can only act through the intermediacy of matter, although it is non-material. And hence it is limited by matter. It can only suspend interaction between energy levels which have been created by material means in the organism. Therefore, as the various potentialities, suspended, as it were, in the egg, become released in development, the power of the Entelechy becomes progressively less. In the higher animals the only regulation possible in the adult stage is the repair of wounds. But in the simpler forms even the adult organism can perform remarkable feats of regeneration. For example, if the leg of a newt be cut off, a perfect new limb will be regenerated. Further, it does not matter at what level we make the amputation; the missing part will

The Idea of the Soul in Western Philosophy and Science

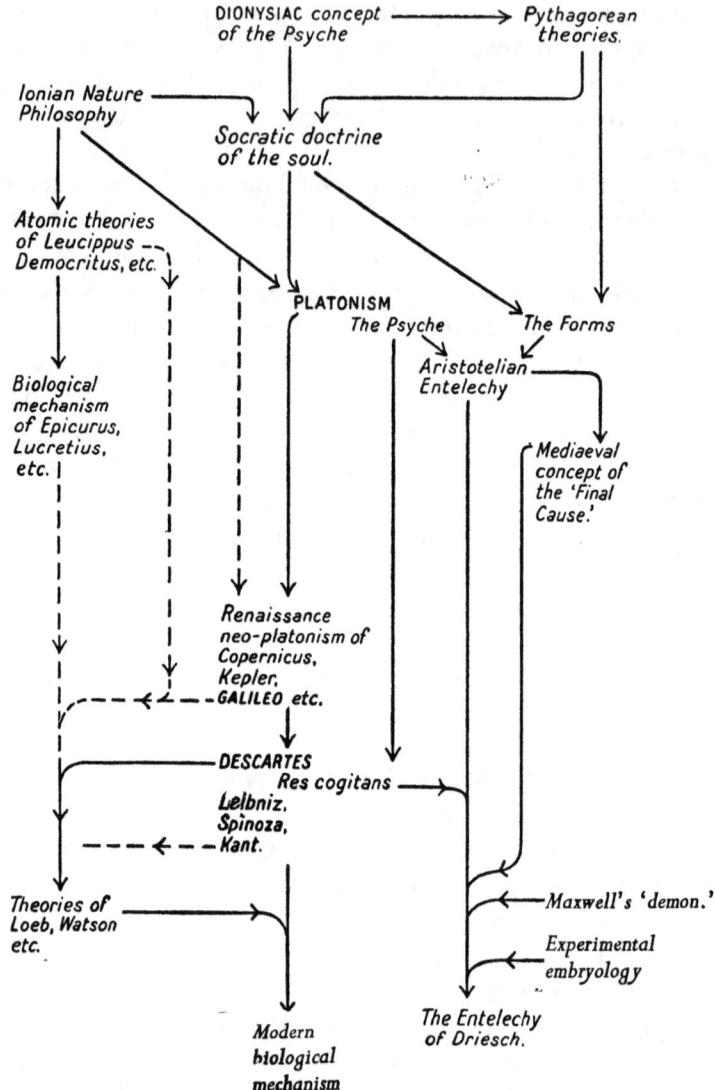

DIAGRAM XXIV.

The Drieschian Entelechy

always be exactly replaced. Or, in Driesch's terminology, the Entelechy will choose just the right prospective value required for the regeneration of the missing part.

In spite of their originality and the comparative novelty of their subject matter, Driesch's conceptions have a history which goes back to the origins of Greek thought. This, as we have emphasised throughout, is true of all our philosophical and scientific ideas, although Driesch's theories happen to provide an especially striking instance of the continuity of thought. It is in fact literally true that Driesch's Entelechy is the lineal descendant of a strange being, who, thirty centuries ago, danced into Thrace from somewhere in the East. We refer to the god, Dionysos. Possibly his twentieth-century epiphany, in the egg of the sea urchin, is stranger even than any known to his worshippers in bygone times.

Diagram XXIV shows in diagrammatic form some of the more obvious affinities, with Greek and Renaissance thought, both of Driesch's vitalism and of contemporary 'mechanistic' conceptions.

"Non Angli sed angeli."
SCHOOL HISTORIES, attributed to Gregory the Great.

CHAPTER XVIII.

The Physical Schema of Entelechy: Axial Gradients

WE have described Driesch's neo-Aristotelianism at some length, for two reasons. First, in order that the reader may in some degree appreciate the peculiar and complex nature of the facts which the biologist must handle, and the consequent difficulty of describing such facts in mechanistic terms. Secondly, in order to show that it is the very difficulty of the mechanist's task which makes that of the vitalist so easy. To find a mechanistic, or as we should prefer to call it, a natural explanation of a biological process, may call for years of difficult laboratory work which may yield little of significance in the end. But anyone of moderate intelligence may sit in his study and evolve half a dozen highly plausible supernatural explanations in the course of an afternoon. By a supernatural explanation we mean one which abandons the attempt to describe observed relations in terms of things 'perceptively known' and uses aetiological entities, such as the Drieschian Entelechy, which cannot be investigated through perceptively knowable relations. Driesch's explanation of ontogeny is really of the same kind as that which ascribes lunacy to the action of an evil spirit. Such an explanation can never lead to a real understanding of the causes of lunacy, simply because the 'spirit' being in principle unobservable, automatically acquires just those properties which are necessary to explain everything included in the term lunacy. Because it explains so much, it really explains nothing at all. Similarly, Driesch's Entelechy

Physical Schema of Entelechy

does everything necessary to bring about development: it guides development with all the solicitude and efficiency which the angels of the schoolmen lavished on the guidance of the planets. And since the angel, or Entelechy, does everything, and may in any case be presumed to know much better than we do, it would be futile, even impious, for us to worry our heads any further over the matter. Fortunately for astrology, Galileo, Newton and others refused to leave everything to the angels. It is the study, not of angels, but of angles, masses and accelerations which has given us the law of gravitation. And fortunately for experimental embryology, modern biologists have refused to sit back and let Entelechy do all their work for them.

The work of the American biologist, Child, has shown the way towards an extremely simple 'natural' explanation of the facts which led Driesch to invent, or resuscitate, his supernatural Entelechy.

In order to give a clear account of Child's theory of ontogeny, it will be necessary to describe the most fundamental of all the functions of living matter, its *metabolism*. To the unsophisticated eye, an organism appears to be quite distinct from its environment; to the physiologist the distinction is arbitrary, for the reason that the environment is continually flowing into the organism, and the organism back to the environment. The organism is a kink or eddy in a metabolic stream of which the most fundamental and obvious feature is the activity called respiration. Oxygen is constantly flowing into the organism, carbon dioxide is continually flowing back to the environment. Similarly, food and water must continually enter the organism from the environment, to return to it as nitrogenous excretion, sweat and so forth. Hence the fixity, or rather, the permanence, of a frog, an amoeba, or of a man is quite different from the fixity of an inorganic object such as a book or a mountain. The permanence of the mountain is static, that of the organism is dynamic, like the illusory fixity

The Idea of the Soul in Western Philosophy and Science

of a fountain. The organism is a Herakleitan flux, because its essence, like that of the fountain or the Herakleitan Real, is in its fluency. If the respiratory, nutritive, or any other part of the metabolic flow be cut off, the organism dies, for the same reason that a fountain collapses if the water be cut off. Like the Herakleitan Real, the organism *rests by changing*, for

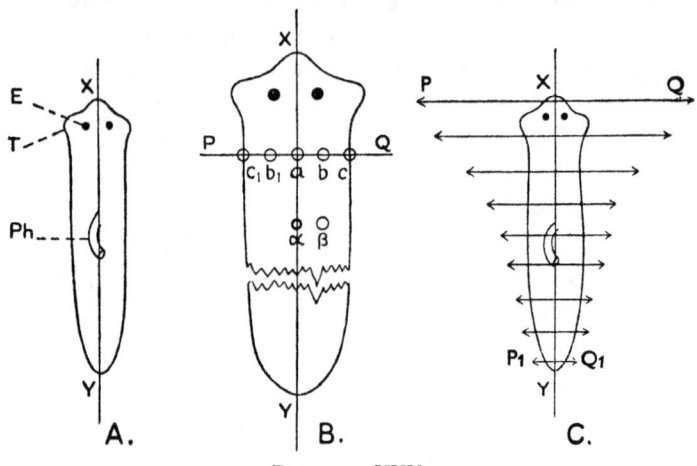

DIAGRAM XXV.
A. E = Eye. T = Tentacles. Ph = Pharnyx.
B. Diagram to show bilateral metabolic symmetry. See text description.
C. Diagram to show metabolic gradient. See text description.

the organism does not burn fuel merely in order that it may do work, like a petrol engine or a locomotive. Even when living matter is performing no work, it is essential for it to respire. If it does not respire, it dies; in order to persist, it must consume itself. '*It is*,' said Herakleitos, '*the opposite which is good for us*': we may go further and say that it is the opposite which is essential for us, the necessary condition of our being.

Now Child discovered a peculiar and fundamental fact about the metabolic stream. The discovery was made on a small flatworm, Planaria, and we shall therefore describe it in relation to that organism. Planaria (Diagram XXV, A) is a creature

Physical Schema of Entelechy

about half an inch long, having tentacles, eyes and a pharynx visible externally, and a rather complex internal structure. Like many organisms, it is bilaterally symmetrical; that is, it can be divided by a line XY, which we will call the morphological axis, into symmetrical right and left halves. Child's discovery, like most fundamental ones, is simple. He found that the metabolic rate is different in different regions of the animal, and that the pattern of metabolic rates, like the structural pattern, is symmetrical about the morphological axis. So that if we draw a line PQ across the animal at right angles to the morphological axis (Diagram XXV, B), we shall find that the region a, on the axis, has a greater rate of metabolism than b, to one side of the axis, and b in turn, has a greater metabolism than c at the edge. And if b', on the other side of the axis, is at the same distance from it as b, it has a metabolism equal to that of b; similarly c' has a metabolic rate equivalent to that of c. Underlying the visible morphological symmetry, then, is an invisible metabolic symmetry. Further, as we move down the animal, away from the head, the metabolism of all parts decreases. Thus α has a lower metabolism than a and the metabolism of β is less than that of b. Hence, if we draw lines at various levels, proportionate in length to the metabolism at each level, we shall get a pattern like that shown in (Diagram XXV, C) where PQ represents the high metabolism at the head end, $P'Q'$ the low metabolism at the posterior end. The head of the animal, which dominates the animal functionally, is also the dominant part of the metabolic gradient. Such a gradient of metabolism is called by Child an *axial gradient*. So much for the facts. Underlying the symmetry of form, the morphological pattern, is a metabolic pattern, a symmetry of metabolism.

From these facts, Child makes the following simple hypothesis: the metabolic pattern is the *cause* of the morphological, or structural, pattern. For example, the reason why Planaria has a pair of eyes, equidistant from the morphological axis,

The Idea of the Soul in Western Philosophy and Science

is simply that it has a symmetrical pair of metabolic rates, each of which, acting on the originally undifferentiated protoplasm of the embryo, brings about the differentiation which we call an eye. The eyes arise just where they do, and nowhere else, simply because they are formed by a given metabolic rate which occurs at just two regions in the metabolic pattern. Other metabolic rates, at other points in the pattern, cause the differentiation of other kinds of structure.

Now this hypothesis, if it can be substantiated, is an extraordinary triumph for the Pythagorean method in biology. For a metabolic rate can be written simply as a number . . . x calories of heat, or y grams of oxygen metabolised, per unit of time. And in the sense that the form of the organism, its morphological pattern, can be predicted from a knowledge of the purely numerical metabolic pattern, the number is the cause of form.

Compare this with the Aristotelian, or scholastic, explanation by reference to final causes, which would run somewhat as follows. The reason why Planaria has eyes is that it requires to see, and the Entelechy of the eye, in order to effect this consummation, draws part of the matter of the organism into the form of an eye, 'as a loved one draws a lover.' The soul or Entelechy of the eye is vision, and this, acting as a *telos* or final cause, makes an eye out of undifferentiated protoplasm, which therefore stands in relation to the perfected eye as matter to Form, potential to actual.

Now it is without doubt *in some sense* true that Planaria has eyes because it is the 'purpose' of Nature that the creature shall enjoy vision. But it does not by any means follow that the purpose of the eye is vision, *in exactly the same sense* that the purpose of a watch, say, is to show the time, since that would mean that Planaria was created by a finite being, as watches are. For to ascribe purpose to an infinite Being is a contradiction in terms; purpose implies desire, and desire implies limitation, finitude. And to the sophisticated religious

Physical Schema of Entelechy

instinct, a finite Creator is almost as absurd a conception as the purposeless world of the crude materialist. So that even the religious mind, to which such an explanation makes the most immediate appeal, must be extremely wary of thinking of Nature in terms of final causes. Moreover, even if it were demonstrably true, the explanation by reference to final causes would be useless to the scientist, since the phenomenon to be explained, in this instance the presence of eyes, is described in terms of entities which are perceptually unknowable. The supreme merit of Child's 'Pythagorean' explanation is that it is entirely in terms of entities which cannot only be perceived, or immediately deduced from perception, but accurately measured.

The importance of Child's hypothesis in relation to Driesch's experiments is that in the egg or embryo of any animal there is a metabolic gradient similar to that of the adult Planarian. This gradient, the primary axial gradient, is initiated by causes external to the egg. In mammalian development, for example, one side of the egg receives a richer oxygen supply than the other, and becomes the apex of the axial gradient. Diagram XXVI represents an egg having a metabolic rate of one hundred units at one end, grading off to sixty units at the other end. Consider any two regions, A and B, in the egg. If development is allowed to proceed normally, A is going to differentiate into, say, nervous tissue, and B into kidney. In Driesch's language, the prospective value of A is nervous tissue, and of B, kidney. But if, by operating on the egg, we interchange A and B, then A will form kidney and B nervous tissue. That is, although A 'normally' forms nervous tissue, it also has the prospective potency of forming kidney, and conversely for B. Reversal of the relative positions of A and B has also led to a reversal of their prospective values. Why is this? We have seen Driesch's answer. The Entelechy selects the right prospective potency, in each instance, which will enable A and B to collaborate with the rest of the egg in the formation of a perfect embryo. Otherwise the animal would have excretory tissue where its brain should be, and vice versa. Let us see if, in the light of Child's hypothesis, a 'natural' explanation cannot be substituted for that of Driesch.

Now the real value of Driesch's analysis is that it shows that the egg is initially homogeneous. The facts of regulation really do preclude the idea that the egg is a complex arrangement of parts which produces an embryo as a sausage machine produces sausages. No such machine could have in

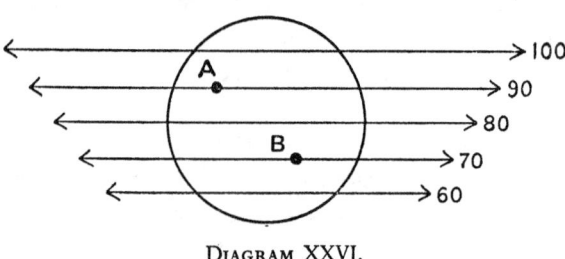

DIAGRAM XXVI.

any part a prospective potency greater than the prospective value of that part, much less the almost infinite prospective potencies which exist in all parts of the egg. Initially, the only difference between A and B is one of *position*, relative to the other parts of the egg. So that our question now becomes, how can a mere difference of position, in an initially homogeneous egg, lead to the heterogeneous collection of parts (nervous system, excretory system) and so on, which develops in the embryo and adult? And the answer is simply, because there is an axial gradient of metabolism in the egg. A metabolic rate of ninety units, acting on A (Diagram XXVI) produces nervous tissue; a metabolic rate of seventy units, acting on the same raw material at B, produces excretory tissue. If we interchange A and B, we reverse their position in the axial gradient, so that B is now acted on by a metabolic rate of ninety units, and therefore differentiates as nervous tissue, while A, now acted on by a

Physical Schema of Entelechy

rate of seventy units, gives excretory tissue. The prospective values interchange, because it is the position of a region in the egg, not its material constitution, which is the differential condition determining its ultimate fate. *Ein jedes jedes kann*, not because there is an Entelechy selecting prospective potencies, but simply because prospective values are determined by position in the metabolic pattern. A devastatingly simply physico-chemical description of the facts which led Driesch to invent his monstrous supernatural apparatus of Entelechies.

One of the most important and interesting tasks of contemporary experimental biology is to fill in the details of this epigenetic theory. Here the discovery of *organisers* is of fundamental importance. The direct determination of prospective values by the axial gradient, such as we have described, is now known to be subordinate in importance to an indirect determination through the formation of organisers. The axial gradient produces in the originally homogeneous egg a substance called an organiser. This substance is responsible for the formation of certain primary organs, and these now become secondary organisers for the next set of organs, and so on until development is complete. If the egg be cut into two before the appearance of the organiser, a region of primary organiser forms in each half, and development proceeds normally. If the division be made later, after the appearance of the organisers, each half will develop only those organs for which it has the appropriate secondary organisers. Driesch was very fortunate in choosing to work on an egg, that of Echinus, which forms its organiser at a comparatively late stage in cell division, so that, before this stage, it has the extraordinary powers of regulation which we have described. But the eggs of many other animals form their organisers before they have even divided into the first two blastomeres. In such instances the first two blastomeres, when separated from each other, each gives rise, not to a small perfect embryo, but to one half of a large embryo. Now Driesch would have to say that the eggs of some animals are provided with a more efficient Entelechy than those of others. Moreover, the presence or absence of the properties ascribed to Entelechy would, on Driesch's theory, be an absolutely arbitrary occurrence, for since the Entelechy is non-spatial, there can be no perceptual criterion of its presence or absence. But, on the theory of organisers, the behaviour of the egg is quite simply determined by the relative rates of cell division and of organiser formation. And these are numerical quantities which may be perceptually determined.

> "... to-day there is less basis for vitalistic theory than ever before ... and, while many other attempts will undoubtedly be made in future to demonstrate the indispensability of some sort of vital principle, the analysis and synthesis of science, proceeding step by step, testing and retesting the supposed facts, adopting and discarding hypotheses, will continue to be the basis of our advance in knowledge."
>
> CHILD

CHAPTER XIX

The Future of the Neo-Pythagorean Method

DRIESCH'S vitalism is, for several reasons, the most instructive of the 'supernatural' or vitalistic philosophies. First, because of the really extraordinary nature of the facts on which it is based. The regulatory powers of the organism, especially in the early stages of development, are so striking, and so closely simulate the workings of some kind of supernatural agency, that it seems at first sight inconceivable that a natural explanation of ontogeny should be discoverable.

Secondly, because Child's explanation lays bare the error which is fundamental to all vitalistic theories, namely, that they ignore the dynamic nature of living matter, which is its most significant attribute. In attempting to account for regulation, Driesch fails to notice the fundamental fact that Nature is perpetually flowing through the organism as a metabolic stream. But it is in virtue of the fact that it is a flux that the organism regenerates. Just as the particles flowing in a river will gradually repair a cavity dredged in its bed, restoring the original shape, so the metabolising tissue flows into and regenerates any mutilation of its pattern. Because he ignores the fluent nature of the organic pattern, Driesch not unnaturally concludes that organic activities are directed by something outside Nature, the Entelechy. For although he asserts that Entelechy is in Nature, Driesch also affirms that it is not in space, but 'acts into space.' It could not, of course, be spatial, since it is perceptually unknowable. Therefore we must conclude that it is really outside Nature, in the same sense that Descartes' *res cogitans* is outside Nature.

Thirdly, the theories of Driesch and Child are relevant, in a curious but significant manner, to a question which at first sight seems quite unrelated, the question, namely, whether animal behaviour requires for its explanation a vital principle.

It is for this reason that we have until now postponed all discussion of the various objections which have been brought against the mechanistic description of behaviour. There are certain objections which may be dismissed immediately. Of such superficial criticisms the most familiar is the assertion that human behaviour is so extraordinarily complex that it could not possibly have a structural basis. Such an objection would not be raised by anyone having even a general knowledge of the structure of the human brain. We have already described how the connections between afferent and efferent neurones mediate the formation of conditioned reflexes. In most vertebrates the neurones of the brain are packed in a solid, three-dimensional mass. But to a small degree in the reptiles, and in the mammalia to a much larger degree, part of the brain has a sheet-like, or cortical, structure. In a part of the so-called 'end-brain' the neurones are arranged in a broad thin sheet called the cerebral cortex. Such an arrangement greatly facilitates the inter-communication of the neurones; the cortex may in fact be compared with a telephone switchboard on which any combination of points can be made. In the higher mammals, particularly in the primates (and among the primates, particularly in man) the area of the cortex is enormously increased by convolutions. The following quotation will give some idea of the size and complexity of the human cortex.

"The number of possible combinations between the neurones is so large that it baffles the power of the mind to grasp it. As an example, one million

Future of Neo-Pythagorean Method

neurones connected together in all possible ways in groups of two neurones each, gives a number of combinations with nearly three million figures in it. There are not far off ten million neurones in the human cerebral cortex."[1]

In fact we may safely ignore all criticisms of the mechanistic theory based on mere grounds of complexity.

Criticism of the principles involved in mechanistic description is, however, another matter. We cannot do better than discuss such criticisms in the light of the simple proposition with which we opened our account of conditioned reflexes. We said that it is a matter of common experience that "a dog knows its master." That, in a few words, epitomises the kind of behaviour which it is the object of the theory of conditioned reflexes to explain. And, in describing how such behaviour could be explained in terms of conditioned reflexes, we made an important tacit assumption. Because '*master*' is one word we assumed that its perceptual counterpart is one stimulus, or one fixed group of stimuli. But the perceptual reality corresponding to the word 'master' is most certainly not a single stimulus, or constant group of stimuli. The difficulty is admirably expressed in the following passage by E. S. Russell:

"The perception of an image or pattern is of course very familiar to us, so much so that we do not realise how extraordinary a thing it is. A dog very quickly learns to recognise his master by sight, even at some little distance; we must assume that he sees an image of his master. Now this image is not a fixed and invariable one; it is different in size according as the master is distant or near at hand; it is different in shape according as the master is seen full face or in profile, standing up or lying down; it varies according to the way the master is dressed. Yet notwithstanding these large variations, the image is recognised as that of the master. What really matters is the whole-perception, the general pattern; the details are quite unimportant save in their relation to the pattern.

"Now it seems very difficult to conceive that such facts as these are susceptible of a physiological formulation. Thus the image as cast on the retina of the dog is not a fixed one, affecting always the same retinal elements; it varies enormously and hardly remains constant from one moment to another. Obviously the individual retinal cell, with its individual nervous

[1] From *Vertebrate Zoology*, by G. R. de Beer.

The Idea of the Soul in Western Philosophy and Science

connection with the cortex, counts for nothing *per se*; any particular retinal element may form almost any point in the retinal image; it is only its position relative to other stimulated elements that gives it any significance, and that significance is a constantly changing one. In other words, what really matters in visual perception is the whole, the pattern, irrespective of what particular retinal elements are stimulated. Somewhere the retinal mosaic must be organised into a whole or pattern, and it seems inconceivable that this can be a purely summative physiological process. From the physiological point of view the relation between stimulus and response must be mediated by chains of neurones extending between the receptor organ and the effector, and each stimulated receptor cell must contribute its own individual impulse. There seems no way of imagining how a pattern, a whole, can be formed, if the physiological formulation is true, and yet it is essentially to patterns and not to a mosaic of physiological stimuli that the animal responds."[1]

It will be seen that the author of this passage maintains, in no equivocal terms, that the recognition of pattern is incapable of description in physiological terms. In this he is going far beyond the evidence; but what his reasoning really does seem to show is that the recognition of pattern cannot be described on a *connectionist* hypothesis. By a connectionist theory we mean one which refers the building up of conditioned reflexes to the formation of specific new paths in the brain. On such a theory the formation of a conditioned reflex would be comparable to the addition of a new wire to a telephone exchange! Now there is no doubt that the formation of connections between afferent and efferent paths plays *some* part in the synthesis of conditioned reflexes. What Russell's analysis shows is that something more than the mere building up of connections must be involved.

The essence of his objection is, in fact, that conditioned behaviour cannot be explained as the result of interaction between a machine-like arrangement of parts. *It is, in other words, essentially the same objection which Driesch brings against the possibility of a natural explanation of regulation in the egg.* Not only is the objection the same, but the fact on which it

[1] From *The Behaviour of Animals*, by E. S. Russell.

Future of Neo-Pythagorean Method

is based is the same . . . the fact, namely, that *Ein jedes jedes kann.*

The stimulus designated by the word 'master' is a whole complex of quite different things, yet any of them is capable of evoking the response pattern which we call 'recognition' of the master. Any cell in the retina can contribute any part to any of the numerous patterns which the dog recognises. This is exactly paralleled by the ability of any part of an Echinus egg to form any component of a perfect embryo. Now if Russell's objection to a natural explanation of behaviour is, *mutatis mutandis*, the same as Driesch's objection to a natural explanation of development, there is at least a presumption that Russell's position is open to the same kind of refutation as the vitalism of Driesch. That is to say, there is a presumption that, for behaviour as for development, some form of gradient theory may prove an adequate natural explanation of the facts. It is a remarkable fact that a 'gradient' theory of behaviour, which as we have seen, seems to follow from a rather abstract analogy with embryonic development, appears also to be indicated by evidence of a very different nature. We refer to the work of the American investigator, Lashley.[1] It is impossible to enter here into the details of his brilliantly conceived investigations; but fortunately it is possible to indicate the gist of his conclusions in a few words. Lashley trained a number of rats, hundreds in all, to run a laboratory maze (see p. 195). Then he operated on the cerebral cortex, removing pieces of all sizes, from very small fragments up to nearly the whole cortex, and of differing shapes. And he found that the effect of the operation on the ability of the rats to 'remember' the maze was quite independent of the locality of the part of the cortex removed. It was for long believed that the various 'psychical' functions of the organism could be assigned to definite regions of the cortex. Thus, such and such an area of the cortex would be the physical basis of, say, visual memory,

[1] Lashley, *Brain Mechanisms and Intelligence.*

another part would be the locus of mathematical reasoning, or of the recognition of grammatical form, and so on. Removal of any given patch in the cortex would result in the removal of one or other of these psychical functions. Lashley's work on rats (and in addition the observation by neurologists of war victims) has quite exploded this notion. The effect of cortical extirpation on the retention of the maze habit was found to be solely dependent on the extent of the extirpation, and, as we have said, not at all related to its position, or shape. A small extirpation has little effect, quite irrespective of its position in the cortex; a large extirpation causes the rat to forget nearly all it has learned. A total extirpation of the cortex causes the disappearance of all conditioned behaviour. Here again there is a remarkable analogy with Driesch's experiments. In the cerebral cortex, as in the developing egg, *Ein iedes jedes kann*. Any part of the cortex, provided it be not too small, can retain the maze habit, just as any part of the egg, above a certain size, retains the potentiality of forming a whole embryo.

So that Lashley's experiments point to the same two conclusions as Russell's reasoning; they provide an experimental basis for the conclusions inferred by him from a different source. First, a connectionist hypothesis is shown to be quite untenable. If an animal can retain its memory of a maze habit in spite of the removal of any portion of the cortex, up to a certain limit of size, it follows that any part of the cortex can take over the function of any other part. This is quite inconceivable on a 'telephone switchboard' theory, or indeed any theory which ascribes conditioned behaviour to the interaction of specific parts, as in a man-made machine. Secondly, our initial presumption that conditioned behaviour may be attributed to some sort of cortical gradient system is now on much firmer grounds. For since we now have definite experimental knowledge that the cortex can 'regulate' in exactly the same manner as a developing egg, we have definite

Future of Neo-Pythagorean Method

grounds for presuming that in the cortex, as in the egg, there are gradient systems in virtue of which the parts may take over the function of the whole. In order to see what the nature of such a system might be, let us again return to the fundamental problem, raised by our proposition that a dog 'knows its master.'

From Russell's analysis it is evident that the dog's act of recognition is not in any sense a mere reaction to a constant perceptual stimulus, or group of such. The single word

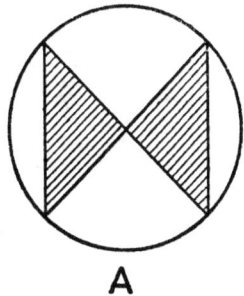 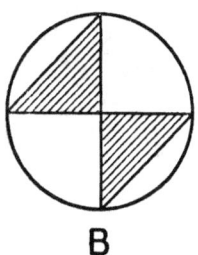

DIAGRAM XXVII.

'master,' or any other substantive, corresponds, as we pointed out at the beginning of this book,[1] to a perceptual manifold, or if we prefer it, to a retinal manifold, an infinitely diverse group of retinal patterns. So that in order to find a natural explanation of the dog's act of recognition we must look for something constant within the perceptual manifold constituting an 'object' of experience. It is clear that this constant factor must be sought in the *relations* between the various elements of the manifold. The dog recognises its master's face because the relations between the parts of the face are different from those of other faces, and remain distinct, whatever the orientation of the face on the dog's retina. Suppose, for example (Diagram XXVII), that A is the image of some object on the retina. Then, for a different distance and orientation

[1] See page 38.

The Idea of the Soul in Western Philosophy and Science

of the object, the retinal image might be like that shown in B. With respect to the elements of the retina the image is now quite different, but the spatial relations within it are unaltered, and hence it is recognised as an image of the same object.[1] Hence our problem—how does the dog recognise its master?—really boils down to the abstract question—how does the organism recognise constant *relations* in a perceptual flux? It will be seen that there is more than a superficial analogy

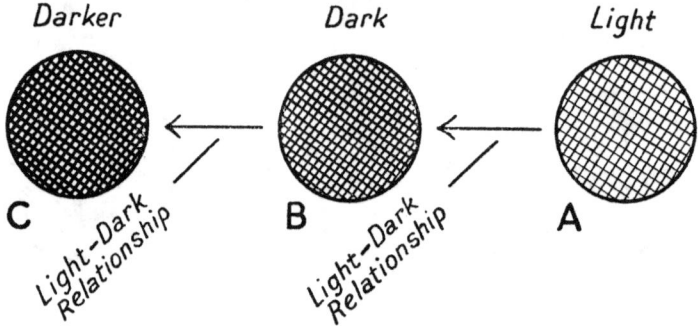

DIAGRAM XXVIII.

between this question and that of the relation between perception and knowledge, which we discussed as it appeared in Plato's philosophy.

The fact that animals do recognise relations is easy to show experimentally. For example, Köhler trained chicks to respond to the darker of a pair of grey discs. In Diagram XXVIII, B represents the darker disc of the pair A B. Now if A is taken away, and the chicks are shown B, together with a still darker disc C, they will go to C and not, as before, to B. Hence it is the 'light-dark' relationship they have learned to recognise, not the pair of discs as such. In other words they are recognizing a perceptual gradient. Here the gradient is that corresponding to the simplest possible kind of visual pattern. More complex patterns, such as that of Diagram XXVII, would

[1] See Appendix, p. 254.

Future of Neo-Pythagorean Method

form a correspondingly more complex gradient pattern on the cortex. Now, as Lashley has shown,[1] a gradient pattern in the cortex is precisely the sort of pattern which would function in spite of moderately extensive injuries to that organ.

In Diagram XXIX, for example, suppose A and B are excitations thrown on the cortex by the light and dark discs. The excitation gradient is shown by the broken lines. Now even if we remove the area (a b c) the gradient still persists

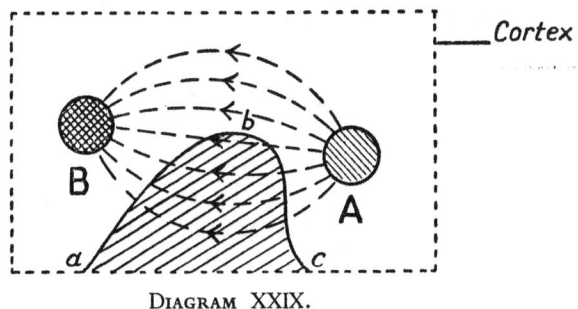

DIAGRAM XXIX.

in the rest of the cortex, and can still excite the appropriate efferent paths in the lower centres of the brain.[2] If, however, there were a very complex gradient pattern, corresponding to the recognition of complex shapes or other perceptual relations, we should expect the removal of a large piece of the cortex, such as (a b c), to dislocate the cortical excitations, bringing about a corresponding diminution in the 'intelligence' of the animal's behaviour. And this is precisely what Lashley found, for the small cortical extirpations, which had little

[1] This discussion is adapted from the theoretical discussion with which Lashley concludes his work, *Brain Mechanisms and Intelligence*. Any defects in the above account, due to the extreme simplification of Lashley's discussion, or to other reasons, are to be attributed to the present writer, not to Lashley.

[2] Even if the extirpated area were to intersect A or B, this would not affect the case. For the connection between retina and cortex is such that a local excitation of the former excites the whole cortex. So that A and B are to be regarded as centres, or maximal areas, of a pan-cortical excitation.

effect on the retention of simple habits, resulted in a serious dislocation of more complex behaviour patterns. Finally, it should be observed that Lashley's gradient theory fulfils the basic requirement that, in the cortex, *Ein jedes jedes kann*. According as the pair of light and dark discs is remote from or near to the retina, it will excite different parts of the cortex. But the nature of the gradient pattern, and hence of the efferent paths excited in the lower centres of the brain, will remain unchanged.

This rather complex discussion has brought us to a concept which is nevertheless quite simple. And it has brought us to the core of biological mechanism. For the essence of intelligent behaviour is that it consists in the perception and manipulation of relations.

Köhler, whose work on the intelligence of apes is classical,[1] uses the term "Insight" to describe certain features of their behaviour. When faced with the problem of reaching a bunch of bananas suspended from a high roof, his chimpanzees rapidly devised the method of dragging a box to a point directly beneath the fruit, so that they could climb up to it. Also, they discovered the interesting variation of using Köhler in place of the boxes, clutching his arm and pulling him to the required position. A similar piece of Insight behaviour was the method of using a stick to reach fruit outside the bars of the cage. They even learned to use two or three boxes, piled on each other, or two sticks, slotted into each other, in situations where one would have been inadequate.

Now in all these instances the 'insight' into the problem was arrived at, not by trial and error, with a steady diminution of error,[2] but quite abruptly, with no unsuccessful attempts. Such behaviour clearly consists in the ability to manipulate spatial relations 'in the mind,' explicit action being suspended until the solution is 'seen.' This brings us to a most important aspect of Köhler's observations, namely that the solution seems

[1] W. Kohler, *The Mentality of Apes*.   [2] Ante, p. 196.

Future of Neo-Pythagorean Method

to be 'seen' in more than the merely metaphorical sense. For the chimpanzees must see both the goal and the instrument (e.g. fruit and boxes) simultaneously in order to see what must be done to reach the goal. So that it is more than a mere play on words to say that the insight only comes when all the relata of the problem are simultaneously in sight. And if Lashley's suggestions are correct, this is just what we should expect; namely that all the relata must excite the cortex simultaneously in order that an effective behaviour pattern may be synthesised.

These observations suggest a fruitful mechanistic approach to the problem of human thinking. It is a commonplace observation that we can only 'think in symbols.' Everyone is aware of the enormous economy of thought effected by the use of mathematical symbols. For example, the solution of the equation $dy/dx = 7x$, a relatively elementary problem in mathematics, would be literally unthinkable without the special symbols of the differential calculus. And we need the symbols for exactly the same reason that the ape must keep the image of the goal and the instrument on his retina together, in order that the relata of the problem may be, as it were, projected simultaneously on the cortex. Compare the statement $dy/dx = 7x$ with the verbal transcription: 'Find the function of a variable such that the ratio of an infinitesimally small increment of the function, with respect to the concomitant increment of the variable, converges to a limit equal to seven times the variable as the numerator of the ratio approaches zero.' Presented thus in verbal fashion, the problem is hopelessly intricate, because the symbols are such that the relations cannot be 'seen as a whole.' This verbal presentation of the problem is analogous with the problem facing the ape before he has seen the two relata in one field of view.

We have entitled this section 'The *future* of the Pythagorean method . . .' because our discussion has been concerned less with accomplished work than with very tentative suggestions for the treatment of problems as yet unsolved. It should be added that, vague as Lashley's theory may be, it is much more definite and promising than any suggestion which could have been made, twenty years ago, for a natural explanation of the facts of ontogenetic regulation. But to pretend that Watsonian Behaviourism, or any other 'natural' theory, has given us a complete description of organic behaviour would be palpably absurd, as absurd as to pretend that modern physis has provided us with a complete description of inorganic events. The biological mechanism of the future will stand in relation to Behaviourism as Behaviourism stands in relation to the crude and tentative biological mechanism of Descartes.

But the really impressive feature of the natural description of behaviour is not that so much, admittedly, remains to be done, but that so much has already been achieved. In principle, Descartes' dream has come true, although this will not prevent vitalists from triumphantly pointing to the obvious gaps in our knowledge. Wöhler's synthesis of urea was, as we have said, the first nibble at the vitalist position, which then, as now, was based on our ignorance, rather than our knowledge. The vitalists of Wöhler's day were forced, of course, to compromise with mechanism. They said that the animal does not have to 'think' about excreting urea, so that perhaps after all it was not *all* living processes, but only those associated with consciousness which required a vitalistic principle for their explanation.

Before the discovery of the conditioned reflex it was of course possible to maintain that only 'unconscious' or 'purely reflex' actions could be explained without the aid of a vital principle. And the vitalists did maintain this, with great vigour. But since it would be so absurd to maintain that a rat learns to run a maze 'unconsciously,' the vitalists have been forced back one stage further. They maintain that the learning of a maze by a rat is not really an example of intelligent

Future of Neo-Pythagorean Method

behaviour, but consists in a mere automatic elimination of error, and that what really requires a vital, or supernatural principle for its explanation is behaviour which is not only conscious but intelligent.

The theories and experiments of Watson have already made great inroads on this position. Also we have pointed out that the discovery of a natural explanation of the facts of regulation has a distinct bearing on this aspect of the vitalistic theory of behaviour. For the remarkable regulatory powers of the developing embryo appear to show that in ontogeny it is not the material cause, but the *telos*, the end or final cause, which determines the means. And this is precisely the sort of reasoning that the present day vitalist advances against the natural interpretation of intelligent behaviour. In intelligent behaviour, it is maintained, it is the goal of the animal's activity, conceived by its mind, which really determines what it does. For example, Köhler's apes did not always move the boxes in the same way in order to bring them into a useful position. Nor did it matter what was the initial position of the box in the cage, or of the fruit on the roof. These could be varied in any way, but the invariable result was that the boxes were brought beneath the fruit. It is only the end, the *telos*, which is constant, just as, in the development of a perfect embryo from a mutilated egg, it is the end, not the processes which lead to it, which remains unchanged. So that the Psyche or mind of vitalistic theory is an end or *telos*-having entity, like the Entelechy of Driesch's theory. And if the physical apparatus which mediates intelligent behaviour were a mere static arrangement of interrelated parts, it would indeed be impossible to conceive of a physical schema of intelligent, or *telos*-having behaviour. Similarly, a static ontogenetic pattern, or a frozen river,[1] or any other sedentary material pattern, would be incapable of 'regulation,' that is, the realisation, through infinitely diverse material configura-

[1] Cf. p. 239.

The Idea of the Soul in Western Philosophy and Science

tions, of a fixed *telos* or end. But only the lower centres of the brain and nervous system are to be regarded as a static pattern, a rigid system of afferent and efferent connections. Deprived of the cortex which controls this system, an animal is indeed a reflex automaton, a slot machine; it is in virtue of the fluent nexus of cortical gradients that the organism as a whole is no mere slot machine, but a teleological unity, as

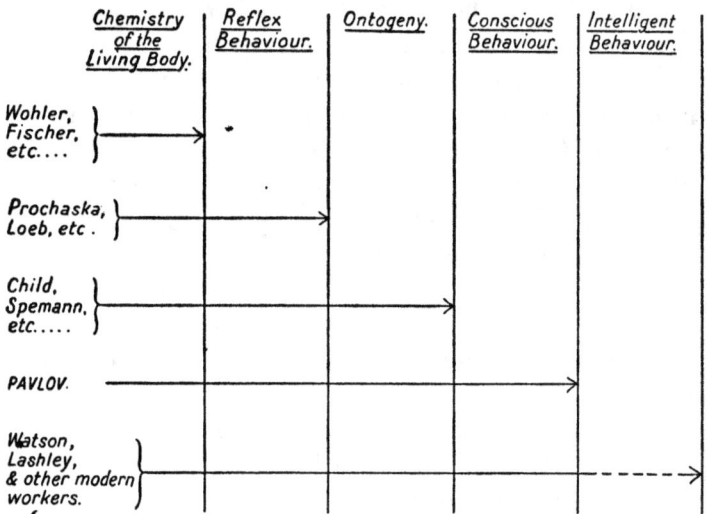

DIAGRAM XXX.

the ontogenetic process is teleological in virtue of the axial gradient of metabolism.

Diagram XXX shows the successive 'fronts' on which vitalism has taken its stand, and their successful occupation by various aspects of mechanistic analysis. We have shown that the mechanistic method is now rapidly invading the domain of 'intelligent' or 'insight' behaviour, the last front of the

Future of Neo-Pythagorean Method

vitalist.[1] It is difficult to see what sort of position can be left for the vitalist of the future to defend. The lines of the future extension of mechanism seem already to have been laid down by Lashley. That is to say, the most fruitful progress is to be expected from research in which behaviour patterns and cerebral structure are conjointly investigated. The mammalian brain is a vast, relatively unexplored labyrinth in which the mechanist is discovering the very 'bones and sinews' of behaviour, the physical schema, which Socrates so lightly dismissed, of action and passion. But it is quite safe to predict that the mechanist will not discover, lurking in the mysterious passages of the brain, an Entelechy, Psyche, or any other supernatural Minotaur. In principle, Descartes' dream, the dream which Socrates attributed, long ago, to Anaxagoras, has been realised.

[1] Presumably it is clear that in talking of 'vitalism' we have always had in mind the kind of theory which C. D. Broad calls Substantial Vitalism and distinguishes from Emergent Vitalism. Socrates was an advocate (indeed the inventor) of the former type of theory, and it is this which we have called the Socratic type of vitalistic theory. Similarly, the biological mechanism which we have advocated is not what Broad calls Pure Mechanism. That is, we have simply implied that the behaviour of the whole organism is 'determined by the nature and arrangement of its components' but *not* that it could necessarily 'be deduced from a sufficient knowledge of how the components behave in isolation or in other wholes of a simpler kind.' Since, however, the argument of the subsequent chapters of this book is quite compatible with either Pure Mechanism or with Emergent Vitalism (although not, of course, with Substantial or Socratic Vitalism), it has not been thought necessary to discuss the idea of 'emergence.' The reader is referred to Broad's *The Mind and its Place in Nature*, from which the above quotations are taken.

The Idea of the Soul in Western Philosophy and Science

APPENDIX TO CHAPTER XIX

For simplicity, the effect of a change of orientation in the third dimension, involving foreshortening, has been ignored. Foreshortening does, of course, affect the spatial relations of the parts of a visual object. Tilted away from the observer, the object shown in Diagram XXVII might take on some such appearance as this:

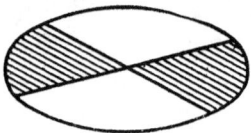

But foreshortening seldom involves a radical change of visual relationships, such as could not be accounted for by a moderate degree of irradiation of the conditioned visual stimulus. When foreshortening is so extensive that it does bring about a radical change in visual relations, we may and do fail to recognise a familiar object. Those who are familiar with Ucello's famous battle scene will recollect the bizarre and disquieting appearance of the extravagantly foreshortened warrior in the foreground.

> "*Bring out number, weight and measure in a year of dearth.*"
> BLAKE

CHAPTER XX

Physis, Psyche and Mechanism

THE LIMITATIONS OF MECHANISM

BUT, it will be urged, none but a very naïve person would look for the Psyche in the brain, or in fact any*where* else, either in the organism or outside it. The Psyche is not in the organism as the heart or the brain is, but we are nevertheless aware of its existence because, to borrow Descartes' phrase, it acts into the organism. That is to say, we find the Psyche, by which we mean our own private stream of consciousness, our own sensations, thoughts, emotions and volitions, not by poking about in the brains of rats, or for that matter in those of men, but simply by immediate introspection. However thoroughly we explore the brain, we shall find only . . . the kind of tissue called brain. But this fact cannot throw the slightest doubt on the reality of the stream of consciousness which we call the Psyche. In fact it is in some sense quite certainly true that the entities which the physiologist calls brains and glands are together with all other material things, a part of the Psyche.[1] In short, the mind and the body are known in quite different ways. The body of an organism is something which is known perceptually, while its Psyche can only be known, introspectively, by the organism itself. To expect to find the Psyche, or anything else non-physical, by investigating physico-chemical relationships within the organism, would be a confusion of thought of the worst possible kind.

[1] Not necessarily in the Berkeleian sense, however, still less in the even more radical sense in which Leibniz took the physical world to be a construction of the Psyche.

Nothing more than this, however, is properly implied in the mechanistic position. It cannot be too strongly emphasised that biological mechanism is not a theory of the nature of consciousness, or in any sense at all a metaphysical theory: it is simply the scientific theory which asserts that the exploration of the physico-chemical constitution of the living organism will reveal nothing that is not physico-chemical. Stated thus, the mechanistic attitude might almost seem to be based on a tautology; yet, as we have seen, it is just this statement which the vitalist is at pains to deny. The vitalist, in fact, maintains that in exploring the physico-chemical nature of the organism we shall find something which is not physico-chemical, the Mind, Psyche, Psychoid, Entelechy, or what not. It is possible, even without a wide knowledge of formal logic, to see that a statement which contradicts a tautology must also be self-contradictory. But, of course, no vitalist would formulate his beliefs quite in this way. He would say that, in investigating the physics and chemistry of the organism, we shall find something non-physico-chemical, the Psyche, not as it is in itself, but by its physico-chemical effects. That is to say, it will be found that in the living organism the laws of physics and chemistry are different from the laws which hold outside the organism, and it is this discontinuity in the physical realm which must be attributed to the Psyche. No doubt, if such differences could be discovered, the vitalist would have some grounds for attributing them to the Psyche, although the psychical nature of such differences would not, as most vitalists appear to think, be an immediate logical consequence of their existence. There is really no need, however, to discuss this question, for the simple reason that such differences are unknown. Wöhler's synthesis of urea was, as it were, a point which has broadened out into the ever-widening cone of knowledge now called biochemistry. To-day the results of original biochemical investigations are published in such numbers that it would be almost a whole-time occupa-

Physis, Psyche and Mechanism

tion to read them as they appear. Yet, in spite of all this activity, no one has succeeded in discovering in living matter a single exception to the natural laws of chemistry, the laws of chemistry as exemplified in test tubes. Did such exceptions exist, the probability of their having been discovered by now would be overwhelming. Until vitalists can produce a single instance of supernatural chemistry, all discussion of the complexities of human and animal behaviour will remain a little beside the main point.

We are now in a position to give the following brief definition of the mechanistic position: to every event in the organism which is perceptually knowable, it is possible to assign a causal description in terms of antecedent events perceptually known; it is never necessary, in describing any perceptually knowable abstraction from organic behaviour, to have recourse to introspective analogy.

The mechanist does not say, or at least there is nothing which entitles him to say, that events introspectively known may be explained or described in terms of events perceptually known. What mechanism purports to do, and what, it is so triumphantly doing, is to apply the neo-Pythagorean method to the analysis of living processes in so far as they are perceptually knowable. More than this it may never attempt to do. In the following discussion we shall endeavour to show that, from the philosophical point of view, this limitation is of extreme importance. Also we shall show that it is a limitation inherent in the nature of mechanistic description, and not in any sense a consequence of limited factual knowledge.

THE PYTHAGOREAN ORIGIN OF THE LIMITATIONS OF MECHANISM

Repeatedly, in our account of the historical background of mechanism, we have emphasised the fact of its Pythagorean origin. And, although the refinement and complexity of

The Idea of the Soul in Western Philosophy and Science

modern science are beyond anything that Pythagoras could have envisaged, it is nevertheless true that his famous acoustical discoveries contain the essential features of all subsequent mechanistic or 'natural' descriptions.

It will be recollected that these discoveries showed the relation between the length of a vibrating string and the pitch of its note. Now Pythagoras had no technique for measuring the rate of vibration of a string, so that he was unable to give a direct numerical description of auditory phenomena. But he was able to circumvent this difficulty by his discovery of the numerical relationships of the octave and other intervals. The strings of the Greek lyre were of equal length, being tuned by keys altering the tension, so that there was nothing in the construction of this instrument to suggest the association of the intervals with numerical proportions. As we have explained, it is probable that Pythagoras discovered these proportions by means of some sort of monochord, having a movable bridge by which the length of the string could be varied without altering its tension. The ratio of the octave, as everyone knows to-day, is 2 : 1. By putting this in the form 12 : 6, Pythagoras was able to express the smaller intervals in integral ratios; thus the fifth is 12 : 8, the fourth 8 : 6, and so on.[1] The genius of Pythagoras' discovery lay in the peculiar insight which led him to express in numerical form something which at first sight seems to have no numerical aspect at all, namely, the musical interval. It is precisely this kind of insight which makes a great natural philosopher to-day, and which has led to all the fundamental discoveries of physical science in the past.

And this is so in all the natural sciences which have progressed beyond the merely classificatory stage. The odorousness of a chemical laboratory, to the uninitiated its most striking aspect, is just the aspect of his subject which the chemist ignores, together with all other qualitatively perceived pheno-

[1] For a full account of Pythagoras' acoustical discoveries, see Burnet's *Greek Philosophy, Thales to Plato*.

Physis, Psyche and Mechanism

mena. What the layman would describe in some such terms as these: a yellowish bitter liquid was poured on a white tasteless powder, with the result that the powder disappeared and the liquid fizzed; the chemist would express as follows: $2HCl + CaCO_3 = CaCl_2 + H_2O + CO_2$. Unless one happens to have learnt the elements of the atomic theory, the above formulation appears very erudite indeed. Nevertheless, the abstractions made by the modern chemist are of the same nature as the arithmetical entities abstracted by Pythagoras from musical phenomena. For the concrete experience called 'perceiving chalk,' the chemist substitutes the formula $CaCO_3$, which is his shorthand for a fairly elaborate series of numerical data obtained by means of the chemical balance. These data are expressed in terms of ratios called atomic weights, signified by the symbols Ca, C, etc. The fact that the chemical formulae express ratios is of fundamental importance. If we say 'twelve pounds of apples' we are referring partly to a numerical abstraction (twelve units of weight) and partly to a concrete fact, the existence of apples. But if we say 'the ratio, twelve pounds of apples divided by three pounds of apples,' we are left with . . . 4, not four pounds or four apples, but the pure ratio or number, 4. By reducing his data to ratios the chemist rids them of the last trace of perceptual concreteness. That he does this is due to the fact that Pythagoras, the father of mechanism, treated his data in the same way. We do not, of course, mean that this is just an arbitrary fashion which Pythagoras happened to start. On the contrary, the method of numerical abstraction is now universal, because it is the only method which could be used in scientific investigation. Its usefulness lies in the fact that reasoning about pure numbers is valid, irrespective of what the numbers stand for. That is why numerical abstractions can be used as a basis of prediction. In every fundamental scientific hypothesis we find the same principle used, the substitution of numerical ratios for concrete perceptual experience. Thus the undulatory theory of light replaces colours by numbers called wavelengths. Although the undulatory analogy is no longer wholly tenable as a description of optical phenomena, the numbers associated with it are retained, and a set of numbers, derived from the quantum theory, is fitted to the phenomena which will not go into the older hypothesis.

We have seen that biological mechanism arose in modern Europe by an extension of the methods of physical science to living matter, much as physics and chemistry had arisen from the extension of neo-Pythagorean from celestial to terrestrial events. It is therefore hardly necessary to point out that, like the physics and chemistry of which it is a special application, biological mechanism is a system of numerical abstractions. Owing to the peculiar complexity of its subject matter, biology is only now, in the twentieth century, beginning to develop appropriate means of mathematical expression. Nevertheless, many of its fundamental concepts are implicitly mathematical, even though they are not expressed in mathematical form.

In particular, the concept of the conditioned reflex is essentially mathematical. Consider the building up of a conditioned reflex. First there is the unconditioned stimulus, S_1 say, which elicits a response of the type R. Let us write this, $S_1 \to R$. Then there is the stimulus to be conditioned, which we shall call C. At first this gives no response of the type R. This may be written, $C \to R_0$. After, say, two presentations with the unconditioned stimulus S, C elicits a small response, let us say a response one-tenth as great as that elicited by the unconditioned stimulus; that is, $C_2 \to R_1/10$. After two further repetitions the response is larger, say one-fifth of R: $C_4 \to R/5$. For the concrete judgment that 'the dog recognises its master' the behaviourist is in effect substituting a series of equations of the type $C_x \to R/y$, together, of course, with more complex but essentially similar equations describing reflexes of the second and higher orders, and still other equations describing irradiation and differential inhibition. No one, or no one but

Physis, Psyche and Mechanism

a solipsist, doubts that the dog feels joy in the recognition of its master. But that does not come into the equations; from the nature of the case it cannot. No doubt, too, Pythagoras was moved by music, as we are to-day, to exaltation and sadness. But this emotional, or Dionysiac, element of his experience had no part in his equations connecting lengths and intervals, for the simple reason that it was not part of the data that was put into the equations. For this reason it would be absurd to suppose that any conceivable reasoning based on such equations could tell us anything about the nature of emotions, or indeed about any kind of *concrete* experience, which is necessarily prior to the mathematical abstractions of science. And the fact that the behaviourist can, in a sense, abstract numbers even from emotions, does not really alter the position.

I have no doubt that, given sufficient knowledge, a behaviourist could describe all the physico-chemical changes in my body in physico-chemical terms. It would be absurd to expect him to describe them in terms of anything else. For example, I am now sitting at a table writing this book. Considered from the only point of view which is possible to an external observer, the perceptual point of view, my literary activity consists of a pattern of muscular contractions in my wrist and fingers, so interrelated that they produce a series of curves on a white sheet. These muscular patterns are, of course, caused by other events in the efferent nerves of my arm, which are in turn caused by physico-chemical events in the various centres of my brain. And these present events in my brain are causally related to previous events, back to my earliest infancy, in my brain and outside my body, through the intermediacy of conditioned reflexes. Notice that there is absolutely no mention here of the experiences I am having as I write. Nor could any conceivable advance in natural science bridge the gap between the observer's perceptual experience, which he is describing in terms of numerical relations, and

The Idea of the Soul in Western Philosophy and Science

my introspective experience. For that matter there is (in spite of much glib talk about the 'public' world of the scientist) a gap equally unbridgeable between the observer's perceptual experience and mine. Mechanistic description is therefore doubly an abstraction from the concrete wholeness of experience. It is an abstraction, first because it ignores all that part of experience which we have called *Dionysiac*, all our emotions, thoughts and volitions. Secondly, the mechanist disregards nearly everything even within the limited part of experience, the perceptual part, to which he deliberately confines himself. Concretely experienced, the perceptual world is the world in which are exemplified such qualities as redness, loudness, sweetness and smoothness. But redness, as such, will not go into an equation, so the physicist squeezes his red light through a pair of hair-fine slits, catches it on a screen, measures the diffraction bands, and hands us a formula in which the distance between the slits and the periodicity of the bands are related as argument to function. This, it will be seen, is rather a complex modern version of the old Pythagorean trick. Being loath to admit that his formula is not redness, the physicist tells us that since waves on a pond also make an alternating pattern when they go through a pair of gaps, then light is 'really' an undulation, and therefore his formula is 'really' redness after all. So that the man in the street, poor ignorant creature, is quite deluded when he thinks he sees a red colour; he is really seeing an undulation which can be characterised by a pair of numbers. In fact, some of our more mystically inclined physicists have almost dared to go as far as saying that he really sees a pair of numbers. It is only fair to add that modern physics is tending to discard such absurd hypostatisations of its numerical symbols. But natural science continues, and must continue, to deal with numerical abstractions, and biological science is no exception to this limitation. The consequences of this limitation, from the philosopher's point of view, will be the subject matter of the next part of this discussion.

"*Now extension must be the affection of something extended.*"
LEIBNIZ

CHAPTER XXI

The Limitations of the Neo-Pythagorean Schema: 'Philosophical' Behaviourism

NAÏVE EPIPHENOMENALISM

BUT, the behaviourist might retort, while it is no doubt true that my descriptions are in terms of abstractions from experience, that does not really limit the scope of my method, because I can explain the whole of experience in terms of my abstractions. When I describe certain changes in your blood pressure, in the activity of your endocrine glands and so forth, I am admittedly not describing your emotion as you experience it. But the physico-chemical events which I describe are nevertheless the cause of your emotion. Similarly, when I describe the effect of light of a given wavelength on your retina, I am not describing the sensation of, say, redness as you experience it, but I am describing the cause of your sensation. And similarly with all the other aspects of your experience. For each of your experiences, either introspective or perceptual, I can assign a physical cause.

This view, that the 'psychical' or 'mental' world is an effect of which the 'physical' or 'material' world is a cause, we shall henceforth refer to as *philosophical behaviourism*. It should be clearly realised that this is a metaphysical theory, because it is an attempt, a very crude one indeed, but nevertheless an attempt, to elucidate the nature and grounds of experience. Indeed, it is a neo-Socratic theory (although the philosophical behaviourist would be unwilling to admit this) since it is really an attempt to re-define the ontological status of the Socratic notion of the spiritual Psyche. It should on no account be confused with the various *scientific* theories designated by the term 'biological mechanism.' Such theories make no attempt to explain the nature of experience; they simply take it for granted, and confine themselves to the exploration of relationships within perceptual experience.

The view which we have called philosophical behaviourism is really a special instance of the more general philosophical theory known as epiphenomenalism. On this theory, of which Cartesianism is the first example, perceptions, thoughts, emotions and volitions are by-products of physico-chemical events in the brain. Only these cerebral events are 'real,' or in any way effective in determining our actions, so that our mental life is no more than an illusory glow around the physics and chemistry of the brain, a mere phantasmal essence, 'secreted by the brain,' as a celebrated physiologist has put it, 'as the liver secretes bile.' Of course, Descartes did not say that mental events are either 'unreal' or 'by-products.' Whatever his philosophical sins, he never descended to mere silliness. Nevertheless, modern 'physiological' epiphenomenalism is undoubtedly an offshoot of his metaphysics. And although epiphenomenalism in its naïve or 'brain-secretion' form has not been taken seriously by any competent thinker, we shall nevertheless find that a brief discussion of it will form a useful introduction to a more serious inquiry.

First, let us try to understand, as clearly as possible, what it is that the epiphenomenalist maintains. I am looking at some object in the 'external' world, let us say the red patch which seems to have become a ritualistic symbol in all philosophical discussions of this kind. A 'physiological' epiphenomenalist would describe my perception of the red patch in some such terms as the following: "Light, reflected from the object," he would tell me, "strikes your retina, in which it induces a photochemical change, thus causing an impulse to pass along your optic nerve and bring about an excitation of your brain. All these changes are real physico-chemical changes which I

Philosophical Behaviourism

can observe with my galvanometers and other instruments. But now the excitation in your brain causes a mental event, which you call 'seeing a red patch.' I know that this is a mental event, and not a real, or physico-chemical occurrence, because if I were to open your skull and look at your brain when you think you are seeing a red patch, I would not find a red patch anywhere in your brain, but only action currents and the various other physico-chemical events associated with nervous tissue. These physico-chemical events recorded by my instruments are all that is really taking place in your brain; your sensation of a red patch is merely a mental addition, a sort of illusory glow around the real, or material events."

Now we must enquire of the epiphenomenalist how he knows that I have a retina, a brain and an optic nerve. Because, he replies scornfully, he can see them. But, on his own showing, the experience which he calls seeing my brain is a mere mental addition to the 'real' physico-chemical processes in his brain. It is perhaps hardly necessary to explain that the logical consequence of this theory is that nothing 'really' exists at all, since everything is an epiphenomenon of an epiphenomenon of an epiphenomenon . . . *ad infinitum*! The full absurdity of such a theory may be brought out by supposing that the epiphenomenalist is looking at his own brain, by means of a mirror, say. He would then be in the terrifying predicament of having a brain which was an epiphenomenon of itself.

Although we have tried to define physiological epiphenomenalism as clearly as may be, it is obvious enough that it cannot even be stated in a manner free from confusion and self-refutation. For any kind of physiological epiphenomenalism necessarily involves a causal view of perception. And, in maintaining such a causal theory, the physiologist is, *ipso facto*, admitting that in perception we have knowledge, not of physical objects, but of the effects of physical objects in the mind of the observer. Hence, not only brains and nerves, but also the lenses, galvanometers and all the other instruments used by the physiologist are, on the epiphenomenalist view, the mental effects of physical objects, not the physical objects as they are in themselves. It should be carefully noted that we are not saying that lenses and brains are 'mental' entities, but simply that *if* causal epiphenomenalism is true, then lenses and brains, as given in perception, are the mental effects of (unknown) material objects. Now it is obviously meaningless to define matter as that which is given in perception, and then to say that matter is the cause of perception. For if lenses, brains, chairs and mountains are the mental effects of physical causes, they cannot at the same time be the physical causes of mental effects. In so far as it may be clearly stated at all, causal epiphenomenalism may be defined as the theory which tries to maintain both of these views! And the origin of this confusion of thought is obvious enough: the naïve epiphenomenalist is really assuming that *his* perceptions are 'real' or 'material' objects, but that the perceptions of everybody else are an 'unreal' or 'mental' glow around material events. It is also obvious that what we have said of the epiphenomenal theory of visual perception also holds for any theory which purports to explain emotions and thoughts in an analogous way.

At the risk of undue repetition, it must again be pointed out that the function of 'scientific' theories is to explain the perceptively known in terms of the perceptively known. As soon as the philosophical behaviourist calls the perceptively known world (or rather, certain abstractions from it) the 'physico-chemical' world, and then tells us that he can explain experience in terms of the physico-chemical, he has embarked on a task which metaphysics may or may not be able to achieve, but which science, from the nature of the case, cannot even attempt. For the fact of perceptual knowledge cannot be grounded in the perceptively known. Any attempt to find the ontological ground of perception in the perceptively known is a project, like that of lifting oneself by one's own bootstraps, doomed to self-refutation.

Philosophical Behaviourism

But the behaviourist, now becoming more philosophical, may retort that what has really been refuted by the above argument is not epiphenomenalism, but the theory known as naïve realism, and that philosophical behaviourism need not be associated with this theory. That is to say, for naïve or causal epiphenomenalism he would substitute a critical epiphenomenalism, critical in the sense of being associated with a more critical theory of sense perception.

Now it is certainly true that naïve epiphenomenalism is closely related to naïve realism, and in a sense, the doctrine which we have criticised is that known as naïve realism. That is, we have imputed to the behaviourist the belief that coloured patches, and other perceptual phenomena, belong 'absolutely' to the surfaces of physical objects, even when no one is looking at them. Our refutation consisted in pointing out that this belief is incompatible with the causal view of sensation which is implied in physiological epiphenomenalism. But the behaviourist may now try to save his epiphenomenalism (some form of which is necessary for any kind of philosophical behaviourism) by adopting a different view of the nature of perception, and of physical objects.

CRITICAL EPIPHENOMENALISM

This revised form of the epiphenomenal theory is based on the view that in the 'real' or 'physical' world there are only 'primary' qualities, such as extension and weight, and that the 'secondary' qualities, such as redness, sweetness and loudness, are 'psychical additions,' caused by the action of the external world on our sense organs, but having no independent existence in that world, the world of extended bodies. This, it will be recalled, is the neo-Democritan doctrine which was revived in modern Europe by Galileo and others.

Let us see if it is possible to understand, on these terms,

how the physical world could 'cause' the mental or psychical world. Our philosophical behaviourist would now have to give some such account of perception as the following: "As I look at your brain I see certain patches of colour interrelated in such and such a way. But these patches of colour are not really in your brain; they are psychical additions, created by me, or rather in the physico-chemical processes in my brain, in the act of perceiving. I know, however, that you have a brain, whether I am looking at it or not, and that it consists of colourless, but extended objects such as atoms and electrons. These, and their various motions, are all that really exist in your brain, and all perceptions of colour, sound and so forth, are psychical additions caused by these real objects and their motions." It will be seen that what we have here is a revised epiphenomenalism differing from the naïve form in that its definitions of physical and mental have at least an appearance of distinctness. What the epiphenomenalist is now saying is that something which is merely extended is causing me to perceive an extended patch of colour.

But this assertion is hardly less absurd than the assumptions of naïve realism. For it is meaningless to talk of something being extended unless we can say what it is an extension *of*. An extension of colour is just an irreducible fact of experience with which we are all acquainted. But it is impossible to separate the colour and the extension; they form a unity as indivisible as a body and its motion. One can, of course, talk about redness without reference to any specific red shape, because red light has certain properties which are independent of the area of its source. Similarly, all circular patches have certain geometrical properties independent of their colour. But we must never forget that such notions as redness and circularity are abstractions from concrete experience.[1] To

[1] Of course, the concept of *circularity* may well be, as Plato thought, grounded in knowledge of a Form transcending perception. We are not concerned, however, to determine the ontological status of universals, but simply to point out *individual* circles cannot exist except in substantial union with 'secondary' qualities.

Philosophical Behaviourism

attempt to conceive motion, extension and the like as self-subsistent entities is like trying to separate the grin from the Cheshire cat. In short, extension is always an extension of a secondary quality; the two cannot really be separated in thought, still less in perceptual experience. So that what the critical epiphenomenalist is really asserting is that an abstraction from perceptual experience (i.e. extension) is causing perceptual experience, the perception of extended bodies. Hence his alleged explanation of experience assumes the very thing to be explained.

And further, if the philosophical behaviourist tries to save his metaphysical theory by reference to 'scientific' theories, such as the atomic theory or the undulatory theory of light, he only makes matters worse by trying to support his initial paralogism on a paralogism of the second order. He may aptly be likened to the Indian sage who, having explained that the earth was supported on an elephant, and the elephant on a tortoise, relapsed into silent meditation when asked what supported the tortoise. For the existence of atoms and such like can never be more certain than the facts of concrete experience (coloured patches, sounds and so forth) from which the existence of atoms is inferred. And since epiphenomenalism necessarily implies that thought, as well as the appearances given in perception, is an epiphenomenon of matter, no epiphenomenalist can believe in the atomic theory, in behaviourism or in any other scientific theory. For all such theories depend for their truth on the validity of human thinking. So that what the epiphenomenalist is asking us to believe is that thinking is in some sense unreal, and that only matter is real, because thinking tells us that matter causes thinking.

It should be noted that we are not here questioning the validity of the atomic theory, or any other *scientific* theory. That is to say, given the requisite extension of our powers of vision we could no doubt see that macroscopic material bodies are composed of countless swarms of the smaller material bodies called atoms. Indeed, this extension of our vision has been in a sense achieved, for we can see, not atoms, but their shadows, by illuminating crystals with suitable rays. Oddly enough, the very fact that the physicist can bestow a quasi-visibility on his ultimate particles is in itself a refutation of epiphenomenalism. For it will be immediately obvious that the fact that atoms are objects of perceptual knowledge can never explain perception. If atoms had been some millions of times larger than they are, so that they could be detected by a comparatively trivial magnification of our visual powers, no one would have dreamed of supposing that they could be the 'cause' of perception. This illustration shows, too, that our critical epiphenomenalist is really groping towards a valid principle of some sort, for it is the very invisibility of atoms which gives epiphenomenalism a specious appearance of credibility. In fact, the principle which is imperfectly realised in his theory is that which has formed the main theme of our argument, namely, that if percepts are caused by something in the external world, then that something (or it may be, "those somethings") must be in principle perceptually unknowable. We are not here maintaining that perceptions are caused by something perceptually unknowable, or even that they are caused at all, but simply that if they are caused, then they are caused by something perceptually unknowable. There is still the possibility, of course, that perceptions are not caused by an unknown thing in itself, and that matter consists of percepts and of nothing but percepts. At present, however, we are concerned only with the implications of the view, which is an essential tenet of philosophical behaviourism, that perceptions, and all other happenings in our minds, are caused by material events (whatever these might be: we have seen that epiphenomenalism can give us no idea of what they are). Because atoms are very small, so that they can only be perceived by means of a very difficult technique, the epiphenomen-

Philosophical Behaviourism

alist is tacitly assuming that they are, in principle, perceptually unknowable.[1]

It does not necessarily follow from our principle that the cause of perceptions is mental, as so many idealists have maintained. Indeed, this assertion is as meaningless as epiphenomenalism. But it does follow that if there is any meaning in the notion of objects as they are in themselves, or *noumena*, which exist unperceived, then these noumena must be perceptually unknowable. And since, in Kant's phrase, space or extension is the form of all perceptual knowledge, anything exemplifying this form being perceptually knowable, then the noumena cannot be spatial.

It will be seen that all epiphenomenal theories of perception boil down to the assertion that perception is caused by a spatial noumenon, and it is this assertion which we have shown to be self-refuting.

We have chosen to discuss visual perception, in preference to other forms of experience, because everyone is to some extent familiar with the fact that retinae and optic nerves constitute the physiological basis of vision. (And no part of our argument, of course, is in any way affected by this fact). It is clear, however, without further argument, that visceral changes, as perceptually known, cannot be the cause of emotion, or laryngeal events the cause of thought, for the reasoning by which we have shown the untenability of visual epiphenomenalism is destructive also of what we may call emotional and ratiocinative epiphenomenalism. In fact, the fallacy involved in visual epiphenomenalism is, *a fortiori*, a fallacy in the realm of introspective experience, for, owing to the essentially private nature of emotion and thought, it is only possible to conceive these as epiphenomena by analogy with perceptual or 'public' experience.

[1] The epiphenomenalist might here take refuge in the assertion that the atom of modern physics is no longer a little lump of matter. But then, of course, if it is not material, it can hardly be extended or perceptually knowable. Presumably it would be a concept, if not a percept, and matter would then be an epiphenomenon of concepts, which is hardly what the epiphenomenalist is trying to maintain.

The Idea of the Soul in Western Philosophy and Science

THE PYTHAGOREAN ORIGIN OF EPIPHENOMENALISM

And it will now be readily appreciated that this fallacy, which is inherent in all forms of philosophical materialism, is to be traced to an illegitimate extension of the Pythagorean principle. Extension and motion are numerical abstractions from perceptual experience; it was entities of this kind that Pythagoras abstracted from his perceptual knowledge of vibrating strings. He then showed that certain of his abstractions (lengths) were numerically related to certain others (intervals). And that is all that mechanistic explanation can ever do, namely to exhibit the numerical relations between numerical abstractions from experience. The mechanist must take experience as a going concern, and explore the relationships given *within* it. There is no reason to suppose, as vitalists do, that there is any field within perceptual experience which is not open to mechanistic description.

But if the biological mechanist, turning pseudo-philosophical, tries to explain experience in terms of his abstractions from it, he becomes involved in the bottomless mystifications of epiphenomenalism.

THE POSSIBILITY OF A DUALISTIC EPIPHENOMENALISM

It seems quite certain, therefore, that entities such as extension, figure and motion, the so-called 'primary' qualities of Galileo, Locke and others, cannot be the 'cause' of secondary qualities. Our discussion has not, however, disposed of the idea that there is, on the one hand, a material world in which only primary qualities would inhere, and on the other hand a mental or psychical world which would consist of secondary qualities only. What we have shown is that the former, if it exists, cannot be the cause of the latter. It is clear that these two worlds are none other than the two worlds of Cartesian philosophy, the *res extensa* and the *res cogitans*. And it will be

Philosophical Behaviourism

recollected that it was a fundamental tenet of Descartes' thought that there could be no interaction between the extended and the psychical, between the neo-Democritan spatial schema and the Socratic spiritual Psyche. Given Descartes' initial concepts and premisses, this conclusion is certainly sound, although of course the reasons which led him to it were rather different from those which we have submitted in favour of a similiar position. It is in any case obvious that if, for philosophical purposes, such modes as length and colour are hypostatised as independent substances, they must, since they are different in kind and not in degree merely, remain really and wholly independent in the sense that they may never be reunited by a causal relationship. So that Cartesian philosophy teaches us one valuable principle, if no other, namely that a consistent epiphenomenalism must be rigidly and uncompromisingly dualistic. No doubt our modern 'scientific' epiphenomenalists would find this conclusion somewhat surprising, if not quite unpalatable. It is certainly to be regretted that philosophical behaviourists do not deign to read Descartes, who worked out the implications of their position three centuries ago. They would then be saved the embarrassment of professing a metaphysical doctrine which they would certainly not accept, if they understood it.

THE INCREDIBILITY OF DUALISTIC EPIPHENOMENALISM

If the contention be accepted, that a spatial noumenon cannot be the cause of the mental or psychical world, it follows that Cartesianism, which denies the possibility of causal connection between the physical and the psychical, is the only form of epiphenomenalism which is not self-refuting. Unfortunately, like many other doctrines which are perfectly consistent with themselves, it is quite incredible. It is doubtful if this doctrine has won the unqualified belief of any great thinker since Descartes' time, and it is fairly certain that Descartes himself was not entirely successful in persuading himself of its truth.

We have seen, also, that like the Renaissance philosophers, he was led to the idea of spatial noumena, devoid of secondary qualities, by emotional rather than purely rational considerations. Like Pythagoras, Kepler, Galileo and his other spiritual forbears, he was in love with mathematics. He was drunk with Number, as Spinoza was drunk with the idea of God, and his conception of Nature as a collection of extended, or purely numerical things-in-themselves is in the last resort an expression of his emotional conviction of the primacy of Number. Of course, we are not adducing this emotional attitude as evidence for the falsity of the conclusions to which it led him. No doubt there are truths vouchsafed to drunkards and lovers which are withheld from the sober and unloving. But in discussing Cartesian epiphenomenalism, it is as well to keep its emotional bias in mind.

We have said that this doctrine is incredible, and in fact most of us find it so. And its incredibility is not entirely grounded in the fact that if it were true the universe would be a very queer sort of nightmare, a vast calculating machine inhabited with ghosts infected with illusory actions and passions. The fundamental objection to Cartesianism seems to be this: if, owing to the entire disparity of the *res cogitans* and the *res extensa*, there is no communication between object and subject, then why is it that sensations resemble objects *in any way at all*? On Descartes' own showing, percepts are copies of objects in so far as they reveal their extension, although all else given in perception is illusory. But, why, if there is no real communication between the material and the psychical, should our percepts resemble material objects even in appearing to be extended? Descartes, presumably, would have answered, because of the success of mathematical physics in predicting the events of the material world. Now this answer, and it is difficult to see how else Descartes could meet our

Philosophical Behaviourism

objection, is based on a very obvious *petitio principii*. For if, by hypothesis, the material world is not given in perception, how do we know what the material world is like, and hence, how can we know that by mathematical physics, or by any other means, we can predict events in it?

So that the Cartesian account of the relation between Physis and Psyche rests, ultimately, on faith. We are asked to believe that the resemblance between objects and percepts is just a miracle, a miracle continually performed by God. Descartes was, of course, aware of these implications, for he himself has to fall back on the 'veracity of God' to establish the reality of the primary qualities.

Now it is not a refutation of a doctrine to point out that it rests on faith in a miracle. But no philosopher will accept such a doctrine unless there are very good reasons for supposing that nothing but a miraculous 'explanation' can, from the nature of the case, cover the facts to be explained. And in Cartesianism it is impossible to discover any such reasons, except in so far as the 'Pythagorean' nature of Descartes' emotional outlook may be said to be the reason for his dualism.

It will now be convenient to recapitulate the results of our discussion, as far as it has gone. We have distinguished between scientific and philosophical behaviourism, pointing out that the latter is really a special form of the philosophical doctrine known as epiphenomenalism, which maintains that perception is caused by the perceptually known, or by abstractions from the perceptually known. But this assertion, whether in its naïve or critical form, is self-refuting, and only a mind-matter dualism of the most uncompromising type, a Cartesian dualism in fact, can save epiphenomenalism from internal contradictions. But if philosophical behaviourism results in a dualism of this kind, in which mind and matter are separate substances between which there is no real connection, it can no longer purport to be 'explaining' the mental in terms of the material.

The Idea of the Soul in Western Philosophy and Science

Obviously, dualism is the last thing the philosophical behaviourist really wishes to support. So that in any case, philosophical behaviourism refutes itself. Finally, we have maintained that the Cartesian dualistic epiphenomenalism, although not inconsistent with itself, is not consistent with any rational grounds outside itself, and therefore cannot claim our acceptance.

THE HISTORICAL BACKGROUND OF DUALISM

Although Cartesian dualism is now almost universally repudiated, its basic assumptions are still deeply rooted in modern thought, especially in popular and 'scientific' thought. We shall do well, therefore, before proceeding with our argument, to consider the nature and origin of these assumptions.

We have said that modern dualism springs from emotional, rather than purely rational grounds, namely from Descartes' intense preoccupation with Number. And in the ancient world, also, dualism arose from an overwhelming interest in one aspect of experience. To the worshippers of Dionysos, the emotion of the dance so exceeded in intensity anything which they experienced in everyday life that they attributed the dance ecstasy to a supernatural principle. Thus they were led to make the fatal abstraction which has haunted European thought down to our own day. They did not merely distinguish the dance ecstasy as a special part of their experience; they abstracted it and set it up as a substantial essence, a supernatural Psyche which led its own independent life and descended, at intervals, into everyday existence. Or, alternatively, the Psyche was regarded as something which, normally asleep in the body, soared up to Dionysos in the heavens when released by the kathartic power of the dance. Possibly the two views, although inconsistent, were both held by the worshippers of the god. Such is the syncretic power of the human mind. But, on either view, the result was the same.

Philosophical Behaviourism

Something which was an integral part of human experience, a heightening, in fact, of ordinary experience, was hypostatised as a separate, self-subsistent principle. This hypostatisation is the father of all subsequent dualism.

It was the father of Pythagorean dualism. The mysticism which in the cult of Dionysos centred around the emotions of the dance was transferred by Pythagoras to the worship of Number. And Pythagorean dualism was the father of Socratic dualism. We have already described the somewhat elaborate synthesis, in the Socratic concept of the soul, of Dionysiac, Pythagorean and Ionian ideas. By combining the Orphic hypostatisation of the Psyche with the Ionian idea of the soul as an animating principle, Socrates invented the concept which permeates every part of modern thinking, the concept of the twofold nature of man, of man as a union of the active, or spiritual, with the inactive or corporeal; the concept, in short, of the organism as a dead carcass actuated by a living ghost. Even if we repudiate this idea, we are still half dominated by it, so deeply does it underlie our pattern of culture. Later we shall have more to say of the Socratic form of the Dionysiac dualism. Here it is sufficient to remind the reader that Cartesian dualism, although deeply influenced, like everything else in European thought, by the Socratic tradition, was essentially a modern restatement of the dualism of the Pythagorean school.

Here also we must draw attention to a very peculiar aspect of this historical sequence. The worshippers of Dionysos, by associating certain ecstatic experiences with a super-mundane Psyche, were in effect asserting the supernatural origin of these experiences. That is to say, the perceptions and emotions of everyday life were supposed to be in Nature, but the extraordinary perceptions and emotions of the dance were believed to come from something outside Nature. The Pythagoreans, taking over this fundamental distinction between the natural and the supernatural, then associated the natural with Number.

The Idea of the Soul in Western Philosophy and Science

The neo-Pythagorean doctrine of primary and secondary qualities, suggested to the Renaissance physicists by Democritan atomism, was therefore an extension of the ancient Pythagorean doctrine of Number, for it implied that Nature, as it existed when not being perceived, was nothing but Number. In the philosophy of Descartes this view is, of course, quite unequivocally stated. Now if Number is explicitly defined as the essence of Nature, it follows immediately that everything not numerical is supernatural. Hence the original Dionysiac belief that certain perceptions and emotions are supernatural has now, by a long and very odd evolution of ideas, become transformed into the Cartesian belief that all perceptions and emotions are supernatural.

Descartes would no doubt have been annoyed if told that his dualism was a modified form of Dionysos worship, but this conclusion seems nevertheless difficult to avoid. Now, as we have already pointed out, even the numerical aspect of Nature is only given in inseparable union with all those 'secondary' qualities which Descartes wished to push into the supernatural *res cogitans*. Hence the Cartesian distinction between the natural and the supernatural is really quite as arbitrary as that of the worshippers of Dionysos. The fact that Descartes, perhaps unwisely, preferred mathematics to dancing does not make his philosophy any more convincing than the Thracian cult from which it is derived.

THE NATURE OF PERCEPTUAL EXPERIENCE

Our discussion has brought us to the brink of that alluring, but engulfing, philosophical morass, so beloved of modern thinkers, usually referred to as the Theory of Perception. Or rather, the theories of perception, flitting like a hundred will-o'-the-wisps over the welter of controversy. Since we believe that the subsequent trend of our argument does not depend for its truth on any particular theory of perceptual

Philosophical Behaviourism

knowledge, we may at once assure the reader that we do not intend to invite him into the morass, even to the extent of asking him to accept any of the current theories; still less do we intend to burden the world with a new theory of perception, could such a thing be. Nevertheless, the nature of perceptual experience is obviously a question very near to our subject, so that some discussion of general issues is unavoidable.

Fortunately, it will be enough for our purpose to point to certain fixities which may be discerned beneath the endless flux of contending theories. We may even say that all competent theories of perception seem to belong to one of two quite well-defined types.

First there are those theories which maintain that perceptual knowledge, knowledge of 'phenomena,' is in some way related to an unknowable noumenon or thing in itself. We have maintained that such a noumenon must be non-spatial. Such theories may regard the phenomenal world as an effect, of which the thing in itself is the cause. Others, following Kant, hold that the thing in itself is so completely unknowable that it is meaningless even to predicate a causal relationship between it and the phenomenal object.

Secondly, we have those theories, very fashionable at the present time, which keep as near to naïve realism as is possible without inconsistency. Pure naïve realism, which may be defined as the belief that perceptual qualities, such as colour, belong *absolutely* to the surfaces of physical objects, is at once refuted by the existence of 'illusions,' such as colour blindness, or by any of the innumerable facts which show the dependence of sensations on events in the observer's body. Hence it is clear that if we hold that *any* sense data are 'really out there,' irrespective of whether or not we are looking at physical objects, we must, to be consistent, hold that *all* sense data have the same independent reality. There is no criterion which would enable us to say that certain sensations are real and others unreal, for all sensations are really experienced, and they are known only as given in perceptual experience. Hence if we are going to reject the idea of a noumenon, and say that matter consists of perceptual data and of nothing but these, we shall have to say that each observer, in looking at any given object, 'selects' one set of perceptual data out of the infinity of such sets of data of which the object consists. Thus the independent reality of sense data is reconciled with their dependence on events in the observer's body, by conferring on the latter a merely selective, as distinct from a genetic rôle.

In England this type of theory is, or rather was, especially associated with the name of Bertrand Russell, that Casanova of the intellect, who has flirted, not to say bedded, with every philosophical theory known to the human mind. It may at first sight seem very odd to hold that an object consists of patches of colour, sounds, smells and so forth, even when no one is looking at it or otherwise perceiving it. Such unsensed sense data are called by Russell *sensibilia*. It seems odder still to say that the object consists, not only of the immense number of sensibilia which have already been sensed (whether by fishes, colour-blind persons, insects or drunkards) but also of the infinite number of sensibilia which could be perceived by any being in the future, no matter how strange his sense organs. But one cannot reject this, or any other philosophical theory, simply on the grounds of its oddity. Russell's theory is no odder, in any case, than many of the universally accepted conclusions of mathematics and natural science. Although it seems so strange to say that a physical object consists of an infinitely complex manifold of divergent shapes, colours, sounds, etc., we must not forget that that is how the object is really given in experience, and that the idea of a *single* physical object is bound to be an inference from actual experience of such a manifold. In some sense it is quite certainly true that a physical object is, in Stout's felicitous phrase,

Philosophical Behaviourism

'a plurality of experiencing individuals.' The selective theory simply differs from other theories in saying that physical objects consist of *nothing more* than a manifold of facts given in perceptual experience. In fact, since it says that the object is just the kind of thing it seems to be, the selective theory is in a way the simplest possible theory of perceptual knowledge. But such theories, of which Whitehead's theory of Multiple Location is another well-known example, lead to enormous difficulties when we attempt to work them out in detail, and the present writer is by no means in the minority in believing them to be untrue. They are not, however, just obviously untrue, and our reasons for believing them to be so are not relevant to the present argument.

What we do wish to maintain, however, most emphatically, is that any theory which attempts a compromise between the above two types is obviously untrue and in fact meaningless. And any theory which distinguishes between 'primary' and 'secondary' qualities is an attempt at such a compromise. Either everything given in perceptual experience is in Nature, or nothing is; either the thing in itself is completely exemplified in perception, or not at all.[1] Any reasoning which shows that the essence of secondary qualities lies in their being perceived necessarily shows that the same is true of the primary qualities. If the former exist only in perception so do the latter, for extension is always extension of a secondary quality, and it is therefore impossible to assign a meaning to the statement that extension causes the perceptual quality which we call colour.

And this brings us back to the general principle which we have reiterated in our discussion of philosophical behaviourism, namely that it is meaningless to abstract this or that element from experience, and then to declare that this example of experience is the cause of experience.

---

[1] Although not, even on selective theories, in less than an infinite number of acts of experience.

The Idea of the Soul in Western Philosophy and Science

'MIND' AND 'MATTER'

Although we have discussed at some length the epiphenomenal view, that perception, thought, and the other activities of 'mind' are caused by 'matter,' we have refrained from any explicit definition of either mind or matter. This omission has been deliberately made, in order to show that epiphenomenalism only succeeds in appearing plausible by refusing to say precisely what it means by these words. Our refutation has in fact consisted in asking the epiphenomenalist: What do you mean by matter? If you mean the appearances given in perception, your assertion is meaningless, because perception is precisely what you purport to be explaining. And if you mean something extended in space, but having none of the other qualities given in perception, your theory is still self-refuting, since extension is merely an abstraction from perceptual experience. And if, alternatively, by matter you mean the 'matter' of scientific theory (e.g. electrons, quanta and so forth), your theory is more confused and meaningless than ever, since the entities of scientific description are quite certainly the creation of human minds. They may indeed have some sort of reality independent of our thinking, but what kind of reality that might be can still only be discovered by the activity of our minds, so that unless we believe in the independent reality of mind we cannot possibly believe in the independent reality of anything.

The philosophical behaviourist who admitted the force of the arguments which we have just summarised, and yet desired to cling to some form of the epiphenomenal theory, might of course define matter as the unknown thing in itself which causes phenomena. He could then maintain that certain activities in my 'noumenal' retina, my retina as it exists unperceived, cause in me certain sensations (e.g. the perception of a red patch) and in him certain other sensations which he calls 'seeing my retina.' This would be a legitimate and

Philosophical Behaviourism

reasonable metaphysical expression (although not, of course, the only possible one) of the physiological fact that the retina subserves the function of vision. But if the cause of perceptual experience is placed in a noumenal world, it can no longer be maintained that the nature of this cause is 'material' as opposed to 'mental.' What our behaviourist would now be maintaining is that both mind and matter are aspects or modes of something more ultimate than either. He would in fact be advocating a psycho-physical parallelism like that formulated by Spinoza. We have already explained why we cannot accept a dualistic epiphenomenalism of this kind. What we wish to emphasise here, however, is that on this new definition of matter, the only one which can lend any plausibility to epiphenomenalism, matter and mind are no longer related as cause and effect, but as complementary effects or modes of some more ultimate cause or substance.

It is now apparent that the statement that 'matter causes mind' does not make sense unless we are very careful to define just what we mean by matter and by mind. Further, it is difficult to see how we can define what we mean by 'matter' except on the basis of some epistemological theory, e.g. the theory that phenomena are caused by unknown 'things in themselves.' And to anyone who happens to hold a different theory of perceptual knowledge, our definition of 'matter' will be meaningless. Hence the mere fact of our using the terms mind and matter tends to degrade any discussion of the psycho-physical problem into a mere squabble over verbal forms. Nevertheless, most of us feel that this is a real problem, even if we cannot easily put it into an acceptable verbal formula.

Many thinkers have of course supported a position which is the exact converse of epiphenomenalism, namely, that the 'mental' world causes, or is in some way prior to, the material world. If we were now to say to an idealist: What do you mean by 'mental'? . . . Is a percept, for example, an instance of what you mean by a mental entity? . . . we should find ourself refuting idealism by arguments which would be the mirror image, as it were, of the refutation of epiphenomenalism. We should discover that idealism differs from materialism only in its verbal definitions of mind and matter.

> "Man has no Body distinct from his Soul; for that call'd Body is just a portion of Soul discern'd by the five Senses, the chief inlets of Soul in this age."
>
> BLAKE

> "The philosophical I is not the man, not the human body or the human soul of which psychology treats, but the metaphysical subject, the limit—not a part of the world."
>
> WITTGENSTEIN

CHAPTER XXII

Nature and the Organism

LIKE the word 'soul' the words 'mind' and 'matter' are wearing out their welcome. And indeed the use of such words more often than not leads to mere verbal quibbles. Yet no one, or no one but the most infatuated positivist, can seriously doubt that these terms, deeply overlaid though they are with metaphysical lumber, have a very real significance, and that the psycho-physical problem which they suggest cannot be lightly dismissed as a mere pseudo-problem, even though its precise nature is difficult to define.

We say that a human being, or a cat, 'has a mind,' but that a chair, or a mountain, is of a purely 'material' nature. If we adopt the current definition of a metaphysical statement as one not susceptible of empirical verification, then the distinction just referred to is certainly a metaphysical one. (Hence the solipsism latent in contemporary empiricist thought.) The statement that 'so and so has a mind' is in fact a *specification* of a transempirical world.

> "How do you know but ev'ry Bird that cuts the airy way,
> Is an immense World of Delight, clos'd by your senses five?"

The poet's question is an epitome of the questions to which

positivism must turn a blind eye. Hence it implies a definition of metaphysics.

Although, in dismissing all metaphysical statements as senseless, positivistic philosophers commit themselves to palpable absurdities, it cannot be doubted that it is always proper to exclude metaphysical questions from scientific method. (Positivism is a misplaced application of scientific method.) Hence, for the biologist the valid distinction is not between 'mind' or 'spirit' on the one hand, and 'matter' on the other, but simply between living and non-living systems. It is in fact the purpose of biological theories of the mechanistic type to elucidate this distinction in non-metaphysical terms. We have shown how, in principle, this has been achieved.

And although there are borderline cases, it is in general very easy to make this distinction. A chair, we say, is a non-living object; a cat is a living organism. Behaviouristic arguments may show us that the cat's 'mind' is much more 'material' than we might think; idealistic arguments may show us that the chair is much more of a 'mental' entity than we naïvely took it to be. But neither the behaviourist nor the idealist can shake our conviction that the cat is a living thing and that the chair is not. Of course, the plain man, or for that matter the biologist, might have considerable difficulty in giving a satisfactory verbal definition of life. But in individual instances the biologist has no difficulty in deciding whether or not he has to do with a living organism.

It can hardly be doubted that the exclusion of metaphysical ideas from the science of life was a necessary preliminary to the development of modern positivism. But for the successful elaboration of a non-metaphysical method for the description of organic processes, positivistic theories of the kind now in vogue could not be given even the appearance of plausibility. It would in fact be a matter of great interest to trace the historical connection between Cartesian mechanism and modern empiricist philosophies. Presumably it would be admitted, by

Nature and the Organism

positivists as well as by their opponents, that modern positivism owes very little to the Positive Philosophy of Comte and a great deal to the Critical Philosophy of Kant. Although there is little enough of positivist logic in the Critical Philosophy, it was the first systematic attack, in the modern spirit, on metaphysical thought. Hume, of course, was even more uncompromising than Kant in his opposition to metaphysics. But Hume had only his scepticism to offer; he built up no systematic alternative to metaphysical thought such as we find in Kant. Paradoxical though it may seem, it was just this aspect of Kant's thought, its positive as distinct from its merely sceptical aspect, which entitles him to be called the father of modern positivism. For unlike Hume, and like modern positivists, Kant was above all concerned to provide a firm conceptual foundation for mathematics and the natural sciences. But it is this, the constructive part of the Critical Philosophy, which is so closely derived from Descartes' neo-Pythagorean schema of the material world.

But, whatever plausibility may be conferred on positivism by the Cartesian exclusion of metaphysics from biology, it cannot seriously be doubted that the notion of 'mind' or 'consciousness' is essentially metaphysical, in the sense defined above. It is possible that in the case of organisms such as plants, which presumably do not enjoy consciousness, any conceivable significant statement about them could be put into physico-chemical or other non-metaphysical terms. We may express this in another way by saying that the concept of life (provided it is not taken to include that of consciousness), does not appear to have any non-empirical reference. But the notion of consciousness is, from the nature of the case, metaphysical. It is true that we have constantly implied, in dealing with biological mechanism, that scientific behaviourism is able to offer a satisfactory empirical criterion of consciousness. Later we shall have occasion to give more explicit expression to this assertion. But this does not really

The Idea of the Soul in Western Philosophy and Science

mitigate the metaphysical implications of the word 'consciousness.' For let it be granted that it is possible to give a complete 'physico-chemical' (that is, perceptual), description of the activity of a conscious organism. After we have given such a description, the organism remains, as it was before, an empirically inaccessible world, closed by the 'senses five' of the observer. When we say—the cat is conscious, but the chair is not—we know, unless we are a positivist, that we have made a statement with a perfectly real metaphysical significance. Such a statement means that the set of sense data collectively referred to as 'the cat' is the perceptual mark, in the observer's world, of a world ulterior to his own, namely that of which the cat is aware.

This discussion, then, has led to a distinction between the concept of life and the concept of consciousness. In the concept of life nothing of a metaphysical nature is necessarily implied. The concept of consciousness is essentially metaphysical. Since the time of Socrates the concept of consciousness, the meeting point of all metaphysical concepts, has been the major preoccupation of philosophers.

Quite apart from the presumed absence of consciousness in the lower organisms, the distinction between life and consciousness is obvious enough. For example, the cat is not always conscious; sometimes it is asleep. But most of us would hesitate to say that the cat is not alive when it sleeps. And were we to say that the cat is alive, although not conscious, when asleep, because it retains the possibility or potentiality of consciousness,[1] we should immediately involve ourselves in difficulties. It is in fact always a dangerous manœuvre to drag in potentiality as an aetiological principle. How do you know, it might be retorted, that similar *potentialities* do not lurk in the chair? In a sense it might be said that they do. Some of the carbon atoms, of which the chair is largely composed, might at some future time form part of the brain

[1] Cf. the Aristotelian notion of the soul as 'first' Entelechy.

Nature and the Organism

of the cat. (E.g. if the chair were burnt on the gardener's heap and thus entered into the metabolism of a plant, which were then eaten by a mouse, which in its turn were devoured by the cat.) Of course, this illustration, savouring as it does of the House that Jack built, is fantastic, but not in principle absurd.

Also, it might be asked, are we really so certain that the chair, as it is in itself, is devoid of consciousness? An idealist would argue that the mere truism that the phenomenal chair enters into our consciousness is sufficient proof that it partakes in some way of conscious experience. Of course even an idealist would admit, presumably, that 'entering into the consciousness' of a living organism is not quite the same thing as 'having a consciousness' into which chairs and other phenomena enter. But what of the 'ultra-phenomenal' chair?[1] The mere fact that it is *ultra*-phenomenal would appear to preclude our knowing anything at all of its inner nature, still less whether consciousness is a mode of that nature.

Nevertheless, it seems indubitable enough that we cannot impute consciousness to the chair in exactly the same way that we impute it to the cat. For we do in fact find that the kind of behaviour with which we associate animal consciousness is always accompanied by certain special and complex physico-chemical conditions, e.g. the presence of protein molecules in dynamic equilibrium with a characteristic environment of electrolytes. And from our own experience we know that the slightest interference with these conditions, such as may be induced by drugs or anaesthetics, is sufficient to extinguish consciousness temporarily or permanently.

Yet, as we have shown, consciousness cannot be a mere epiphenomenon of such physico-chemical *differentia*, since, whatever the ontological ground of these may be, they themselves are only given, as phenomena, in conscious experience.

[1] This term which is, I think, due to A. E. Taylor, is better than 'noumenal' in a discussion of this kind.

The Idea of the Soul in Western Philosophy and Science

Therefore if we accept the natural, or neo-Pythagorean, description of living processes, we are faced with a twofold dilemma.

That mind is not an epiphenomenon of matter is indeed more certain than any 'scientific' truth, for it follows, not from observations which may at some time be belied by more extensive or more careful observation, but simply *from the nature of the case*. Any assertion to the contrary is not merely untrue, but meaningless, as the contrary assertion of 'equals of equals are equal' would be meaningless. And it should be noted that such self-evident 'common notions,' derived through Euclid's κοιναὶ ἔννοιαι from the common predicates or κοινά of Plato's theory of Forms, are quite as fundamental to the mechanistic descriptions of modern science as its technique of observation and experiment. For without such conceptual principles, no amount of mere observation or experiment would be of any use to the scientist, since he would have no notions by which his separate data might be co-ordinated and schematised. We know then, with apodictic certainty, that 'mind,' whatever it is, is not epiphenomenal to the physical world. But we must on no account allow this principle to blind us to the, apparently contradictory, empirical fact that what we call consciousness arises only in conjunction with certain highly specific material configurations. That is one aspect of our dilemma.

And in another aspect it presents itself in even more pressing form. For, quite apart from any rational and abstract refutation of epiphenomenalism, we are all 'intuitively' convinced that our thoughts, perceptions, emotions and volitions are 'real': we find it simply impossible to believe that our perceptions and our mental life do not really enter into and determine our physical actions. And yet it is almost as difficult to doubt the general validity of the 'mechanistic' or perceptual description of human and animal behaviour, although such a mode of description, a description, that is to say, in terms of the

Nature and the Organism

physics and chemistry of the body, seems to leave no room for the psychical life which is disclosed in our deepest intuition as the very essence of our being.

And this, although it is presented to us so clearly and in so uncompromising a form by modern biological theories, is no more than the dilemma implicit in the famous speech of Socrates awaiting death:

"As a young man I fell in love with science. It must, I thought, be a wonderful thing to know the causes of everything, why each thing comes into being, why it exists and why it ceases to be. Thus I tormented myself with all kinds of problems, such as whether it is blood that makes all things possible, or whether it is air or fire, or perhaps none of these things, but rather that the brain produces knowledge from the various perceptions that it generates. And I meditated on the transience of all these things, and on the spectacle of the heavens and the earth, only to become convinced in the end that I had no aptitude for such speculations. Indeed they seemed merely to cloud my mind, so that I became involved in confusion even over the simplest questions. . . .

"But one day I heard a man reading from a book, written, he told me, by Anaxagoras, in which it was asserted that everything is ruled by Intelligence. Now here was an idea which enchanted me; in Anaxagoras, I thought, I have really found what I am after. For if it be true that Intelligence orders all things, it will order all things for the best, and he who would elucidate the cause of a thing, why it is produced, why it exists, and why it ceases to be, must therefore ask himself in what way it is best that it should exist, suffer or act. Such knowledge, of course, would necessarily include knowledge of that which is less than the best. So I expected great things of Anaxagoras. I hoped he would use the principle, that all things are for the best, to deduce the shape of the earth, whether it were flat or round; and I hoped that by the same principle he would explain the motions of the sun and the moon, and of the other heavenly bodies. Not for anything in the world would I have given up these hopes, and in the greatest excitement I procured his books, and raced through them in order to discover what is best and what is less than the best.

"But I was doomed to a great disillusionment. For, as I read through the works of this man, I found that he made no use at all of a ruling Intelligence, but purported to explain everything in terms of air, ether and water, and similar infantile notions. It is just as if someone were to say, 'The actions of Socrates are ruled by his Intellect,' and were then to describe my behaviour

The Idea of the Soul in Western Philosophy and Science

at the moment by saying 'Socrates is now sitting here because of the properties of his bones and sinews, of which his body is constructed. The bones, sinews and sockets are arranged in such and such a way, and the nerves, by relaxing and tightening the bones, have brought him into his present posture.' Or again it were as though he should explain in the same way the reason why I am talking to you now, saying that it were all due to sound, air and acoustics, and completely ignoring the real reason, namely that the Athenians have seen fit to condemn me, and that it seems to me best that I should submit to their sentence. For, heavens above, these bones and sinews of mine would long ago have been in Megara or Boeotia, propelled there by the concept of that which is best, had it not seemed to me more just and honourable to submit than to run away. Of course it is perfectly true to say that I could not put my desires into action without my bones and sinews and such like. But to say that it is in these things, and not in my reason, that the causes of my actions are to be found, would be the most utter contradiction in terms, for any explanation whatsoever depends on the primacy of reason, without which nothing could purport to be an explanation at all."[1]

And although it is almost impossible not to believe that Socrates is right, we cannot dismiss Pavlov as easily as Socrates was able to dismiss Anaxagoras. Sometimes, when conflicting evidence leads us into a predicament of this kind, we may be content to leave the two sides of the dilemma in temporary suspense, as it were, hoping that in the future an increase in our knowledge will clear up the difficulty. But it is scarcely conceivable that the contradiction with which we are concerned could be resolved by any increase, however great, in factual knowledge. For even if the advance of biological science should reveal an impasse, beyond which the categories of physics and chemistry were no longer applicable to the study of living things, the dilemma would not, as vitalists appear to hope, simply disappear. For it can hardly be doubted that *some* forms of conscious behaviour have already been schematised in terms of things 'perceptively known,' or, as a behaviourist might put it, 'reduced to mechanistic terms.' Hence, even if a limit to natural description were to be

[1] *Phaedo*, pp. 96–99, abridged and freely paraphrased.

Nature and the Organism

discovered, say, in some aspect of the behaviour of man and the higher apes, our dilemma would not, in principle, be affected. Nor may we be content to leave such a contradiction permanently in suspense, as those who profess to believe in psycho-physical 'parallelism' are content to leave it. (We have in any case seen that such a parallelism, or dualistic epiphenomenalism, is just as absurd as any other form of the epiphenomenal theory.) The dilemma must be resolved, for since both sides of it seem equally well grounded in self-evident principles, to leave it unresolved would be to throw doubt on the validity of those very principles, without which rational thought of any kind would be impossible.

"*Thus there is not only life everywhere, joined to members or organs, but there are also infinite degrees of it in the monads, some of them more or less dominating over others. But when the monad has its organs adjusted in such a way that by means of them the impression they receive, and consequently the perceptions which represent them, are distinguished and heightened . . . this may amount to sensation, that is to say, to a perception accompanied by memory, a perception, to wit, of which a certain echo remains to make itself heard on occasion. Such a living being is called an* animal, *as its monad is called a soul.*"

LEIBNIZ[1]

CHAPTER XXIII

Nature and Psyche

It will now be maintained that the psycho-physical dilemma is only an apparent one, in the sense that if we accept both sides of it we shall be led into beliefs which, although perhaps unexpected, are not contradictory.

Incidentally, it may be pointed out that one of the most notable developments of modern science, namely relativity mechanics, is the outcome of accepting both sides of such an apparent dilemma. It seems contradictory to say that the velocities of all observers, whatever their relative motions, are identical in relation to the velocity of light. But the results which follow, although odd, are not self-contradictory.

Now if it be true that 'mind' is really ingredient in our actions and also true that the 'material,' or perceptively known aspect of these actions falls entirely within the realm of physico-chemical description, the conclusion seems inevitable that 'mind' or 'spirit' is in some sense present to the whole of the physico-chemical realm, not merely to that part of it which happens to form our bodies. The qualification, 'in some sense,' is clearly important.

[1] From the translation by Mary Morris.

Nature and Psyche

The dilemma raised by biological mechanism is really only a dilemma if it be implicitly assumed that mind is *uniquely* revealed in man (and other animals) and that only these are in any sense psychical beings. The so-called psycho-physical dilemma always, in fact, reveals itself as an opposition between Cartesian mechanism and the Socratic theory of the soul, the theory that spirit is a supernatural substance present to Nature only in the material configurations called 'living' bodies. Therefore it is not merely fortuitous that Socrates is associated with the first appearance in European thought of the conflict between teleological and mechanistic conceptions. For it was he who first explicitly defined the Dionysiac belief in the rigid duality of human nature. It was because he conceived himself as two beings, a corpse or puppet on the one hand, actuated by a detachable ghost on the other, that Socrates found behaviourism unthinkable.

Here again the historical parallel with relativity mechanics is significant. The assumption that inorganic nature is a being devoid of soul is not a necessity of thought but a legacy from the seventeenth century, from the Cartesian form of the Socratic 'puppet and ghost' theory. In the Middle Ages the converse assumption, that Nature is alive, seemed the obvious and natural one to make.[1] Now the unconscious belief which makes it so difficult, at first, to grasp the theory of relativity, namely the belief in the 'absolute' nature of space and time, also dates from the seventeenth century, from the philosophical foundations of the Newtonian cosmology. When this assumption is abandoned, the conception of the velocity of light as a limiting velocity ceases to be a paradox.

Similarly, the psycho-physical dilemma ceases to be one if we reject the Cartesian view of the Psyche as a principle

---

[1] Of course, mediaeval theology completely identified itself with (it was in fact a special development of) the Socratic concept of the separable ghost. And in popular thought Nature was conceived to be a body, comparable with the human body, with a private ghost of its own, the World Soul. This is not, however, the sense in which we shall maintain Nature to be a psychical being!

The Idea of the Soul in Western Philosophy and Science

confined to the biological realm. Later it will be necessary to develop the implications of this statement. Here it will suffice to reiterate the general argument, that since organic activity is both spiritual and physico-chemical, the Socratic theory is false, and in some sense, spirit must be immanent in Nature. In what sense, we shall attempt to show in the sequel. (Doctrines of the same general import as this have often been held—any value which this argument may have lies *only* in the sequel.) It may, however, be well to point out at once certain things that will not be implied. It is not implied that the world exhibits no heterogeneity of the kind proclaimed by the words 'material' and 'spiritual.' Nor is it implied that this heterogeneity is not essentially metaphysical in nature. Indeed, the metaphysical nature of the concept of consciousness has intentionally been emphasised. The implication is that this heterogeneity does not involve an ontological disjunction between a 'natural' and a 'supernatural' realm. Nothing more than this is intended in the use of the word 'immanent.'

If spiritual activity occasions a real heterogeneity in the world, but not a Cartesian scission, then it enters into the world *hierarchically*. It will be convenient to mark off the following (more or less arbitrary) grades in the spiritual hierarchy: animation, life, consciousness, self-consciousness.

The concept of 'inanimate' Nature is one of the more unfortunate notions which have come down to us from Cartesian philosophy. Herakleitos had a truer insight when he said that the most fundamental aspect of Nature is its fluency, its ceaseless change and animation. The clouds and the wind, the tides sweeping under the moon, are in some very real significance of the word, animated. The earth and her sister planets pursue their courses, it would seem, without guidance from angels or other anthropoid agency. Every schoolboy knows that under certain conditions a piece of sodium may leap into the most dangerous animation.

Nature and Psyche

These examples are not to be taken as vague poetical analogies. Nor is the word animation to be understood in any equivocal sense in this context. The animation of a cat, or of a human being, is in fact a special instance of a wider animation which pervades all Nature. For the movements of living things are the outcome of chemical activities (in muscles, glands and so forth), which differ in no respect from the familiar chemical processes of the inorganic world. It is indeed a commonplace of science that the sun, since it is the furnace from which every plant derives its powers of chemical synthesis, is the source of all animal activity, the fount, as it were, of all organic animation on this planet. Equally with the motions of our atmosphere and other terrestrial motions, our actions are an integral part of a nexus of cosmic energy exchanges.

One is indeed tempted to say that Nature is alive, although that would be doing some violence to the common usage of the word. For the distinction between animation and life, the next grade in the hierarchy, is less sharply defined than might be imagined. It has already been pointed out that the concept of life does not necessarily involve that of consciousness. And here, in talking of 'life,' we mean 'mere life,' not conscious life.

It is apparent that the difference between 'non-living' Nature and the living organism is in no sense a difference between something animate and something inanimate. Of course, the animation of a living thing is co-ordinated in an extraordinarily complex manner, and a vitalist would distinguish this as an unique attribute of living matter. But the peculiar unified complexity of organic activity, its elaborate co-ordination for certain ends or purposes, such as reproduction and the capture of food, cannot be made the basis of any ontological division of Nature into 'physico-chemical' and 'biological' parts. For the existence of organic teleology implies the existence of teleology in the non-living world. It has often, for example, been pointed out that life, or anything sufficiently resembling terrestrial life to merit the name, could only arise in a most specific and elaborately organised environment. If the depth and composition of the atmosphere, or the orbit of the earth in relation to the sun, had been even slightly different, the higher forms of life could not have arisen on this planet. But for the unique physico-chemical properties of water, no life of any kind could have arisen.[1] So that if, as Socrates urged, the existence of living things is to be taken as evidence of teleology in the universe, the manifestations of the teleological order cannot be regarded as confined to living organisms alone. In order that life might appear, teleology must also have been at work, in inorganic Nature, before its advent. Hence teleology cannot be differentially exemplified by living things.

Any other attempts to find a sharp discontinuity between life and the rest of Nature would have the same result; in attempting to demonstrate discontinuity we should reveal continuity between the organic and the inorganic realms. For example, it might with considerable show of truth be said that the essential *differentia* of the living being is that it exhibits a state of dynamic fixity, that it 'rests by changing,' to use the Herakleitan phrase, in virtue of its metabolic exchange with the environment. But such a distinction, although in one sense well founded, is double edged. The very fact of metabolic exchange serves to assimilate the organism to Nature, rather than to effect a separation. If it be true to say that the special mark of the organism is its state of dynamic interchange, it is as true to say that the special mark of the environment is its dynamic interplay with the organism. The relation of dynamic interchange is 'symmetrical,' in the sense which modern logicians have given to the word.

It is true that Nature as a whole cannot be in dynamic equilibrium with an environment, for by definition the whole of Nature has no environment. This, however, merely proves

[1] Cf. Henderson, *The Fitness of the Environment*.

Nature and Psyche

that Nature as a whole is not (as Stoic and popular mediaeval thought took it to be) an animal, since dynamic interchange with an environment seems to be an inseparable accompaniment of animal organisation.

All this, of course, is not to say that the organic is not easily distinguished from the inorganic. Except for certain borderline phenomena (e.g. viruses), the distinction is usually patent enough. We have merely been concerned to show that the distinction does not (any more than that between chalk and cheese, say) imply a fundamental disjunction in Nature.

So we come to the next grade in the hierarchy. Surely, it might be urged, the existence of consciousness implies just such a disjunction? In discussing the place of mind in Nature we encounter the following difficulty at the outset. Since we can know Nature only as it enters into our consciousness, we cannot discover by direct inspection whether or not consciousness enters into this or that part of Nature. But if there were some formal perceptual mark of consciousness, this would provide a means of discovering its extension in the natural realm. The conditioned reflex is just such a perceptual or 'external' manifestation of that inner world revealed only to the conscious subject. Perceptually known to an external observer, consciousness is the exhibition of conditioned reflexes. Wherever we find behaviour which, on analogy with our own, we call conscious behaviour, we find that the perceptually knowable aspect of that behaviour can be analysed into a system of conditioned reflexes. Now conditioned reflexes have been found wherever they have been looked for in the animal kingdom, even in the 'lowest' forms of life, and nothing resembling a conditioned reflex has been discovered outside the animal kingdom. Hence it seems that consciousness is an invariable accompaniment of animal life (although presumably not of plant life) and is absent in the inorganic world. Here it must again be emphasised that the existence of a clear distinction within Nature does not imply an ontological disjunction of the Cartesian type.

Let us recall exactly what is meant by a conditioned reflex. When we say that an animal has simple or unconditioned reflexes, we mean that it reacts to a stimulus, that is to say, to any environmental change such as may be occasioned by light, heat, touch and so forth. When we say that it has conditioned reflexes we mean that it 'learns by experience,' e.g. that the dog recognises its master. And by this is meant that the reaction to a given stimulus *now* may be quite different from its reactions to exactly the same stimulus in the past, and different again from its reactions to the same stimulus in the future. That is to say, the perceptual manifestation of consciousness is that the 'sensitivity' of an organism does not remain fixed, but depends on the previous history of the organism. A conscious being is one whose sensitivity is conditioned by its history. Alternatively, it may be said that a conscious being is one which reacts, or is sensitive, not merely to the immediate present, but also to events in the past. The 'inner' aspect of this historical extension of sensitivity is, of course, memory. Later it will be apparent that memory and consciousness are to be regarded as identical. Now it is clear that without sensitivity there can be no consciousness. Sensitivity is a component of consciousness. This is one aspect of the hierarchical nature of spiritual activity.

And it is a fact of primary importance that sensitivity is not in any sense a special property of 'living' organisms, but a universal attribute of all material things. There is no reason to suppose that there is any difference between the simple or unconditioned reflex sensitivity of an organism and the sensitivity of a non-living object to its environment. The sensitivity, for example, of wax to the fire or of a photographic plate to a distant star. The sensitivity of a living organism depends, as we have seen, on the transmission along nervous

Nature and Psyche

tissue of a wave of physico-chemical change,[1] comparable with the transmission of a flame along a train of gunpowder. The wave of neural activity consists of a transference of ionic changes in no way differing from the ionic changes which were first discovered in inorganic media. The changes induced in an eye by light are photochemical changes, as those in a photographic emulsion are photochemical changes.

Hence, when we compare the 'sensitivity' of an animal with that of inorganic bodies, we are using the word in more than a figurative sense. We mean, in the most rigid and literal interpretation which can be put on this statement, that animal sensitivity is identical with the physico-chemical sensitivity which pervades the whole of the material universe.

When it is said of a thing that it is sensitive, it is usually implied that it is purely passive, that it "feels quickly or acutely,"[2] that, in relation with other objects it is acted upon, not active. But the sensitivity of an object really implies its activity just as much as its passivity. Thus, to take one of the most striking examples of physical sensitivity, an iron filing is sensitive to the presence of a magnet. Because the latter is large in relation to the former, it is convenient to regard the magnet as active and the filing as acted upon, or passive. But this is no more than a convention, and in reality the relationship is in all respects mutual. If, for example, the iron filing were fixed and the magnet freely suspended, the magnet would move towards the filing, and it would then be said that the magnet was sensitive to the filing. Instead of a minute filing one might have a lump of iron of the same size as the magnet, and if these were suspended near each other, each would move towards the other with the same speed. It is clear, in the light of this example (for which the reader may easily find parallels in gravitational or electrostatic attraction,[3] in mechanical

---

[1] Or through undifferentiated protoplasm where a specific neuro-motor apparatus has not been evolved.
[2] *Oxford English Dictionary*.   [3] Cf. Newton's third law.

impact, or indeed in any instance of physical sensitivity) that sensitivity always implies an exact equality of action and reaction.

Therefore it would be desirable to replace 'sensitivity' by some more generalised terms having the implication of mutual interaction rather than of mere passivity. We propose to use the word *reciprocity*. Instead of saying that the iron filing is sensitive to the magnet, or vice versa, we shall say that the magnet and the filing reciprocate each other. If any two objects (events, if one prefers the modern idiom) reciprocate each other, then the reciprocity of A, regarded from the point of view of B, is active, but from the point A, passive. It will be seen that the idea of reciprocity does not imply the metaphysical notion of cause, or transeunt influence.[1]

Every spatio-temporal change, whether it be the transmission of a nervous impulse, or the 'influence' of the moon on the oceans, the photochemical change in a human eye, or in a silver emulsion or in a green leaf, is an instance of this universal reciprocity. A living system differs from inorganic nature in being a delimited teleological system of reciprocities. A conscious organism differs from one that is merely alive in that its reciprocity is historically conditioned. That is to say, the conscious organism reciprocates, not merely the immediate present, but also its past history. The past *endures* in the living organism. The internal aspect of this historical endurance is memory, its external aspect the conditioned reflex. This is one sense in which sensitivity, or reciprocity, is a component of consciousness. We must now go further into the implications of this.

[1] The notion of reciprocity is similar to Lotze's concept of 'immanent operation.' Lotze, it will be recalled, maintained that the notion of transeunt 'influence' is untenable. For what can we mean by saying that A 'influences' B? That the 'influence' leaves A and goes off in search of B? (Why not in search of Y or Z?) And if A can only be conceived to act on B through the intermediacy of this third thing, this influence I there must be further intermediaries between I and A and between I and B, and so on to infinity. Lotze might well have added that since action always implies reaction, there must be a second set of influences going in the reverse direction, from B to A!

Nature and Psyche

Imagine an organism which had powers of perception similar to our own, but which could only 'remember' its perceptions in little bursts of short duration, say of five minutes, with a hiatus of complete oblivion between each short stretch of continuous remembering. Such an unfortunate creature would not be one organic individual, but many successive individuals. It would be as many individuals as there were five-minute intervals in its life. Viewing it from the perceptual or behaviouristic point of view, one would say that its conditioned reflexes were divided into five-minute 'quanta.' All the creature's experiences during one five-minute period would be completely obliterated in the hiatus before the next interval. Throughout the duration of one of the five-minute periods, it would be a conscious being, a 'metaphysical subject,' and throughout the succeeding interval it would be another, different conscious being, and so on.

Now imagine the lengths of its little quanta of remembering to be progressively reduced to smaller and smaller dimensions, its powers of perception within each quantum remaining, however, undiminished in clarity. Imagine further that this process be allowed to approach arbitrarily near the limit (in the mathematical sense) where the duration of each quantum is zero. Then our hypothetical creature would still have perception, in the sense of reciprocity, but no consciousness or cognition. For suppose any arbitrarily small period of time be assigned, say one-millionth of a second. Then by carrying the process of quantisation far enough the creature could be deprived of the power of remembering what it experienced even such a short time before.

Here it will be convenient to make a distinction between *perception* and *sensation*. (Such a distinction has in fact been implied.) In a well-known passage, Bacon defined perception as "the being affected by an object without contact, though consciousness is absent."[1] An iron filing *perceives* the magnet.

[1] *Oxford English Dictionary*.

The Idea of the Soul in Western Philosophy and Science

We shall use perception in this sense, and distinguish it from sensation, by which we shall mean, perception accompanied by consciousness.

The quantised organism would still have perception, but not sensation. Within each 'quantum' of course, it would have sensation. But its consciousness could be reduced by the process described to as low a level as desired: 'in the limit' there would be perception without sensation. And if *conation* be defined as that which stands in relation to volition as perception to sensation, there would be conation but not volition.

Perception and conation, it is clear, are aspects of that which we have called reciprocity, for such a quantised organism would react only to the 'instantaneous' present, not to the events of its past history. Having only reciprocity, but not enduring reciprocity, it would have ceased to be a conscious organism. *It would have no previous history*, except in so far as it entered into the consciousness of a conscious organism. History, memory, consciousness, are three names for the same metaphysical concept.

Now it is possible to state more explicitly what is intended by the statement that spirit enters hierarchically into Nature. Because all Nature exemplifies reciprocity, one of the components of mind, of psychical activity, is immanent in Nature. Matter is 'momentary' or 'instantaneous' mind, mind which dies away, as it were, in the instant that it springs to life; it is suppressed or frustrated mind.[1]

In the sense that matter may thus be regarded as epochal mind, all Nature is a psychical being. But in the sense that the physico-chemical component of mind is epochal and not enduring, inorganic nature is spiritual on a 'lower' plane than a conscious organism.

Socrates is not mistaken when he says that it is the concept

[1] Cf. the Leibnizian view of matter, exemplified by the quotation at the head of this chapter. Cf., also, *Philosophische Schriften*, edited Gerhardt, iv, pp. 230 et seq.

Nature and Psyche

of what is best that keeps him in his cell at Athens, when he could so easily have escaped to his friends in Megara or Boeotia. But neither are Anaxagoras nor Pavlov mistaken. For the behaviour of Socrates' body, the perceptually knowable aspect of the being called Socrates, may be described, like that of any other material system, in terms of relations between things perceptively known. Socrates is mistaken only in taking his own account of his behaviour to be incompatible with that of the behaviourist. And he is mistaken because he fails to see that although he, Socrates, is truly a soul, his body is no mere puppet, tenuously strung to a separate spirit world, but the perceptively knowable aspect of his Psyche. The body of Socrates is the epochal aspect of his enduring Psyche.

It has often been remarked that the poetry of all eras and cultures is inspired by a deep feeling of concord with Nature, what a modern philosopher has so aptly called 'aesthetic animism.' To dismiss such feelings as mere anthropomorphic fantasies is easy enough—too easy. When the poet, addressing his beloved, says—

> "Thou swing'st the hammers of my forge;
> As the innocent moon that nothing does but shine,
> Moves all the labouring surges of the world,"

it is possible that he says no more than the literal truth. For if the relation between the spiritual and the material are as we have shown them, then the reciprocity of the moon and the oceans, and the emotional bond between lover and beloved, are both manifestations, one at a lower, the other at a higher level, of the hierarchy of spiritual activity.

It should be obvious that we have hardly begun to develop the implications of the theory adumbrated here. For example, this interpretation of the nature of mind and matter clearly implies an intimate metaphysical relation between time and Psyche. In a sense, time *is* the spiritual activity which enters 'hierarchically' into Nature, transforming the merely epochal into the enduring or psychical.

But this is not the place to pursue ideas of this kind. It is sufficient to have indicated, however tentatively, how a biological concept of life may provide an observational basis for metaphysics. Many in the past, however, have sought such a basis for metaphysical thought. Yet metaphysics still awaits general recognition as an objective enquiry. Therefore the writer's pretensions to achieve what others have failed to achieve should be received with some scepticism.

INDEX

ACTION, purposive, 21, 99
AIR—
  as life-principle, 65
  as Logos, 107
  as primary stuff, 45, 46, 51, 56, 59, 103, 213
Alcibiades, 72
Alexander of Hales, 126
Alexander the Great, 105
Alexandria, 121
Ambrose, St., 131, 208
Anamnesis, 87-89
Anaxagoras, 60, 61, 70, 71, 168, 169, 174, 175, 180, 190, 213, 253, 292, 303
Anaximander, 44-46, 48, 63
Anaximenes, 45, 46, 53, 55, 60, 62, 65, 73
ANIMAL SPIRITS, 152, 156, 157, 159
ANIMATING PRINCIPLE, 18, 21, 22, 277
ANIMATION, 296, 297
ANIMISM, 16-18, 22, 92, 93
  aesthetic, 305
  Platonic, 91-93, 100, 103
ANTHROPOLOGISTS, Victorian, 17, 91-93
ANTHROPOLOGY, 16-18, 22
ANTI-NICENE FATHERS, 78, 118-121, 129, 133, 163
Apeiron, 45, 48, 49
Apollo, 31
Apology, The, 77
APPEARANCE, 32, 36, 40, 81, 84, 95, 136, 162, 282
Aquinas, St. Thomas, 16, 93, 127-129, 168
ARAB SCHOLARSHIP, 120, 127, 128, 131
ARISTOTELIANISM, 56, 96, 100, 106, 112, 120, 131
Aristotle, 60, 68, 78, 95-107, 114, 122-125, 127, 128, 131, 132, 136, 139, 140, 162, 215, 216, 225
ASTRONOMY, 133 ff., 163, 166
ATHEISM, 103
ATOMIC THEORY, 139, 140, 143, 269
  Greek, 37, 46, 59, 60, 65, 139, 141, 144, 168, 278

ATTENTION, 189
Augustine, St., 121-127, 133, 146, 163, 208
Averroes, 127
AXIAL GRADIENT, 233, 235-237, 252

BABY, 198, 199, 201-203
BABYLONIAN CAPTIVITY of the Jews, 110, 111.
BABYLONIAN SCRIPTURES, 106
Bacon, Roger, 131
BEAUTY, 87-89
BECOMING, 33, 35, 37, 42, 43, 45, 52, 62, 81, 84, 87, 88, 102, 216
BEHAVIOUR—
  animal, 151, 172, 174, 175, 177, 179, 180, 188, 191, 192, 195, 196, 214, 240, 241, 243, 247, 289, 290
  conditioned, 244
  conscious, 216, 251, 292, 299
  gradient theory of, 243
  human, 50, 74, 90, 191, 196, 207, 213, 215, 290, 293, 305
  intelligent, 247, 248, 250-253
  moral, 74, 77
  PATTERN, 193, 196, 203, 206, 248, 249, 253
  purposeful, 181, 182, 190
  study of, 184 ff.
  verbal, 200, 205, 206, 208, 210
  visceral, 197-201, 206
BEHAVIOURISM, 71, 169, 175, 182, 196, 200, 207, 208, 212, 213, 250, 261, 263, 287, 295, 305
  Philosophical, 263, 264, 267, 269, 270, 273, 275, 276, 281, 283
BEING, 33, 35, 37-41, 43, 62, 63, 67, 81, 84, 88, 89, 94, 96, 97, 102, 136, 142, 161, 216
Berigord, 133
Berkeley, Bishop, 38-40, 148
BIOCHEMISTRY, 256
BIOLOGY, 36, 260
  Experimental, 174, 191, 192, 213, 237
  Neo-Pythagorean Method in, 213, 214, 234, 249, 257

307

BLASTOMERE, 217–219, 221, 224, 257
BLOOD—
　as life-principle, 28, 29, 42
　circulation of, 152
BODY (as distinct from Soul), 16, 18, 21, 25, 27, 28, 30, 33, 34, 47, 62–66, 74, 76, 99, 101, 104, 123, 124, 127–129, 151, 154, 156, 158–160, 166, 213, 255, 280, 305
Boethius, 125
Bologna, 133
Book of Wisdom, 111, 114
BOUNDLESS, The 45, 46, 48
BRAIN, 30, 152, 166, 181, 240, 247, 255, 261, 264–266, 268
Bridgman, Laura, 208
BUDDHISM, 93, 127
Burnet, J., 77
Byzantium, 125

CARTESIANISM (CARTESIAN PHILOSOPHY), 94, 145 ff., 213, 264, 272–275
Categoria, The, 125
CAUSE, 273, 283, 302
　Final, 32, 234, 235
　of Perception, 263, 265–267, 270–272
CHANGE, 51–25, 55, 56
Charlemagne, 125
Child, G. M., 231–233, 236, 240
CHIMPANZEES, Koehler's, 248, 249
Christ, 111, 113, 116–118, 127, 162
CHRISTIAN PHILOSOPHY and THOUGHT, 53, 78, 117–122, 126, 213
CHRISTIANITY, 92, 111, 113–120, 123
CHTHONIC CULTS, 29
"CIRCUS" MOVEMENTS, 177, 179
Clement of Alexandria, 118, 125
COGNITION, 155, 303
COLOUR, 39, 40, 80, 148, 260, 262, 268, 273, 279–281
Compte, A., 287
CONATION, 304
CONCEPT, Socratic, 17, 69, 70, 72–76, 85–88, 90, 92, 103, 180, 188, 201, 206, 288
CONDITIONING, 184, 199, 201–203, 209
CONNECTIONIST THEORY, 242, 244
CONSCIOUSNESS, 23, 28, 29, 73, 74, 81, 152–154, 161, 175, 177, 179, 205, 255, 256, 287–290, 296, 299–304
　moral, 74
Constantinople, 125, 133
Copernicus, 133 ff., 147, 163, 167
CORTEX, cerebral, 240, 242–245, 247–249
Crawley, A. E., 17, 19, 20, 22–24, 91
CRITIQUE, Kant's, 167, 168

Dalton, 59
Dampier-Whetham, W. C., 137
DANCE, 29–31, 47, 75, 76, 276–279
Darwin, Charles, 63, 168
DEATH, 18, 25, 31, 64, 104
Demiurgos, 126
Democritus, 59, 144, 147
DEMON, Maxwell's, 227, 228
Descartes, 144–160, 163, 165, 169, 172–175, 212–215, 225, 226, 240, 250, 253, 255, 264, 273–276, 287
DETERMINATION, embryonic, 237
DEVELOPMENT, embryonic, 90, 217, 221–223, 231, 235, 237, 243
Diogenes the Cretan, 65
DIONYSIAC CULT, 29–34, 47, 50, 64, 74, 75, 89, 115, 119, 277, 278, 295
Dionysos, 29–32, 47, 166, 229, 276–279
DISCRIMINATION, perceptual, 186, 187
DOG (as experimental subject), 39, 40, 80, 180, 184–188, 193, 197, 260, 261
DREAMS, 18, 27, 31
Driesch, H., 215–218, 222, 225–230, 235–240, 242–244, 251
DUALISM, 32, 33, 43, 47, 50, 60, 92, 94
　Aristotelian, 97, 101, 104, 123, 124, 128
　Cartesian, 158, 159, 167, 275, 277, 278
　Pythagorean, 50, 277

ECHINUS, 218, 221, 237, 243
EFFECTOR ORGANS, 152, 173–175, 185, 193, 242
EGG, 98, 100, 216 ff.
Eidolon, 27, 30
Einstein, A., 36, 44
ELEATIC PHILOSOPHY, 57, 58

Index

ELEMENTS, Empedocles' doctrine of, 59, 60
EMBRYO, 216–225, 234–237, 243, 244, 251
EMBRYOLOGY, Experimental, 217 ff., 225, 231
EMOTIONS, 197–200, 255, 261–264, 266, 271, 276–278, 290
Empedocles, 59, 60
ENDOCRINE GLANDS, 197, 199, 263
ENTELECHY—
   Aristotelian, 99, 102, 151, 162, 216, 234
   Drieschian, 216, 225–231, 235, 237–239, 251, 253, 256
ENVIRONMENT, 216, 217, 231, 298, 299
EPIGENETIC THEORY, 237
EPI-PHENOMENALISM, 264–276, 282–284, 290, 293
   Critical, 267–272
Erigena, 126
ESSENES, 111
ETHICS, 49, 50, 68, 72, 86, 108, 116
Euclid, 49, 52, 83, 131, 290
EVIL, 32–34, 47, 64, 72, 74
EVOLUTION, 46, 63, 168
EXPERIENCE, 69, 184, 203, 204, 245, 261–265, 268, 271, 276–283, 289
   learning by, 181, 185, 186, 300
EXPERIMENTAL METHOD, 37, 47, 59, 60, 168, 170, 184 ff., 192–196, 200, 207, 212, 216, 290
EXTENSION, 40, 141, 148, 154–156, 267–269, 272, 274, 281, 299

FAITH, 118, 275
FEAR, 198–200, 206, 209
FIRE, 46, 59, 103
   as symbol of Herakleitan flux, 52–54
FIRE-LOGOS, Herakleitan, 54, 63, 64, 103, 107, 114
FORM, 48, 49, 234, 271
   Aristotelian theory of, 95, 97–103, 114, 123, 234
FORMS, Platonic theory of, 81, 82, 84–90, 93–97, 100, 114, 115, 122, 126, 131, 135, 290
FOSSILS, 45

Galileo, 59, 132, 134, 136, 139–149, 151, 153, 167, 231, 267, 272, 274
GEOMETRY, 43, 44, 83, 88, 135, 168
GEOTROPISM, 177, 179
GHOST, 18, 26, 27, 277, 295
Gnosis, 118
GOD—
   as ultimate Being, 41
   Christian, 115–118, 122, 126, 129, 274
   Hebrew, 113–117
   in Aristotelian thought, 98, 100, 102, 103
   in Cartesian thought, 146, 149, 151, 160, 275
   in Platonic thought, 91, 119
GODS, Olympic, 25 ff.
GOOD, 32–34, 72–74, 94
GRADIENT—
   cortical, 244, 247, 252
   metabolic, 233, 235–237, 252
GRAVITATIONAL FORCE, 36, 77, 139, 150, 159, 177, 178
Green, T. H. 205

HABIT, 196, 197, 206–209, 248
Haldane, J. S. 215
Harvey, William, 152
HEBREW CULTURE, 110–113, 117
HELIOTROPISM, 176
Herakleitos of Ephesos, 50–57, 63, 64, 79, 81, 85, 106–108, 111, 114, 232, 296
Hesiod, 25, 26
Hippocrates, 131
HOLOPHRASE, 19–22, 161, 203–206
HOLOPSYCHOSIS, 20
Homer, 26–29
Hume, David, 287
Huxley, Aldous, 200
HYLOZOISTS, 42

IDEALISM, 284, 286
IDENTITY IN DIFFERENCE, 33–37, 41, 42, 69, 70, 74, 77, 83, 84, 86, 94, 103
IMMORTALITY, 25, 28, 93, 104, 124, 126, 128
IMPULSE, nervous, 155, 157, 173, 174, 179, 302

INHIBITION—
   differential, 187–190, 193, 198, 199, 202, 209, 261
   external, 189, 290
   internal, 189–191
"INSIGHT" BEHAVIOUR, 248, 249, 252
IONIAN PHILOSOPHY, 35, 42, 46, 51, 58, 62, 63, 65, 67, 70, 74, 75, 83, 89, 90, 103, 107, 133, 145, 162, 277
IRRADIATION, 187, 199, 260

Jahveh (Jehovah), 103, 113
Jesus, 113, 116
John, St., 118
Johnson, Dr., 40
JUSTICE, 68–70, 72, 73, 87

Kant, Emmanuel, 40, 93, 145, 148, 167, 168, 271, 279, 287
Katharsis, 31–33, 47, 50, 75, 76, 115, 276
Kepler, 129, 136–141, 143, 147, 149, 151, 167, 191, 274
KNOWLEDGE, 69, 73, 80, 81, 87, 95, 97, 107, 136, 246, 265, 270, 271, 279, 283
Koehler, W., 246, 248, 251
Kreidl, O., 179

LANGUAGE, 19, 72, 200, 203–206
Laotzu, 127
Lashley, J., 243, 244, 247–250, 253
LATENT PERIOD, 188, 189
Laws, The, 94
LAW, Mosaic, 110, 117
LEARNING CURVE, 195
Leibniz, 16, 44, 167
Leucippus, 144
LIFE, 25, 34, 63, 123, 124, 286–288, 296, 298
LIFE PRINCIPLE, 28, 34, 42, 62, 65, 123, 162
LOCATION, Theory of Multiple, 281
Locke, J., 272
Loeb, Jacques, 175–177, 180
LOGIC, 60, 96, 119, 256
LOGOS—
   Christ-, 116–118, 122, 126, 162
   Fire-, 54, 63, 64, 103, 107, 114, 162

Herakleitan, 53, 54, 63, 64, 107, 111, 114
Philo's doctrine of, 114–120, 129
medieval, 163, 165
Stoic, 107–109, 114–116, 119, 120

MAGIC, 23, 24, 29, 119, 131, 162
Malebranche, 160, 166
MANY, The, 41, 51, 70, 97
MATERIALISM, 42, 108, 128, 235, 272, 284
MATHEMATICS, 49, 82, 85, 131–134, 167, 274, 278, 287
MATTER, 24, 42, 48, 49, 70, 114, 127, 129, 140, 148–150, 155, 159, 160, 165, 169, 266, 269, 270, 275, 282–286, 290, 304, 305
   Aristotelian formless, 97–101, 114, 123, 234
   living, 151, 171, 231, 239, 257, 260, 297
Maxwell, J. Clark, 226–228
MAZE, 194–196, 200, 202, 243, 244, 250
MECHANISM—
   Biological, 168–170, 196, 201, 212–215, 230, 240, 241, 248, 250, 256–260, 264, 272, 286, 287, 295
   Cartesian, 152, 154, 160, 165–167, 215, 250, 286, 295
MEMORY, 196, 206, 244, 300, 302, 304
   associative, 181
   image, 23, 26, 161
   visual, 243
Meno, The, 88
Messiah, 112, 113, 115–118
METABOLIC RATE 233, 236
METABOLISM, 231–234, 252, 289, 298
METAPHYSICS, 263, 266, 283, 285–288, 296, 302, 306
   Cartesian, 147, 156, 159, 160, 163, 168, 213, 264
   Greek, 32, 34, 60, 63, 70, 74, 79, 96, 108, 109, 139
MILESIAN PHILOSOPHY, 35, 51, 55, 63–65, 79, 97
MIND, 23, 47, 67, 94, 104, 107, 149–150, 155, 158, 160, 166, 169, 251, 255, 256, 275, 282–285, 290, 294, 295, 299, 304, 305

Index

Mirandola, Pico dela, 133
MONADOLOGY, Leibnizian, 167
MONISM, 42, 55, 56, 58, 59, 94, 97, 106, 107, 124
MORALS, 33, 73, 74, 76, 77
MOTION, 56, 81, 90, 99, 141, 148, 149, 151, 154, 268, 269, 272
MUSIC, 31, 47, 48, 212, 258, 259, 261
MYSTERIES, Eleusinian, 29
MYSTICISM, 29, 51, 89, 94, 119, 277
MYTHOLOGY, 23, 25, 26, 32, 42, 45, 115, 119, 162

NATURAL LAW, 48, 54, 84, 88, 108, 257
NATURE, 20, 23, 24, 32, 33, 36, 41, 43–46, 48, 51, 57, 62, 67, 90, 101, 108, 123, 124, 132, 145, 151, 169, 192, 205, 235, 239, 240, 274, 277, 278, 296–300, 304–306
NEO-ARISTOTELIANISM of Driesch, 216, 230
NEO-PLATONISM, 94, 125, 163, 167
NEO-PYTHAGOREANISM, 138, 144, 150, 154, 213, 214, 216, 278
NERVOUS SYSTEM, 152, 156, 173, 174, 189, 220, 252, 261
Newton, Isaac, 36, 137, 139, 151, 231
Nicholas of Cusa, 133
NOMINALISM, 126
NOUMENA, 271, 273, 279–282
Novara, Mario da, 133
NUMBER, 48–51, 54, 132, 136, 137, 145, 234, 262, 274, 276–278

OBSERVATION, scientific, 135, 138, 144, 177, 290
OCCASIONALISM, 160, 166
Odysseus, 27, 28
ONE, The, 41, 51, 55–59, 70, 94, 95, 103
ONTOGENY, 216, 224, 225, 230, 231, 239, 251
ORGANISERS, 237, 238
Origen, 125
ORPHICISM, 32–35, 47, 64, 277

PANTHEISM, 108, 167
PARADOX, Herakleitan, 51, 55–57, 79

PARALLELISM, Psycho-physical, 155, 157, 159, 283, 293
Parmenides of Elea, 42, 55–59, 79, 84, 162
Paul, St., 116, 117, 120
Pavlov, I. P., 182, 184–186, 188, 190, 191, 193, 292, 305
Peras, The Limit, 48–50
PERCEPTION, 37–40, 56, 57, 80–82, 85, 86–88, 95–97, 102, 107, 136, 140, 142, 143, 146, 148, 150, 154, 235, 241, 242, 246, 264, 271, 274, 275, 277–283, 290, 303, 304
Theory of 278 ff.
PERSONALITY, 27, 30, 34, 74, 76, 112
Phaedo, 71, 169, 175, 182, 213
Phaedrus, 89
PHENOMENA, 36, 56, 57, 62, 96, 135, 136, 140, 279, 282, 283, 289
Philo the Jew, 113–117, 119, 120, 126, 129
Photius, Patriarch, 118
PHOTOTROPISM, 175
Physis, 42–44, 46, 52, 53, 62, 70, 87, 101, 103, 104, 145, 162, 164, 275
PINEAL GLAND, 156–158, 163, 262
PLANARIA, 232–235
Plato, 40, 47, 50, 58, 68, 74, 78, 80, 82, 84, 86–91, 93–95, 97, 99–103, 106, 108, 111–114, 118, 122–127, 129–133, 135–139, 141, 142, 162, 169, 190, 213, 216, 290
PLATONISM (PLATONIC PHILOSOPHY), 18, 58, 74, 81, 90, 92–96, 100, 103, 112, 119–123, 125–130, 132–134, 140, 145, 163, 215
PLURALISM, Physical, 59, 60
POSITIVISM, 285–288
POTENTIALITY, 288
PREDICTION, Scientific, 85, 177, 181
PRIMARY SUBSTANCE, 42, 44, 48, 49, 51
air as, 46
neutral, 44, 48, 51, 56
water as, 43
PRIMITIVE—
CULTURES, 16 ff., 161
LANGUAGE, 17–22, 161, 203
MAN, 17, 18, 20–24, 161
THOUGHT, 17–24

PROSPECTIVE—
   POTENCY, 221, 222, 225, 235–237
   VALUE, 221, 225, 229, 235–237
Protagoras the Sophist, 67, 79–85, 90, 94, 142
Psyche, 26–28, 42, 43, 46, 53, 87, 93, 94, 166, 169, 251, 255, 276, 305
   Air-, 46, 63, 73
   Aristotelian, 99, 100–104
   Cartesian, 146, 148, 150, 152–159, 165, 213, 214, 275, 295
   Fire-, 53, 63, 64
   Ionian (material), 62–64, 73–75, 90
   Platonic (immaterial), 87, 89, 90–94, 100, 101, 104, 119, 123, 126
   Pythagorean (immaterial), 65, 76
   Socratic, 73–78, 90, 93, 101, 213–215, 263, 273
PSYCHOLOGY, 20, 26, 28, 64, 157
Ptolemy, 131, 133, 134
Pythagoras, 47–51, 54, 61, 108, 118, 147, 174, 258–262, 274, 277
PYTHAGOREAN PHILOSOPHY, 64, 65, 74–76, 103, 111–113, 115, 130–138, 143, 144, 147, 169, 191

QUALITIES—
   primary, 40, 136, 140, 141, 148, 154, 267, 272, 274, 281
   secondary, 136, 141, 144, 148, 149, 154, 267, 269, 272, 278, 281
QUANTA, 163, 282, 303, 304
QUIETISM—
   Christian, 115, 116, 127
   Stoic, 106, 109, 116

RAT (as experimental subject), 193–197, 200, 202–204, 243, 244, 250
RATIONALISM, 29, 47
REAL—
   concept of the, 37, 38, 40–43, 46, 81, 84, 105
   Change as Herakleitan, 51–53, 56, 85, 232
   immaterial, 50, 59, 60, 74, 90, 96, 97, 100, 103, 127, 128, 163, 165, 166, 213
   Pythagorean twofold, 49, 51

REALISM, 126
   Naïve, 267, 268, 279
REALITY, Ultimate, 36–42, 52, 57, 81, 99, 127, 162
REASON, 15, 37, 41, 47, 54, 60, 89, 107, 108, 114, 116, 120
RECEPTOR ORGANS, 154, 175, 178, 185, 187, 242
RECIPROCITY, 302–305
RECOGNITION, 243, 245, 247, 261
REFLEX, 174, 179, 180, 181, 184
   arc, 174, 188
   conditioned, 182, 184–186, 188–193, 199, 201, 202, 204, 240–242, 250, 260, 261, 299, 300, 302, 303
   delayed, 188, 190
   trace, 188–190
   unconditioned, 184, 300
REGENERATION, 227, 229, 239
REGULATION in development, 219, 221, 224, 227, 237, 239, 242, 244, 250, 251
REINCARNATION, 33, 128
RELATIONS, 205, 206
   perception of, 245, 246, 249, 261, 272, 305
RELATIVITY, Theory of, 24, 149, 168, 294
RENAISSANCE—
   Carolingian, 122, 130
   Italian, 130–132, 138
   Platonic, 120, 130, 135
   Thought, 40, 144, 145, 150, 167, 168, 191, 229, 274
Republic, The, 94, 111
Res Cogitans, 154, 156, 163, 166, 225, 226, 240, 272, 274, 278
Res Extensa, 154, 155, 159, 163, 272, 274
RESPONSE—
   conditioned, 192, 195–199, 204, 210
   to stimulus, 181, 184, 185, 193, 194, 242, 243, 261
   unconditioned, 198, 199, 201
   verbal, 201, 206, 210
Roux, 217
Russell, Bertrand, 280

SCEPTICISM, 79–81, 94, 146
SCHOLASTICISM, 122, 131, 133, 234

Index

SCHOOLMEN, The, 131, 135, 139, 140, 150, 163, 231
SENSATION, 39, 140, 152–154, 156, 177, 255, 263, 267, 274, 303, 304
  relativity of, 80, 84, 87
SENSEBILIA, 280
SENSITIVITY, 300–302
SIN, 112, 115
Socrates, 16, 47, 50, 68–79, 82, 86, 90, 92, 101, 118, 130, 145, 169, 174, 175, 180, 188, 190, 213–215, 253, 288, 291, 292, 295, 298, 304, 305
SOLIPSISM, 285
SOPHISM, 67, 68, 79, 96
SOUL—
  active *only* after death, 25, 29
  Aristotelian idea of, 99, 104, 127
  as animating principle, 21, 22, 62, 65, 277
  as breath, 23, 26, 27, 46, 166
  as mental image, 23, 26, 27, 161
  Cartesian idea of, 145, 150, 151, 154, 156, 163, 165, 213
  Christian idea of, 25, 50, 62, 92, 122–124, 127, 129
  Dionysiac cult of, 29–34, 47, 50, 74, 75, 276
  divine origin of, 30, 33, 122
  Greek cults of, 24–34, 73
  Herakleitan idea of, 53, 54, 63, 64
  immortality of, 25, 33, 104, 124, 126, 128
  memory of, 88
  modern concepts of, 16, 213, 285, 305
  not an animating principle, 16, 18, 22, 28, 34
  Platonic idea of, 88–93, 112, 114, 119, 122, 163
  primitive cults of, 23, 24, 93, 162
  primitive idea of, 17, 21–24, 73, 161, 162, 166
  Pythagorean idea of, 64, 65, 115
  Socratic idea of, 73–78, 90, 213, 214, 277, 295
SPACE, 96, 107, 148, 295
Spinoza, 167, 274, 283
SPIRIT, 18, 24, 92, 159, 163, 214, 215, 230, 286, 294–296, 304, 305
STATOCYST, 179, 180

STIMULUS, 175, 181, 185, 193, 194, 197–203, 242, 243, 245, 300
  conditioned, 185–190, 198, 199, 201, 203, 206, 210, 212, 241, 254
  substitute, 210–212
  unconditioned, 185–190, 198, 203, 260
STOICISM, 106–109, 113, 115, 120, 129, 162
Stout, G. F., 280
SUBJECTIVISM, 81, 84, 85, 154
SYMBOLISM, 15, 21, 49

TELEOLOGY, 90, 98, 213, 215, 252, 297, 298
Telesio, 133
Thales, 43, 46, 49, 63, 83, 150, 162
Theatetus, 80, 141, 142
Themistius, 125
Theophilus, Bishop, 121
THOMISM, 128, 162, 163
THOUGHT, 47, 64, 91, 102, 104, 155, 207, 208, 212, 249, 255, 262, 264, 269, 271, 282, 293
Timaeus, 91, 125, 133, 135
TIME, 85, 107, 295, 305
Titans, 32, 33
Torah, The, 110
TRANSMIGRATION, 34
TROPISM, 175, 177, 180, 184
TRUTH, 67, 68, 80–82, 91, 95, 122
Tycho Brahe, 139
Tylor, E. B., 17, 18

UNIVERSALS—
  Plato's theory of, 84–87, 126
  Socrates on, 69, 72
UREA, Synthesis of, 172, 250, 256

VITALISM, 165, 166, 172, 213, 215, 229, 230, 239, 243, 252, 256, 292
VOLITION, 72, 152, 155, 157, 255, 262, 264, 290, 304

Waicuri, 20, 204
WATER—
  as primary substance, 43, 44, 46, 51, 59, 83, 84, 103, 213
  chemical properties of, 143, 298
Watson, J. B., 200 ff., 250–252

WEIGHT, 21, 141, 148, 267
WHEEL OF LIFE, 33, 34, 47
Whitehead, A. N., 281
Woehler, 172, 250, 252, 256
WORLD-SOUL, Platonic, 91, 101, 107, 114, 116, 119, 122, 129, 162

WORLD-SOUL, Stoic, 107, 120
Xenophon, 68
Zagreus, 32
Zeus, 32
Zeno the Eleatic, 168

For Product Safety Concerns and Information please contact our EU
representative GPSR@taylorandfrancis.com
Taylor & Francis Verlag GmbH, Kaufingerstraße 24, 80331 München, Germany

www.ingramcontent.com/pod-product-compliance
Lightning Source LLC
Chambersburg PA
CBHW070750020526
44115CB00032B/1608